The Survey Method in the Social and Political Sciences

The Survey Method in the Social Sciences

The Survey Method in the Social and Political Sciences

Achievements, Failures, Prospects

William L. Miller

Frances Pinter (Publishers), London

© William L. Miller 1983

First published in Great Britain in 1983 by
Frances Pinter (Publishers) Limited
5 Dryden Street, London WC2E 9NW

British Library Cataloguing in Publication Data

Miller, William L.
   The survey method in the social sciences
   1. Social sciences—Fieldwork
   2. Social sciences—Methodology
   I. Title
   300'.723   H61

ISBN 0-86187-316-5

Typeset by Joshua Associates, Oxford
Printed by SRP Ltd., Exeter

Contents

Key to Acronyms

ABC1	the non-manual middle class (Market Research Society grades A, B, and C1)
ACAS	Advisory Conciliation and Arbitration Service
AEI	American Enterprise Institute
AFL	American Federation of Labour
AID	Automatic Interaction Detector
ASL	Audience Selection Limited (London pollsters who specialise in telephone survey methods)
BBC	originally the British Broadcasting Company, now the state run British Broadcasting Corporation
BMRB	British Market Research Bureau (London pollsters)
C2DE	the manual working class plus those on welfare payments (Market Research Society grades C2, D, and E)
CATI	Computer Assisted Telephone Interviewing
CIO	Congress of Industrial Organisations (USA)
CND	Campaign for Nuclear Disarmament
EEC	European Economic Community (Common Market)
FDP	Free Democratic Party (Germany)
FES	Family Expenditure Survey
GB	Great Britain (*not* the same as the UK)
GHS	General Household Survey
IPP	Index of Political Predisposition
IQ	Intelligence Quotient
ITN	Independent Television News (London)
LFS	Labour Force Survey
MORI	Market and Opinion Research International (London pollsters)
NF	National Front (right wing British party)
NFS	National Food Survey
NOP	National Opinion Polls (London pollsters)
OPCS	Office of Population Censuses and Surveys
ORC	Opinion Research Centre (London pollsters—not to be confused with NORC, the National Opinion Research Center in Chicago)
RSL	Research Services Limited (London Pollsters)
SCPR	Social and Community Planning Research (London pollsters who specialise in work for government agencies; currently an SSRC designated research centre in survey methods)

SDP	Social Democratic Party (Britain)
SERL	Socio-Economic Resources Level
SES	Socio-Economic Status
SN1–SN9	Survey Norm characteristics (defined on pp. 6–7)
SNP	Scottish National Party
SPD	Social Democratic Party (Germany)
SSRC	Social Science Research Council (of UK government)
TUC	Trades Union Congress
UK	United Kingdom of Great Britain and Northern Ireland (*not* GB)
WATS	Wide Area Telephone Service (USA)
WIRS	Workplace Industrial Relations Survey

Preface

The Survey Method is popular with decision makers in government, industry, and commerce. By 1979, annual expenditure on survey research in Britain had reached about £85 million—enough to pay for a short interview with every adult in the land. Surveys are also popular with the media. Private polls tell them about their readership or their viewers; public polls give them news headlines. During the 1979 election campaign over a third of the main news stories in the press took opinion poll findings as their theme. Increasingly we view society through the window of survey research.

But the Survey Method has not been universally popular with social scientists. Its findings have been dismissed as unconvincing, biased, trivial, corrupt, a danger to democracy or—if nothing worse—too expensive. Because of these criticisms, I was asked by the (British) Social Science Research Council (SSRC) to consider whether the Survey Method had made an effective contribution to our understanding of politics and society and whether it had exhausted whatever utility it had possessed, or whether we might expect it to do better in the future. Though I had directed election surveys in 1974 and 1979, my main interests had been in the political substance under investigation and in certain techniques of statistical analysis, rather than in the Survey Method itself. Consequently I felt no obligation to defend the Survey Method as such, still less to defend conventional methods for conducting surveys.

Some criticisms of the Survey Method are clearly founded on malice: absurdly high standards are set and surveys denounced for failing to attain them. Others are founded on ignorance: the critic, being unaware of the variety of Survey Methods available, criticises the only method he knows. Still others are founded on sloth, for the criticism contains within itself a solution to the problem, yet the critic finds it more comfortable to criticise someone else's work rather than get down to the tiresome business of improving upon it. But some criticisms are not so easily dismissed, and traditional methods are obsolescent. New technology provides exciting opportunities in survey research, as well as posing radically new problems.

The book is in four parts. The first describes in non-technical language just what I mean by the Survey Method. The second discusses criticisms that have been levelled against it. The third describes three interconnected examples of important survey research traditions, each extending over several decades and many surveys. Finally, the last section looks at what kind of survey we should be doing in the future, and at a revolutionary new technology for survey research. I have drawn my examples mainly from political surveys, which gives them a coherence they would otherwise lack, but political surveys have ranged far beyond voting analyses to focus on topics such as class solidarity, ideology, feelings of identification, reactions to the mass media, spatial processes, direct action, and social violence. Most, if not all, of my criticisms and recommendations apply to surveys in any of the social sciences, in planning or in marketing. Political studies draw on many disciplines and the studies I describe as political science were perhaps as often described by their authors as sociology or psychology as political science.

The book sticks closely to the theme of the Survey Method itself. In particular, I have tried to avoid widening the discussion into too general a consideration of empirical social science. I have also resisted the temptation to say much about statistical methods of survey analysis, since these are not fundamentally different from the methods used to analyse all kinds of non-survey material, and would in any case merit a book-length discussion on their own. The logical structure of analysis and interpretation is often critically important, but I have avoided technical details, and the reader will not find a single equation or formula in this book.

Surveys are too important to be left to specialists. I have kept the student and general reader very much in mind. No prior knowledge, no extensive library facility, no philosophical training, no statistical skills are required. The text will provide methodology students with a useful account of the purposes and potentialities of Survey Methods which will complement other texts on detailed practicalities or statistical techniques. Social science and marketing students should find it helpful in evaluating the survey-based literature in their particular subjects. Non-specialists in government, commerce, or the media who have to commission survey research, react to proposals from market research agencies, or interpret survey findings will find it a useful briefing on what surveys may achieve, and what may go wrong when survey design is defective.

But despite its non-technical style, I hope the book will also be read by survey practitioners who want to step back from the day-to-day problems of particular surveys or particular techniques and reflect on basic questions about the broad structure of the method.

For their help in clarifying my ideas, I am greatly indebted to John Barter of NOP, Martin Collins of SCPR, John Clements of ASL, Gordon Heald of Gallup, Gerard Hoinville of SCPR, Margaret Holmes of Marplan, Peter Hyett of British Telecom, Jim Rothman of Marplan,

Bob Worcester of MORI, and Bob Wybrow of Gallup. Among those who commission or interpret polls for the parties and the media, Linda Anderson at the BBC, Paul McKee at ITN, Keith Britto of the Conservative Central Office, Geoffrey Bish and Donald Ross at the Labour Party, Ian More of the SNP, Ruth Wishart of the *Sunday Mail*, and David Lipsey and Charles Douglas-Home of *The Times* were specially helpful. Matt Spicer and Ken Cargill of BBC-Scotland gave me more than information and ideas—they gave me a budget to try some experiments with new Survey Methods. Among university-based survey analysts, I must thank Hugh Berrington and Martin Harrop of Newcastle, Ian Budge and Ivor Crewe of Essex, David Butler of Oxford, and Donald Stokes of Princeton for their comments and advice.

I am grateful to them all for their time and interest, particularly because their comments usually ranged far beyond their own institutions and specialisations.

PART I

THE SURVEY METHOD

Part I defines what I mean by the Survey Method. Dictionary-style definitions are not very helpful—unintelligible to those who are not familiar with surveys; obscure or unacceptable to those who are. Such is the variety of Survey Methods that any attempt to include them all within a short definition degenerates into vague generalities. Instead of using that approach, Chapter 1 specifies nine features of a simple basic survey model—roughly the model which Dr Gallup and his competitors established during the thirties as the norm for modern survey research. Chapter 2 traces the development of this Gallup norm from earlier, more expensive, or less accurate techniques.

By *surveys* I mean data-gathering methods that approximate the Gallup norm to a greater or lesser extent. Variation and flexibility can go on without limit, however. There are no generally agreed demarcation lines between the Survey Method and other methods of social research. Surveys entail the study and comparison of a large number of objects (usually people). As the number in the survey decreases, there comes a point where the researcher is using a Comparative Method rather than a Survey Method. Similarly, surveys use a very tightly controlled, systematic process for selecting the people to be included in the survey, and an equally systematic method for obtaining information (like attitudes, opinions, reports) from them. As the rules for selecting people and obtaining information are relaxed, there comes a point where the research method should be described as anthropology or journalism, rather than survey research. But an enormous amount of variation around the Gallup norm is possible, while still meriting description as Survey Research.

Chapter 3 looks at the way each of the features of the basic survey model have been varied to suit particular problems or research objectives. It is very important to be aware of the range of possibilities, since many criticisms of the Survey Method are only valid as attacks on an inappropriately applied variant of the method. While I want to convey a concrete, practical notion of what the Survey Method is, I also want to stress its flexibility. My basic survey 'norm' is an aid to understanding, a reference point, not by any means the only correct or pure model for a survey. Chapter 3 closes with a brief description of the variety of analytic strategies appropriate to different kinds of survey data and research goals.

1 A simple model for an election survey

The term *survey* is used so loosely that it can apply to almost any method of data collection or review. I shall begin with a very specific, concrete notion of what I mean by a survey. What I have in mind is a somewhat simplified and idealised version of the method used by Gallup, ORC, NOP, MORI and other pollsters to forecast election results in Britain and America. Once the features of this basic 'survey norm' have been specified we can go on to look at the immense variety of other Survey Methods. This survey norm will serve several functions. It will give a concrete example of a survey, which may be easier to understand than an abstract definition. It will provide a reference point for deciding what is, and what is not, a survey: surveys will be defined as data collection procedures that more or less approximate the survey norm. I will also use it to structure my discussion of alternative Survey Methods, by looking in turn at variations in each of the defining characteristics of the norm. Lastly, it has been the dominant model for survey research since the 1930s, and is therefore a good image to have of any survey unless there are clear, explicit indications that it differs from the norm.

Hyman has suggested that sample surveys have five essential features, namely: (1) a large number of cases; (2) selection by some rigorous sampling criterion; (3) data on the cases collected in normal life-setting situations, rather than in a laboratory or experimental setting; (4) data collection by standardised procedures; and (5) the data consisting of quantitative measurements, including the simplest form of quantitative measure—an indicator of the presence or absence of some attribute (Hyman 1973).

We can use the items on Hyman's list to define a basic survey norm, but his list must be expanded to specify the scope of the survey and the structure of the data. In all, the survey norm has nine features:

Scope
SN1: Geographic scope—national
SN2: Population scope—electorate
SN3: Time scope—at or near to presidential or parliamentary election time

Sample
SN4: Number of cases—2,000
SN5: Sampling criterion—random or quota

Data collection procedures
SN6: Data Collection setting—respondents' homes
SN7: Data collection method—personal, face-to-face interview
SN8: Data measures—fixed choice questions
SN9: Data structure—atomistic

Some of these specifications have a simple and obvious meaning—2,000 cases, for example, means interviews with 2,000 people—but others, especially SN6–SN9, require some explanation.

1.1 *Scope and timing (SN1–SN3)*

Scope specifications are the easiest to understand, though not always easy to implement. If the survey is to forecast or analyse the outcome of an election, it should ideally cover the entire country but be restricted to those who are eligible to vote. Since people change their minds up to the very last minute before they vote, and their memories begin to fail immediately afterwards, the survey should be done as close to the time of voting as may be possible.

The ideal is simple enough. The problems come with the practical application. To begin with geography: the British are perpetually ambivalent about Ireland. Northern Ireland returns MPs to the Westminster Parliament, but Irish politics and Irish political attitudes are so different from those in mainland Britain that they are seldom included in British political surveys. Scots north of the Highland Line are not especially deviant in their political views, but they live in sparsely populated, mountainous territory which makes interviewing in the Highlands and Islands prohibitively expensive. So the geographic periphery of the British state tends to get left out of surveys. Closer to the centre there may be less openly acknowledged 'no-go' areas where the prevalence of crime and violence makes interviewers reluctant to tread.

Neither British nor American elections depend upon a simple popular vote. American presidents are elected by an electoral college whose composition depends upon voting in the different States of the Union; the British Government emerges from a parliament whose composition depends upon voting in parliamentary constituencies. Labour won a majority (simple, not absolute) of the popular vote in 1951, but the Conservatives took most seats in parliament and formed the government. In 1974 the opposite happened: the Conservatives beat Labour in the popular vote, but Labour took the most seats and formed the government. The first of these apparent anomalies installed a governing party for thirteen years, the second for five years. By chance, and chance alone, all recent American Presidents have enjoyed a plurality (i.e. a *simple* majority) of the popular vote, but the electoral system overturned popular majorities three times during the last century and came perilously close to doing so again as recently as 1976. Perhaps the most notorious example of this situation was the 1948 election in South Africa, when an apartheid government was put into office despite losing that election by 10 per cent in terms of the popular vote. So a simple geographic coverage, which takes no account of the geographical mechanisms in the electoral system—and there are several—can produce survey results which are misleading. (See Grant 1982 and Leonard 1968 for detailed descriptions of the British and American electoral systems, including the significance of geography for system behaviour.)

However, these electoral mechanisms are so complex that it can be extremely difficult to incorporate them in a survey design. Hence election polls and surveys in Britain seldom aim at anything but the popular vote. In America, the problem is less severe, because there are relatively few states compared to British constituencies (roughly a twelfth as many) and American polls are sometimes designed on a state-by-state basis, though more usually they too focus on the popular vote throughout the entire country.

Obviously a survey designed to study an election should be restricted to those able to vote, that is to the electorate. In Britain the state has assumed responsibility for registering citizens' right to vote ever since 1918. Almost everyone over the age of 18 has the right to vote and the registered electorate is roughly the same size as the adult population. Electoral registers are published annually. There should be no problem in focusing on the British electorate, since we have an up-to-date list of who they are.

Alas no! Some of those who are entitled to be registered to vote are not registered, and their numbers are compensated by people who are on the register twice though only legally entitled to vote once. This discrepancy may be about 7 per cent. Then there are those who have died, moved away from the areas where they are registered to vote, or are away on holiday or in hospital. Their numbers vary with the seasons and cumulate over the year. So by the end of the year only about four-fifths of those on the register have any practical possibility of voting. In parts of the country like London, or the centres of other large cities, the register is considerably less accurate than 80 per cent, because the rate of removals is high and the areas in which electors are registered to vote are very small subdivisions of the city. Moving across a city effectively disenfranchises a British elector for a year or two, because he or she has moved from one parliamentary constituency to another. Finally, if a survey has to be done to a tight time-schedule—and there is no other way of keeping it close to election day—then many people on the register will be out of the house when an interviewer calls on them and the interviewer will not have enough time to call back sufficiently often to catch the elector at home even if funds are available to pay for repeated visits.

The net result of all these practical difficulties is that surveys cannot be done by selecting people from the electoral register and interviewing them. Some surveys persist in trying to identify registered electors, but often polls and surveys substitute the adult population for the electorate, despite the fact that it is somewhat different from the legally-defined electorate, and very different indeed from the effective electorate.

In America, registration is still the responsibility of the citizen and only about half the adult population votes—slightly more than half in presidential elections, considerably less than half in off-year Congressional elections. Consequently American polling strategy aims at the adult population, but then filters out those who claim they have registered or will register, and may even ask rather pointedly whether the survey respondent knows the location of his polling station (Perry 1979: 320).

The time scope is also easy to specify and very difficult to implement. As we shall see, political polls have performed disastrously when they ceased interviewing even a few days before the vote. Academic studies have shown that memories change rapidly and (even worse) systematically as soon as the vote has been cast. To their dismay, the pollsters have come to realise that 'at or near election time' means election day itself, or the day before, certainly not months or even weeks away from the event. Most surveys may not be concerned to forecast an election accurately. But election polls have shown that *any* survey which aims to discover attitudes, opinions, or feelings must take account of how rapidly these things change. Human feelings are fundamentally different from the inanimate objects or physical processes of the natural sciences. In the social sciences, speed and timing are critically important.

1.2 *Size and sampling (SN4–SN5)*

Surveys are based on sampling: a relatively few cases are selected to represent a much larger population. But although the number of cases is *relatively* few, it must be a fairly large number. The norm is anything between 1,000 and 3,500—say 2,000 in a typical survey. Hyman specified that the cases in the sample had to be not only large but well-chosen. There are two frequently used methods, usually described as *random* sampling and *quota* sampling. In practice they are not so different as at first appears.

Why 2,000? With a sample of 2,000 respondents chosen by a typical random method (*not* a simple random sample however—see below) statistical calculations suggest there is a 95 per cent chance that the survey can estimate to within plus or minus 3 per cent the percentage of the electorate who possess some particular attribute like voting Labour. So, if 52 per cent of the *sample* report a Labour vote, statistical reasoning suggests that in the *electorate as a whole* the odds are 19 to 1 that the percentage voting Labour lies somewhere between 49 per cent and 55 per cent.

Similarly, we can estimate the difference between two groups in a sample. Suppose the 2,000 respondents can be split into two social classes, an upper class of 600 respondents and a more numerous lower class of 1,400. Then the difference between the levels of Labour voting in the two classes *in the sample* should be within plus or minus 6 per cent of the difference between the classes *in the electorate as a whole*. If the lower class in the sample are 30 per cent more Labour than the upper class, then we should calculate that in the electorate as a whole the odds are 19 to 1 that the class difference in Labour support lies somewhere between 24 per cent and 36 per cent (see Butler and Stokes 1974: 440–1 for sampling error calculations in a typical survey).

These estimates of sampling error are sensitive to the size of the sample but not to the size of the electorate. The important point to note is that these same estimates of sampling error apply almost irrespective of the size of the electorate. For any given level of accuracy we need the same size of sample, no matter whether we are investigating politics in Britain or America, or in Scotland or in Detroit. Hence one reason for nation-wide surveys: their findings interest a larger audience, yet their sample sizes need not be any larger than in local surveys. So they are generally more cost-effective.

The second significant point arising from these sampling error calculations is that a sample of 2,000 is adequate for the estimation of levels of attributes throughout the country as a whole, but not really adequate for sub-group analyses nor, what is arithmetically equivalent, for analyses of causes, effects, and influences.

Statistically there is a 19 to 1 chance that we can estimate the true percentage to within plus or minus 3 per cent in the nation as a whole. To double this accuracy we need to quadruple the sample size: thus with a sample of 8,000 respondents we should expect to get only within plus or minus 1.5 per cent of the true percentage. In practice there are many sources of error, and for a given fieldwork force, many of these *increase* with sample size. If we are forced to do 8,000 interviews rather than

2,000, it becomes much more difficult to control the field-force of inter-viewers: poor interviewers are kept on the payroll; interviewers are pressured into more careless work; and the time scale required to do the survey may have to be extended. So it is not entirely surprising that experience with election forecasting in Britain has shown that polls with larger samples have not performed any better than those with smaller samples (Worcester 1980: 37).

However, the standard 2,000 sample is a good deal less satisfactory when it is used to extract subsamples. Labour support in the full sample should be estimated to within 3 per cent, but in subsamples such as those respond-ents in a particular social class or region, or readers of a particular paper, the sampling error rises from 3 per cent in the full sample to 5 per cent in a subsample of 500, and up to plus or minus 11 per cent in a subsample of 100. Unfortunately, once we get beyond the 'horse-race' aspect of electoral analysis and want to know how opinions and votes vary throughout the nation, we quite easily reach down to subsamples as small as 100 from a full sample of 2,000.

Sampling methods vary somewhat from country to country. In Britain the two standard methods are commonly described as *random* and *quota*. The first was favoured by academic statisticians, the second pioneered by market research agencies. Neither is a simple random selection from the electorate, but both are intended to be passable substitutes for one. The objective of any sampling procedure is to produce a representative micro-cosm of the electorate as a whole. If we knew everything about that electorate, we could choose a perfectly representative subset for our sample. But if we knew everything about the electorate, we should not need to do any research and surveys would be unnecessary. The alternative is to select people *at random*, excluding all elements of subjective choice from our selection procedure. Conceptually, we can imagine a gigantic hat with every elector's name written on a piece of paper and placed in the hat. After giving it a good shake, we reach in and pull out 2,000 slips of paper. That would produce a simple, that is to say a pure, random sample. Random samples have the advantage that they should be fairly representative on every known *and unknown* attribute. In addition, statisticians can easily calculate the chances of a random sample being unrepresentative to any given extent. Unfortunately it is uneconomic to spread a sample perfectly evenly across the nation. Interviewers' travel costs would be too high.

Both methods in normal use are based on *multi-stage stratified samp-ling* with a fairly high degree of *clustering* at the final stage. They differ only in the way they select clusters of respondents at the final stage. An example will explain the terminology.

Butler and Stokes' is a good example of the random method. They began by dividing the 618 constituencies of mainland Britain into eighty groups or *strata* on the basis of region, partisanship, patterns of candidature, urban or rural character, and level of unemployment. Within each of these strata they selected one constituency by a random selection procedure which gave larger constituencies a higher chance of being selected. Then thirty-two names were selected from the electoral register in each of the chosen constituencies. About half the constituencies were geographically compact. In these the chosen electors were spread evenly throughout the constituency. A quarter of the constituencies had compact urban cores with rural peripheries. In each of these the urban area was represented by a systematic sample spread evenly throughout, while the rural periphery was represented by a sample spread through just one polling district within the rural area. The remaining quarter of constituencies were sparsely populated. In each of these the polling districts were divided into a wealthier and a less wealthy half on the basis of the proportion of electors qualified for jury service (only the relatively affluent serve on British juries). One polling district was selected randomly in each half and sixteen electors selected, spread randomly throughout the polling district.

The objectives of this *multi-stage* procedure were to ensure that, despite a degree of random selection, all types of constituency would be represented in the sample in the correct proportions (hence the initial division into eighty equal *strata*) and secondly, to minimise costs by ensuring that interviewers had a compact set of addresses to visit (hence the *clustering* of rural respondents within polling districts). Though clustering minimises costs for the full sample, it has a particularly bad effect upon analyses of geographically defined subsamples. One example of a disastrous consequence of clustering is given in Marsh's study of protest potential (Marsh 1977: 71). By chance, one of his clusters was located entirely within a university students' hall of residence.

Even at this stage the selection process in the survey by Butler and Stokes was not complete. The names chosen by the procedure used so far were used to identify only households, not individuals. When the interviewer arrived at the address, she interviewed the selected elector, provided he or she had not died or moved away. Then the interviewer checked who was living at the address. If any new or additional adults were found at the selected address, she chose one of them (randomly) for an additional interview.

Finally, for one reason or another—mainly because respondents were out when the interviewer called, or refused to be interviewed—a sizeable proportion of the attempted interviews was not successful. Even among the final target sample of people actually living at the selected addresses during the interviewing period, Butler and Stokes achieved interviews with only 79 per cent in their non-election year surveys and 69 per cent in their election year surveys. Now in addition to the 31 per cent who did not give an interview at all, others refused to answer specific questions or retreated behind the shield of a 'don't know' response. So when we come to analyse the data, there is a considerable element of self-selection or accidental but non-random selection at the final stage. And let me stress that I have picked the Butler and Stokes series of surveys because they exemplify the best in British survey work, not the worst.

It may have been a little tedious to go through this sample selection procedure in such detail, but it was necessary to underline the difference between the practice of random sampling and the elegant theoretical simplicity of a pure random sample. In practice, the process is far removed from selecting names from a hat and interviewing the named electors.

Quota samples are remarkably similar in construction to the random sample just described. Typically, they also array constituencies into strata, make random selections within strata and random selections of polling districts within constituencies. The difference comes only at the last stage of the selection process. Instead of selecting names throughout the electoral register of the polling district, they select households spread across the physical area of the polling district. Calling at, for example, every tenth house down the street, the quota sampler attempts one interview at each, trying, however, to fulfil an *interlocking quota* of so many respondents with pre-specified combinations of class, age, sex, and employment status (i.e. employed or not). Quota sampling is a bit like pushing stratification techniques one stage further. The design of the quota sample guarantees that the sample contains not only the correct proportions of northern and southern, urban and rural residents, but also the correct proportions of young and old, upper class and lower class, male and female. Where it differs from an extension of stratified sampling is that when the quota sampler selects her quota of young, upper class males at the final stage, she does not make a random selection from *all* the young, upper class males within the polling district—she takes *any* young upper class males from the specified polling district who happen to be available for interview. Quota samples promise a certain specific kind of representativeness and they honour their promise. But as Lady Macbeth found out, a witch's promise may be honoured to the letter yet be profoundly disappointing because expectations go far beyond the letter of the promise: 'Nought's gained, all's spent, when our desires are got without content.' So it is with quota sampling. It guarantees representativeness in terms of the quota; it guarantees representativeness in nothing else. Indeed, the method is very likely to produce distortions towards the readily available and against the less accessible members of the population.

Quota controls guarantee enough old and young people, but they will tend to under-represent the very old and the very young. Quota controls guarantee enough employed people, but they tend to over-represent the transport, distributive, building, and miscellaneous trades while under-representing those who work behind the closed doors of manufacturing industry (see Moser and Kalton 1981: 131). Certainly, known biases can be corrected, though the quota cannot be made too complex or interviewers will be unable to operate it; but correcting for newly discovered biases in quota samples always has the look of solving yesterday's problems, not today's—it is always just too late. Biases in quota polls can be corrected only after they have been discovered (perhaps in previous quota polls). The great virtue of random sampling is that it guards against all kinds of bias without requiring prior knowledge of the significant characteristics of the population under investigation.

There is no easy way of estimating sampling errors for quota samples, but research by Moser suggests they may be substantially higher than with equivalent random samples, so much so that simple quota samples might need to be as much as three times as large as simple random samples to achieve the same accuracy (Moser and Kalton 1981: 136). Even if problems of systematic bias can be overcome, quota samples are inherently more variable and less reliable than random samples.

Against all this it must be said that the methods in current use are neither simple random samples nor simple quota samples. The difference between two multi-stage samples which use random selection at all stages except the final, and only differ in so far as they use random or quota selection at the final stage (within polling districts) will be much less than the difference between pure, single-stage, random and quota samples. Moreover there is an enormous gap between the theory and practice of random sampling when less than 70 per cent of the randomly selected electors actually give interviews. And since quota sampling involves trying alternative people until the quota of interviews has been achieved, rather than repeatedly calling back on selected individuals, quota sampling can be done very quickly in time, even if it requires a large number of interviewers' man-hours. If the pollsters need to do a complete survey in a single day, they can do it by quota methods, using however many interviewers may be necessary. But if they tried the same survey by random methods they would find half their selected respondents were away from home when the interviewer called. If they used as many interviewers as required by the quota method, they would find their interviewers had spent half the day un-employed, while only half the chosen sample had been interviewed—all because no substitution was allowed. Statistics texts fulminate against the dangers of bias caused by substituting one individual for another, but they miss the point: if the selected individual is not available for interview at the right time, we have to substitute another person or another time—there are no other possibilities. Now when attitudes, opinions, and beha-vioural intentions may fluctuate rapidly, substituting another time may be worse then substituting another individual. In the event, the track record of random sample polls in forecasting British election results is no better than the track record of quota polls (Worcester 1980: 37).

1.3 *Data collection procedures (SN6–SN9)*

In the typical survey, as I have defined it, data are collected by a direct one-to-one personal interview between a professional interviewer and the elector. It takes place in the respondent's (i.e. the elector's) home. The format is as neutral as possible: the interviewer tries hard to avoid giving information or encouraging or discouraging any particular response. She shows neither pleasure, disapproval, nor surprise. The presence of other members of the respondent's household is discouraged.

Next, the measurements: these usually consist of the elector's answers to pre-set questions asked by the interviewer. Though there are usually a lot of questions and the interview may take an hour or more, it is not a conversation. It does not ramble from one topic to another. The inter-viewer reads out a list of questions one by one and records the answers. Hence the interviewee is usually described as a *respondent*. Usually the questions are *closed-ended*: the answers are also pre-set and the respondent merely asked to choose between alternatives. However, surveys frequently include a few *open-ended* questions in addition to a larger number of closed-ended. With the open-ended questions, only the question is fixed and the elector is free to give any answer he or she likes. The elector is not provided with even a check-list of possible answers. The interviewer tries to note the gist of the elector's reply. Before analysis, answers given to these open-ended questions are classified in some way, perhaps after the investigators have read through a large number of replies, perhaps according to some pre-set criterion. There is seldom if ever any reference back to the electors to see whether they agree with the way in which their replies have been interpreted and classified—unlike journalists, survey researchers sel-dom give informants the opportunity to object to misreporting!

Hyman's third feature of surveys was that they collected data in normal life-setting situations. Now a person-to-person interview in the home, with third parties excluded from the interview and preferably from the room, is a good deal more of a normal life-setting situation than some psychology laboratory in a university. But it is still not entirely a normal situation for most individuals. The locale is indeed a normal situation—though only one of several normal situations—but the social circumstances are distinctly abnormal. Normally people develop ideas and opinions through discussion with their family, friends, and associates. If they have not done so before the interview, they have no opportunity to do so during it.

A fixed list of pre-specified questions, each with a set of pre-specified alternative answers certainly constitutes data collection by what Hyman would call a standardised procedure. Pre-specified questions ensure that desired topics are covered, but at the cost of preventing a natural evolution of conversation and thought. On the other hand, pre-specified alternative answers have the advantage of giving the respondent a useful check list of possibilities which, in the inevitable haste of an interview, can be a very useful facility for the respondent. They help to ensure comparability between different respondents. They help the inarticulate to express some view, at least, and they give the respondent some control over the classification of his or her answer—the classification scheme is not hidden from the interviewee. But a list of pre-set alternative answers may prompt respondents to articulate feelings and attitudes they really do not possess, or may restrict and channel their responses in ways that do not reflect their real attitudes. I can speak from very personal experience, having been interviewed a dozen times by pollsters, including several of the leading British market research agencies. Closed-ended questions sometimes failed to include the responses I wished to make, while open-ended questions delivered at high speed without a check list made me overlook my preferred response until too late. On one black day I even forgot the name of my favourite beer!

Finally, the data structure: I have described this as *atomistic* because the typical survey merely records each respondent's answer to the various questions; and these questions typically concern only the respondent, and the respondent alone. There are no contextual or relational data.

By *atomism* we mean that each respondent is treated as a completely independent unit in the survey. The term can also be used to indicate that his or her various attitudes, opinions and other responses are also treated as completely separate attributes. What is the alternative? The problem of atomism is closely bound up with the question of additivity. Is a person greater than the sum of his or her attributes? Or to put it another way: is the collection of a person's attributes, viewed as an entirety, something more than their sum? The same question can be raised with respect to people and communities. Is a working class community anything more than a lot of working class people put into close geographic proximity? The answers to questions like these must often be 'yes' and that requires non-atomistic structures of data and non-atomistic techniques of analysis. By using appropriate statistical techniques, we can detect interactions between attributes; by appropriate survey design we can facilitate explicit analyses of interactions between people.

I noted in passing that there are usually a lot of questions in a survey, and interviews could go on for an hour or more. Thus one of the characteristic features of a survey is that it provides a lot of data about each individual. So it permits investigation of a wide range of different inter-relationships between social, attitudinal, and psychological variables; or it permits a very deep investigation into one aspect of attitudes or behaviour. Whichever is the case, the richness of data contained within a single survey is usually striking, especially when data from sample surveys are viewed in comparison with other sources of political data such as election returns or census materials, in which the multiplicity of numbers is accompanied by a paucity of concepts. A natural consequence of this richness of information coupled with the need for a survey to contain large numbers of respondents is that the total quantity of data produced by a survey is very large. Computer processing is almost inevitably necessary to do even the simplest analyses. But once the data have been put into computer-readable form, modern packages of statistical programmes make it as easy to perform complex statistical analyses as to do simple counts and cross-tabulations. So complex multivariate analysis has become almost as characteristic of surveys as the conceptual richness of their data.

Such then has been the norm for political surveys ever since it was established in the 1930s. The possibilities for abuse are obvious. Respondents do sometimes tell explicit, conscious lies, as is shown for example by the difference between two types of Gallup poll, one using open questioning, the other using secret balloting with imitation ballot boxes (see Perry 1979: 317–18). Respondents' memories are fallible and corrupt. Interviewers sometimes make up some or all of the answers they have supposedly elicited from respondents, even when they work for reputable firms and are subject to close supervision. Survey directors sometimes report percentages which are not firmly based on counting respondents' replies. They bias the wording or the selection of their questions, either through incompetence or because they want to please their sponsors by producing acceptable findings. Computers are sometimes programmed wrongly (though their electronic mechanisms seldom cause errors). Clearly, within the broad specifications I have described, surveys can be done very well or very badly. In later chapters I will give examples of the good and the bad. Much depends upon the skills, experience, motivation, and integrity of the large number of people involved in a survey, from the research directors to the interviewers and data processors. Good survey work depends at least as much on personnel management as on statistical formulae.

2   Historical evolution

During the nineteenth century all those groups which were closely connected with the substance of politics—governments, politicians, pressure groups, and the media—developed a keen interest in surveys of one kind or another. Political scientists were slow to join them (Butler 1958: 57). In Britain surveys focused on social conditions relevant to government policy but in America, with its early commitment to mass democracy, surveys also focused on the electoral process (see Butler 1958; Moser and Kalton 1958 and 1971; Teer and Spence 1973; Hodder-Williams 1970; or Abrams 1951).

2.1 *British government and American politics*

The British government itself collected a huge quantity of statistical information by such means as the decennial census begun in 1801, though that was intended to be a full enumeration rather than a sample in any sense. A succession of early British survey pioneers were obsessed with the problem of poverty. Between 1851 and 1864 Henry Mayhew published his four-volume *London Labour and the London Poor*. Henry Mayhew and his collaborators recorded numerous conversations with the street-people of London, along with their own observations of the daily round of life. But he used no formal sampling method, no staff of professional interviewers, and no statistical analysis of his data.

Booth with his seventeen-volume *Life and Labour of the People of London* (published between 1892 and 1897), Rowntree with his *Poverty: A Study of Town Life* (1902) and Bowley in *Livelihood and Poverty* (1915) continued this substantive focus on poverty, but moved away from direct reportage to statistical analysis of quantitative data. As Booth noted in the introduction to his first volume:

> The materials for sensational stories lie plentifully in every book of our notes; but even if I had the skill to use my material in this way, I should not wish to use it here. . . My object has been to attempt to show the *numerical relation* which poverty, misery and depravity bear to regular earnings and comparative comfort.

They also experimented with formal sampling techniques of various kinds, though their basic strategy was to restrict attention to a single town or handful of localities at most. On the advice of Chamberlain, Booth used reports by school board visitors as his source for information about the London working class—an ingenious method of sampling. Even if it made the data somewhat second-hand, it cut the data-gathering operation enormously—yet in a systematic, controlled way. Moreover, Victorian researchers did not trust the poor to tell the truth. Booth's team also interviewed, rather than merely conversed with, the survey respondents, for he wanted quantifiable information.

Rowntree obtained his information by direct interview, using a team of interviewers. Though he carried out a complete, enumerative survey in York, he also did some experimental work on the consequences of selecting incomplete samples of his data at the rate of 1 in 10, 20, 30, 40, and even 1 in 50. Bowley suggested that, in view of a shortage of funds, his 1912 study of working class households in Northampton, Warrington, Stanley, and Reading should be based from the outset on a sample of households and in the following year he published relevant probability calculations in the *Journal of the Royal Statistical Society* (Bowley 1913).

In America, as in Britain, government agencies collected increasing amounts of statistical information and also developed the notion of sampling. From 1866 onwards, for example, the Department of Agriculture Crop Reporting Service made annual forecasts of national crop production and livestock numbers on the basis of a scattered sample of correspondents. (See Bean, 1948.) However, the distinctive feature of surveys in America was their use for election forecasting by the press and by candidates themselves. In July 1824 the *Harrisburg Pennsylvanian* undertook a 'straw vote' poll to measure presidential sentiment in Wilmington, Delaware during the run up to the presidential contest between Quincy Adams and Jackson. In the same year the *Raleigh Star* tried to assess opinion at political meetings. Sampling techniques were crude and uncontrolled in these early media polls, but by the end of the century the *Columbus Despatch* was using trained interviewers and controlling its samples for sex, occupation, and area of residence (Teer and Spence 1973, chapter 1).

In 1896 the *Chicago Record* reportedly spent over $60,000 to mail postal questionnaires to a one in eight random sample of twelve mid-west states, plus the entire electorate of Chicago. The paper received a quarter of a million responses and employed a team of mathematicians to analyse them. They were aware that self-selection could cause bias; so they had asked a question about the respondent's vote in 1892 as well as his voting intention in 1896, and they used previous vote as a basis for statistical controls to eliminate bias. They got the result exactly right to within a twentieth of one per cent for Chicago, but were less accurate in their forecast for the mid-west as a whole (Jensen 1969). They were not to know, as we now do, that memories of previous voting are themselves systematically biased. American political candidates were also quick to take an interest in polls. In 1880, for example, a US senatorial candidate commissioned a poll of all Union veterans in the state of Indiana.

The most famous, later to become the most infamous, of American media polls began in 1916: the *Literary Digest* poll went beyond election forecasting—at which it was notably successful until 1936—and examined public opinion on current issues, an innovation that was quickly copied by other American polls. By the time of the 1928 presidential election there were approximately eighty-five polling organisations, six of them nation-wide, working on political attitudes and electoral prospects (Robinson 1934). The *Literary Digest* poll represented the final flourish of the methodology developed by nineteenth-century American media. It sent out postal questionnaires to a sample of citizens drawn randomly from known listings of the population, principally listings of telephone subscribers and car owners. Under the American electoral system the *Digest* unfortunately had no access to a complete electoral register such as is easily obtainable in Britain. In 1936 the *Digest* sent out over ten million questionnaires and received back almost two and a half million. Until 1936 this method proved accurate, though costly.

In Britain too, the methods and concerns of the nineteenth century continued well into the twentieth. Bowley published *Has Poverty Diminished?* in 1925 as a sequel to *Livelihood and Poverty*; in 1928 Sir Hubert Llewellyn Smith began publication of the *New Survey of London Life and Labour* as a sequel to Booth; and in 1941 Rowntree published *Poverty and Progress* as a sequel to his own earlier study of York. These studies reflected both the substantive concerns and the methodological techniques of their predecessors. In America, studies of voter turnout by Ben Arneson in Delaware, Ohio (Arneson 1925) and by Merriam and Gosnell in Chicago (Merriam and Gosnell 1924; Gosnell 1927) provide other examples of lingering attempts to use geographically limited but basically enumerative, total population survey methods.

Any method that required vast numbers of respondents was inevitably cumbersome to organise and analyse. It was also very expensive. It could only be justified if it proved very much more accurate than methods involving relatively few respondents. In 1935 George Gallup established his American Institute of Public Opinion to conduct weekly polls on current issues, using systematically selected but none the less very small national samples of around 3,000 respondents. A number of other organisations adopted similar methods, including the Crossley poll and the Fortune survey (run by Roper and Cherrington).

2.2 Pollsters' success in the 1936 presidential election

Almost immediately these relatively small-sample polls were faced with a very public test: forecasting the 1936 presidential election outcome. All three forecast a Roosevelt victory, while the *Literary Digest* poll with its two and a half million respondents forecast victory for Landon. In the event Roosevelt won with 61 per cent of the vote, the *Literary Digest* poll was discredited, and the Gallup methodology credited with success.

After the lapse of nearly half a century, it is too easy to dismiss *Literary Digest* methods as pre-scientific and heap unearned praise on Gallup. Gallup style polls did not perform well—Gallup and Crossley both forecast Roosevelt to get only 54 per cent of the vote—though Fortune came very close with a forecast of 62 per cent. Indeed, when all three major polls got the 1948 presidential election wrong, a full scale academic board of inquiry was set up to discover why, though they were in fact more accurate in 1948 than 1936.

However, the *Literary Digest* poll certainly got it very wrong indeed with a forecast of 43 per cent for Roosevelt. Despite its enormous sample, it forecast a landslide for the Republican candidate at a time when there was actually a landslide for the Democrat. Its method was not entirely absurd, since it had proved accurate enough in the past. But by 1936 Roosevelt's New Deal politics had polarised party preference along class lines, with the result that telephone subscribers or car owners, still less the 25 per cent of them who returned *Digest* questionnaires, no longer represented a cross-section of voters for both parties. The events of 1936 clearly showed that an enormously large sample was no guarantee of accuracy, that careful selection of the sample was more important than sheer size. Less obviously, but more important for us today, 1936 showed that the meaning that attaches to *careful selection* may change rapidly, and the selection methods of the past—whatever they are—may not work in the future. We fall into the same error as the *Digest* if we remain too attached to the methods that became conventional in our fathers' days.

Following his success with the presidential election forecast, Gallup set up the British Institute of Public Opinion in 1937 as one of an international chain of Gallup organisations. In 1938 it correctly forecast Edith Summerskill's victory in the Fulham by-election, and this persuaded the *News Chronicle* to publish regular Gallup findings. After the war almost all the commentators agreed that the Conservatives would win the 1945 general election, especially in view of the public enthusiasm that greeted Winston Churchill wherever he went. Gallup, however, forecast a Labour victory. No one paid any attention: its forecast was ignored until proved right by the event.

It would be wrong to attribute the invention and development of the survey norm (a carefully chosen national sample of 2,000 or 3,000, personally interviewed according to a strictly defined questionnaire) to Gallup or to the 1936 presidential election campaign. (Gallup actually used mainly postal methods in 1936, only supplemented by interviews, and their sampling methods were crude at first.) The method had been used before and would probably have achieved prominence without the help of the 1936 experience. Even if samples of 2,000 had produced worse results than samples of two million, considerations of cost would have encouraged the switch; and statisticians had already convinced themselves, if no one else, that huge samples were unnecessary.

But 1936 certainly helped establish the modern survey norm in laymen's eyes, it clearly discredited the expensive old nineteenth-century methods, and it conveniently marks the time when traditional Gallup-type methodology became the norm in political surveys, a norm which is only now being superseded.

2.3 *Surviving failure*

Though the celebrated successes of 1936 and 1945 encouraged the use of Gallup-style methodology, equally celebrated failures in 1948, 1970, and 1974 have done little to hinder its wider adoption, and a failure in 1951 scarcely achieved public visibility.

In 1948 all three major American polls predicted victory for the Republican candidate Dewey, though Truman, the Democrat, won. The American Social Science Research Council mounted an official inquiry which recommended improvements in sampling and interviewing techniques plus continuity of interviewing right up to election day (Mosteller *et al.* 1949). But 1948 was not a landslide election like 1936, and in contrast to the *Literary Digest* poll, the new techniques had a more solid theoretical justification, based on probability theory. They did not rely so much on 'getting it right' for their only justification. Their method had an internal rather than purely external logic.

In Britain, Gallup was joined by two similar polls in 1951, run by the *Daily Express* and by Research Services. All three forecast a Conservative victory. In the event, Labour had a margin of 1.5 per cent of votes over the Conservatives, but because of the way these were distributed across constituencies, the Conservatives took more seats in the House of Commons and the pollsters' universal failure to forecast the national vote was ignored. Conversely, they were somewhat unfairly criticised after February 1974 for predicting a Conservative victory. The Conservatives won more votes, but fewer seats than Labour. In addition the 1974 polls slightly over-estimated the Conservative lead in terms of votes. So their forecasts of a substantial Conservative lead in terms of votes cast constrasted badly with the advent of a Labour government.

Nineteen-seventy was probably the worst year for British polls, prompting a committee of inquiry on 1948 American lines. Throughout the campaign and in their final forecasts almost (but not quite) all the polls had forecast a Labour victory, yet the Conservatives won a clear majority of votes and seats. The polls could not excuse themselves on the grounds of a narrow result, nor on the grounds of sampling error. Too many polls had been taken which proved too far wrong in percentage terms. Something had gone systematically wrong. An inconclusive post-mortem suggested late changes in voting intention had not been caught by polls which closed their fieldwork too early (see Craig 1976 for a complete record of forecasting attempts; Butler and Pinto-Dushinsky 1971 for the 1970 debacle; Market Research Society 1971 for the official inquiry).

Since 1970, however, the performance of the polls has been reassuring. Criticism in February 1974 was based on false premises, and the polls were reasonably accurate in forecasting the results of the 1975 EEC Referendum, the 1979 Scotland Act Referendum, and the 1979 General Election. There was some evidence of an anti-bandwagon effect: the political side which was initially ahead in the polls seems to have lost ground towards the end of the campaign in 1970, February 1974, October 1974, the EEC Referendum, and the Scotland Act Referendum. In 1979 this pattern recurred until polls suggested that the original underdog might win, whereupon support rallied to the Conservatives once more. Such an effect, if it really exists, makes it even more difficult to forecast accurately, and the media polls take special measures, including late re-interviews, to check the continuing validity of their forecasts. But despite late swings and anti-bandwagon effects, the performance of media polls has been sufficiently good to encourage widespread acceptance of their methodology. Indeed, by 1979 British media polls were able to turn in a very convincing performance, using a very slimmed-down version of the survey norm. Five polls made final forecasts. Every one of them used a quota sample rather than a random sample. None used a sample anywhere near Gallup's original 3,000 respondents: two had samples of around 2,000, while three had samples of roughly 1,000. Small quota samples at least had one critical advantage over large random samples: they could be interviewed very close to election day. By 1979 that meant interviewing the whole sample only the day before the election (Worcester 1980; Rose 1981).

What makes the election forecasting polls conducted by the media such a convincing test of the methodology and such good publicity for it is their need to publish their findings before the actual election results are known. There are all sorts of reasons why forecasts might be wrong even if the method were basically sound: late swing by the electors, or sloppy work by an over-stretched fieldforce working to tight deadlines, for example. So failure would be easier to explain than success. No after-the-event poll, whatever degree of accuracy it claims, can be such a convincing test of the methodology. The test would be even more convincing if the figures presented by the media polls were based on simple counts of responses to their interviews. Alas, this is often not so: in 1979, for example, most media polls adjusted their raw figures without publishing any indication that they had done so.

3 Methodological variations

Sample surveys, even within the limited field of politics, have been used to study an immense variety of topics. I shall say something about that variety later on, but in this chapter I want to note some of the ways in which the *format* or *methodology* of survey investigations has departed from the survey norm described in the first chapter. To a considerable degree the topic defines the method, but my focus here will be firmly on the method, rather than the topic as such. It is vitally important to appreciate the variety and flexibility of Survey Methods, because critics often attack the only variant of the method they know when, if they were better informed, they would be aware that their objections have already been understood and accepted by survey researchers and special methods developed to meet the objections.

This chapter will complete the definition of a survey which I began in Chapter 1 by specifying the survey norm. The full definition requires a description of both the norm and its variants. I will use the features of the norm, SN1 to SN9, to structure my description of the variations. I will give references to practical examples of each variation on the Survey Method, and wherever possible I have drawn the example from the survey traditions described in Chapters 7, 8, and 9. How well these different variants of the Survey Method performed their ultimate task of contributing to understanding can therefore be judged when I come to those later chapters.

3.1 *Variations in scope and timing (SN1–SN3)*

The geographic scope of the norm was national (SN1). National (country-wide) electorate surveys serve two functions: they provide information about the *whole* electorate, which is always important; but they also serve as a basis for comparison, a bench-mark against which findings about other areas or groups of people can be judged. Thus many local or specialised studies would be uninterpretable without background knowledge of the national electorate which serves as a universal *control group*. Nationwide American electoral surveys have been undertaken since 1948 by a team at Michigan University, and in Britain since 1964 by workers at Nuffield College, Oxford and later Essex University.

But apart from its bench-mark function, a national survey is appropriate only if the nation *as a whole* is the main focus of investigation. If we are interested in patterns within the nation, then it is important for statistical analysis that we have sufficient respondents from each of the relevant subgroups. Now in a total sample of only 2,000 representing a nation of many millions it is perfectly possible that important subgroups contribute too few respondents to the sample for reliable statistical analysis. In a UK sample of 2,000, for example, there would be about one hundred respondents from Wales and fifty from Northern Ireland, yet we might wish to contrast English, Welsh and Irish attitudes.

One simple, general, but expensive solution to this problem is a very much larger sample, perhaps of the order of 10,000 to 20,000 respondents; but where the subgroups are geographic and can be pre-specified beforehand, it is particularly easy to use the *booster* method, that is to oversample the sparsely populated geographic areas of interest. Thus, the 1952 Michigan survey of the American electorate doubled the rate of sampling in the American West (Campbell, Gurin, and Miller 1954), the 1974 Essex survey of Britain boosted its Scottish sample fivefold (W. L. Miller 1981a) and surveys within Wales frequently double the rate of sampling in the sparsely populated but culturally significant north and west. Notable examples of a fully regional survey design include the Kilbrandon Commission's survey on devolution, which consisted of a dozen regional samples of comparable size (*Commission on the Constitution*, 1973) and Kovenock's study of attitudes and voting in different states of the USA (Kovenock, Prothro *et al.* 1973). Geographic boosters are a modest step towards a factorial survey design in which the object is to achieve equal numbers of respondents in each analytically relevant subgroup of the sample. Boosting the sample in certain areas is, of course, very different from mounting separate surveys in different areas, because the data collected remain the same throughout the entire sample. The survey aims to compare the scores of different areas on the same variables or model parameters, that is to examine *quantitative* differences. Hence British surveys usually exclude Northern Ireland from their samples, rather than boosting the number of Irish respondents, just because Irish politics are considered more than quantitatively different from mainland politics (Butler and Stokes 1974: 14).

Completely separate surveys in limited geographic areas have been justified for a variety of reasons, some of them mutually contradictory. Universal principles can be studied anywhere: the principle of the lever does not require reassessment in every physics laboratory on the globe. Then there is the case-study philosophy—let us discover a possible general principle in one locality and let others check it out in a handful of other places. In contrast, a particular locality can be studied because it is specially interesting, and hence by definition unrepresentative of other localities.

Its peculiarities may be interesting in themselves, or because they make it a critical case which, although unrepresentative of other localities, deviates from them in a known and extreme way. Sometimes there has been no other justification that 'needs must'—it may be cheaper to do a local survey.

Work by the Leeds centre for media research (Trenaman and McQuail 1961; Blumler and McQuail 1968) falls into the universal category, while the pioneering surveys by Lazarsfeld and Berelson in America and the Greenwich and Bristol teams in Britain fall somewhere between the universal, the case study, and the cheap (Lazarsfeld, Berelson and Gaudet 1944; Berelson, Lazarsfeld and McPhee 1954; Benney, Gray and Pear 1956; Milne and Mackenzie 1954 and 1958). Surveys in Scotland, Wales, and Ireland simply cover localities which are interesting in themselves (W. L. Miller 1981a; R. Rose 1971). Other local studies like those in Glossop, Cardigan, and Glasgow seem intended to produce findings applicable to areas wider, but perhaps not a great deal wider than the areas surveyed. Glossop represented 'small towns', Cardigan represented 'rural Wales', while parts of Glasgow did duty for Scotland as a whole (Birch et al. 1959; Madgwick 1973; Budge and Urwin 1966). Similarly the Community Relations Commission has sponsored surveys in a handful of constituencies which were taken to represent areas of high immigrant concentration (Anwar and Kohler 1975; Anwar 1980).

McKenzie and Silver (1968) organised one survey in six urban centres in England, and another in English marginal constituencies, in part to reduce the range of variation in variables that were irrelevant to their analytic concerns.

Goldthorpe et al. (1968, 1969) provide an outstanding example of a critical case study. They wished to attack a theory which predicted political change by so-called 'affluent workers' in areas dominated by certain types of new industry. So they chose an area which had all the characteristics required by the theory and organised a survey to show that the predicted changes were not occurring.

Paradoxically however, single community studies often cannot be used to show the political effects of the locality, because our theories do not entail the presence or absence of effects: they are instead about the size and power of various influences. To evaluate such theories, a multicommunity study is required. Kovenock's voting-in-the-states study is one example. Another outstanding example is Butler and Stokes's investigation of the influence of the local class milieu. They took over 120,000 respondents who had been interviewed in a succession of NOP monthly opinion polls and divided them into 184 separate constituency samples. Then they were able to test whether similar people in different communities were politically different, to quantify that difference, and relate the differences in individual behaviour to measurable aspects of the constituency environment (Butler and Stokes 1974: 134–5).

At the other extreme, the scope of a survey may be widened to include respondents in several national states. There are, for example, regular surveys of the EEC as a whole, the Eurobarometer surveys, but the classic example of a cross-national political survey spread its sample much more widely—through Germany, Italy, Britain, the USA, and Mexico (Almond and Verba 1963) with a later follow-up study in Austria, India, Japan, the Netherlands, Nigeria, the USA, and Yugoslavia (Verba, Nie, and Kim, 1978). Obviously there is a severe problem of question correspondence in such widely differing localities but, as the Kilbrandon survey found with questions about devolution, the short distance between Edinburgh and Norwich is sufficient to raise that problem.

The focus of surveys can also be varied in non-geographic ways. The population scope of the norm was the electorate (SN2). Selecting respondents from a restricted subset of localities is, of course, particularly easy, but other subsets of the population can also be sampled without enormous cost. One simple method has been to change the make-up of the quota interviewer's quota—for example, requiring only young people, only women, only working class, only Roman Catholics, or whatever. Another method is to use the very large number of short interviews conducted by the commercial polling agencies, like Gallup and NOP, as a recruiting base for a special survey. Harrop et al. (1980) cumulated 43,537 interviews from six months of regular NOP surveys. Of these, 270 had told NOP that they intended to vote for the extreme right-wing National Front. Without any further interviewing, Harrop et al. analysed these National Front supporters in terms of the standard social background variables asked in all NOP surveys. Nordlinger (1967) cumulated six NOP surveys to give about 11,000 respondents, from whom he selected a sample of roughly 500 urban working class males who were all party loyalists in the sense of intending to vote again for the same party they had voted for in the past. Moreover he adjusted his selection technique to ensure that although all the sample were working class urban males, two-thirds were Conservative partisans. Then he used the British Market Research Bureau (BMRB) to reinterview this subsample of NOP respondents in an attempt to discover the motivation behind working class support for the Conservative Party.

Captive, or at least well-documented subgroups have been easy targets for political surveys, despite forming small fractions of the population. Schoolchildren provide a base for studies of political socialisation (see

Himmelweit and Bond 1974; Himmelweit *et al.* 1981; Hess and Torney 1967; or Jennings and Niemi 1968), and there have been political studies of the intelligentsia using students, school teachers, and university teachers. Political élites of all kinds have been sampled, using official sources as a means of sample selection. Delegates to political conferences or conventions have been approached directly when they gathered for the congress. Thus surveys have covered relatively low level political activists (Benny *et al.* 1956; Birch 1959; Budge *et al.* 1972; Eldersveld 1964; McClosky *et al.* 1960; Denver and Bochel 1973); British Members of Parliament and American Congressmen (Kavanagh 1970; W. E. Miller and Stokes 1966; Searing 1978); civil servants (Putnam 1973; Halsey and Crewe 1969); and the military (Stouffer *et al.* 1949; Janowitz 1960).

Sometimes survey investigators have dropped much pretence to random sampling in order to contact sufficient numbers of respondents in elusive subgroups. Parkin (1968) contacted Campaign for Nuclear Disarmament activists as they walked along in the annual Aldermaston protest march. Community Relations Commission interviewers contacted members of ethnic minorities by selecting ethnic-looking names or faces (Anwar and Kohler 1975). Goldthorpe *et al.* (1968) selected 'affluent workers' by choosing 'critical case' firms in a 'critical case' locality and taking male employees in shop-floor jobs, aged under 46, married and cohabiting with their wives, living in the locality, earning relatively high wages, and working in selected departments of three factories—in short, a very tightly defined sample, as different from a random sample of the full national electorate as any coterie of cabinet ministers, somewhat inadequately described by such a general term as 'affluent worker'. A particularly bad choice of sample has been made by the use of coupons published in the press. This generates huge samples subject to enormous unquantifiable biases caused by newspaper readership patterns and by self-selection. To my knowledge this has been used at least four times in Scots devolution polls—by the *Express* and the *Record* in 1932 before the *Literary Digest* debacle and by the *Scotsman* in 1969 and the *Record* in 1976. On the last two occasions the press used academics to comment on and analyse the results, but by then the faults of the method were so well known that it should never have been repeated, with or without academic apologists.

The time focus has also varied (SN3). Some surveys, like that by Goldthorpe *et al.* have been done at non-election times by chance. Others, like McKenzie and Silver's have expressly avoided election times in the hope of detecting a truer, deeper expression of political attitudes. Surveys have also been keyed to political events other than parliamentary and presidential elections—off-year Congressional elections in the USA, or the EEC and

Scotland Act referendums in Britain. Keying a survey to the annual Easter march of protest to Aldermaston (Parkin 1968) or an American nominating convention (McClosky *et al.* 1960) has determined not only the personal and geographic focus of the survey but its time focus also.

3.2 *Variations in size and sampling (SN4–SN5)*

My survey norm had a sample size of 2,000 (SN4) and the respondents were selected by a multi-stage stratified sample, clustered at the final stage, using random selection at all stages except the final stage, and either random or quota selection at the final stage (SN5).

As I indicated earlier, a size of 2,000 might be reasonable for estimating overall partisanship in the total electorate, but really is insufficient for more refined analyses. Regrettably, academic surveys whose research objectives require samples larger than 2,000 have often been constrained by their budgets to make do with fewer than 2,000. Prior to Butler and Stokes, most academic surveys in Britain followed Lazarsfeld's 1944 American example and used samples of between 500 and 1,000. I have done the same myself. The practice is totally indefensible—except on the grounds that anything is better than nothing, and no more funds are available.

With samples so small, statisticians are wasting their time inventing significance tests and confidence intervals for us to use. We know from the start that anything other than the known and the obvious is likely to be statistically insignificant, and I cannot applaud the one team of British academics who preserved their statistical purity by announcing the statistical insignificance of their findings as a conclusion.

British academics have never been able to obtain sufficiently large funds or find sufficiently cheap methods to mount their own political surveys with large samples. However, they have made increasing use of cumulated media poll data to get access to large samples even if they had to be second-hand samples. Bonham (1954) cumulated a sequence of Gallup surveys that totalled over 18,000 respondents so that he could look at finely divided strata within the middle class. Butler and Stokes (1974) cumulated NOP surveys to provide a sample of over 120,000 respondents so that they could look at finely drawn geographical divisions. Harrop *et al.* (1980) cumulated NOP polls to give a sample of over 43,000 so that they could look at a very small political group—supporters of the extreme right-wing National Front. Rose cumulated Gallup polls in the weeks before each general election since 1964 to get samples of over 10,000 each time, so that he could apply the Automatic Interaction Detector (AID) technique, a system of analysis that requires large data sets (R. Rose 1980a). Dunleavy

(1979, 1980a, 1980b) did the same as Rose, in his case in order to apply complex interactive methods of log-linear analysis, which also require large data sets.

Governments by contrast sometimes use gigantic samples, not primarily to permit subtle analyses, but in order to make very precise estimates of small but politically sensitive quantities like the unemployment or inflation rate. The German government, for example, has used regular samples of over 600,000 for this purpose. Quite properly they call it a 'micro-census'. But unless we can find radically cheaper ways of doing surveys, only those with bottomless purses will enjoy the luxury of deciding what sampling error they can tolerate, and letting that determine the sample size.

I discussed some variations in sample design when I defined the survey norm because both random and quota methods have been very widely used, though increasing awareness of the need to do polls *quickly* has led to increasing use of quota methods. In 1970 a majority of British polls still used random selection for such important and visible work as forecasting the election result. By 1974 only a third were using random selection, and by 1979 they had all switched to quota samples.

Other important variations in sample design include panel and relational designs, which are described in section 4 of this chapter. But one important set of variations is not discussed elsewhere and has not yet been fully applied to political research. These are the methods of *multi-phase* and *replicated* or *interpenetrating* samples, and their logical extension into *sequential* sampling. New technology for political polling has increased the relevance of these methods.

The basic idea of an interpenetrating sample design is that instead of drawing a single sample of a certain size (2,000 say), we draw a set of several smaller samples—say ten samples of 200 respondents each. The method is equivalent to subdividing the original sample of 2,000, but subdividing it in a very special way: namely, in such a way that each subsample of 200 has the same structural design as the original 2,000, except for smaller size. Thus if the original sample was a random sample of the whole nation, each of the ten subsamples must be chosen to be a random sample of the whole nation—they must not, for example, be geographic subdivisions of the original, nor must they be carried out by different personnel.

Statisticians like interpenetrating samples because they provide one of the best, empirical ways of determining sampling errors. By comparing the ten separate estimates of the percentage of Democrat supporters, each based on a random sample of 200 respondents, statisticians can easily calculate not only the best estimate (which is simply the average of the ten separate estimates) but also the likely range of inaccuracy associated with that estimate (basing their calculation on the observed variation between the ten separate estimates derived by idential procedures).

But interpenetrating samples have other virtues. There may be some variables that are very important to our theories, or which need to be measured very accurately. In that case we include the appropriate questions in *all* of the subsamples. Other variables may be less important, or may require only rough quantification. Questions on these topics need only be put to *one* of the subsamples.

There are two variants of this technique. Using a *multi-phase* design, the full sample is interviewed once, answering only the most important questions. Then we return to one of the subsamples with a list of supplementary questions, perhaps derived in part from ideas that arose during the initial analysis of the full sample. However, if we knew in advance all the questions we wished to ask, then we could use a *split-sample* design, putting some of the supplementary questions to one subsample, some to other subsamples. The advantage of multi-phase and split-sample techniques is that they shorten the interview, since no respondent is asked the complete set of questions. Alternatively, for a given length of interview, split-sample methods allow more questions to be asked. Butler and Stokes (1974) used this method, dividing their sample into two randomly split halves.

New techniques of telephone interviewing allow us to transform this approach into *sequential sampling*. All the interviewing is done by a team of interviewers working from a central location. Because they are all together in the same room, and because they make contact with respondents electronically, the interviews can be done in any sequence. There is no need to do all the St. Louis interviews at the same time, no need even to assign them all to the same interviewer, since no travel is involved. Consequently the sample can be arranged into a random sequence. Let me give a concrete example. For my telephone survey of the Hillhead by-election (W. L. Miller 1982) I began with a stratified random sample of 1000 households. This consisted of a pack of 1,000 cards, each with an address and phone number on it. Then I shuffled the pack (computerised random selection would be easier and better). I now had a *random stream* or *random sequence* of 1,000 addresses which had several useful properties.

By dealing out cards to my interviewers off the top of the pack, I could be sure that any differences between interviewers in, for example, refusal rates were caused by the interviewer and not by the set of interviews assigned to her, since each interviewer had a random subset of the sample to interview. Continuous monitoring soon brought deviant interviewers into line. Secondly, I was able to issue cards from the top of the pack until I had enough interviews to guarantee sufficiently small sampling errors on important variables, or until my interviewing budget ran out. Irrespective of when I stopped issuing cards, my sample of interviews would still be a random sample. Thirdly, I could treat successive hundreds (say) of cards as interpenetrating samples, or as split-samples. So questioning about some unimportant variables could be discontinued after the first one hundred interviews, allowing the interviewers to get on faster thereafter and increase the overall sample size. Fourthly, I could treat the first hundred interviews as a pilot study to test particular questions, then put revised versions of these questions to the remainder of the sample. Naturally I should report percentages based only on use of the revised question. Both my pilot study and my remaining sample would automatically be random samples. Piloting would have reduced my effective sample size by one hundred on the questions that were changed, but it would produce no distortion or bias in the remaining sample.

Sequential samples can thus be very powerful tools for political research. They have been used for a long time for industrial quality control where mass production lines produce random streams of perfect and defective items. But until the advent of centralised interviewing factories based on telephone contacts, sequential samples were impractical for political or attitudinal research.

3.3 *Variations in data collection procedures (SN6–SN8)*

The standard life-setting for surveys was defined as a one-to-one interview in the respondent's home (SN6); but this too has varied. Convention delegates have been interviewed at conventions, MPs at Westminster, ordinary electors at polling stations, sometimes using a 'repeat ballot' format with an imitation ballot box in which to deposit secretly recorded responses to a printed questionnaire. (On one occasion when I used this technique in a British parliamentary election, the Official Returning Officer protested that my ballot forms were turning up in his ballot boxes—on such a small scale, it is to be hoped, that neither my poll nor his election was unduly affected.) These settings may be atypical of the usual life-pattern of the respondent yet typical of his political life-pattern, since for many electors their political lives may be discontinuous, with only a shadow of existence for most of the time.

Goldthorpe *et al.* used two different interview situations which reflected their belief in the importance of work-place and family. They interviewed respondents first of all at work, then at home in the (actively encouraged) presence of respondents' wives. This procedure is sometimes taken a step further and the interview with a single respondent replaced by a 'group discussion' between a dozen or so respondents assembled together. Group discussions unfortunately involve an unnatural physical environment and tend to produce data that are not easily quantified. In Britain they have been used more by the political parties than political scientists. They are a good technique for stimulating the investigators' thoughts and prompting ideas that can then be researched more extensively and quantitatively in a normal survey.

When Gallup first introduced sample surveys to Britain, using a format which roughly conformed to my survey norm, Mass Observation put forward a coherent range of alternative methods. Mass Observation recruited a large panel of volunteer interviewers who provided five sorts of data: first, replies to standard survey type questions; second, reports on loose casual conversational style interviews; third, reports on relevant remarks overheard in the street, the bus, the pub, or elsewhere; fourth, direct observations on relevant behaviour; fifth, relevant autobiographical statements. Overall, a quasi-anthropological approach, similar to the methods used in Jahoda, Lazarsfeld, and Zeisel's haunting study of unemployment in Marienthal (1933). These methods provided a wealth of anecdotal material which could be used to illustrate and interpret statistical findings. Mass Observation was criticised more for its sloppy application of these methods, rather than for the methods themselves. Without rigid control there is a danger of the anecdotes obscuring the backbone of research findings, rather than putting flesh on the bones and bringing the animal to life. Overheard, chance remarks often prove shallow and uninformative, for all the realism of the life-situation in which they occur. (Mass Observation 1938; Firth 1939; Harrison 1978; see also the critique in Abrams 1951.)

Even within the standard life-setting of the home, various procedures for eliciting information have been used. Interviews have been in person, by post, or by telephone. They have ranged from requests for yes/no answers to a couple of questions right up to thirty-hour probing conversations (with an occasional break for sleep). Though telephone interviewing has so far been largely confined to the USA, where special conditions have made it peculiarly appropriate, postal questionnaires are a standard means of approaching élites (Kavanagh 1970) and have also been used in mass electorate surveys. Levine and Robinson (1976) used a postal survey for an early academic study of New Zealand political attitudes. Teams at Essex and Strathclyde did postal surveys of the British and Scottish electorates at the times of the referendums on the EEC and the Scotland Act (Särlvik et al. 1976). However, in both referendum studies they were recontacting by post, respondents who had already been interviewed in person. The self-selection element involved in response to mail questionnaires produced a strong middle class bias in the New Zealand survey.

Depth interviews with an emphasis on probing, free format replies, and even free progression from topic to topic are frequently used as a preliminary stage in helping to design a questionnaire (R. Rose 1971) and more occasionally as a follow-up device to help interpret the statistical patterns revealed by the main survey (McKenzie and Silver 1968). The method was taken to an extreme by Brewster-Smith *et al.* (1956), who interviewed respondents for thirty hours each about their outlook on Russia. Not surprisingly, they interviewed only ten people.

The data measurements have also varied. While the norm (SN8) is undoubtedly a free choice from a fixed range of pre-set answers to a pre-set question, other data measures have also been widely used. Interviewers have been asked to *rate* the respondent's sex, race, age, and socio-economic status. Respondents have been *tested* or used in experiments both within and outside the context of the interview. Thus the IQ ratings and school reports of children involved in political surveys have been added to the data provided by their answers to questions (Himmelweit and Bond 1974). Rowntree did not trust the poor to tell him their earnings. So for his second study of York he used his contacts with fellow employers to get payroll information on 60 per cent of his sample, and estimated the income of the remainder from a knowledge of their occupations and standard rates of pay for those jobs.

Respondents have been asked to mark the positions of parties on graphical representations of ideological or semantic differential scales. They have been asked to give parties and personalities 'marks out of ten', or mark the warmth of their feelings towards reference objects (the police, the BBC, the Queen, etc.) on 'feeling thermometers' (Butler and Stokes 1974, Chapters 15 and 16; see also Lodge 1981 or Doorn *et al.* 1983 for improved methods of 'magnitude scaling'). They have been shown pictures of politicians and asked to name the person and his party (W. L. Miller *et al.* 1981). They have been told stories without endings and asked to imagine suitable story-endings. Frequently they are asked to rank a number of objects in some way, or rate the pairwise similarity of various objects. For example, they have been presented with the names of twelve countries and asked to rate each pair out of the twelve on a scale of similarity. From this scant information it has proved possible to investigate the dimensions of world ideology (Kruskal and Wish 1979).

Respondents, like interviewers, have been asked to *inform* rather than express. They have been asked about their spouses, their parents, their workmates, their friends, and their neighbours. Congressmen have been asked about their constituents, and constituents about their Congressmen (W. E. Miller and Stokes 1966). However, there is considerable ambiguity about the meaning of such report-type data. Obviously it can be treated as perceptions or assertions, that is as attributes of the respondent himself. But there is fairly strong evidence that it cannot be regarded as objective factual information about the persons reported upon. Direct questioning of both husband and wife or both parent and child shows that report-type information is often highly inaccurate and biased. Indeed, repeated interviewing of the same respondents has shown that they are incapable even of accurately reporting their own political attitudes and behaviour in anything but the present tense. Since we know that they systematically misreport their own political behaviour at the election before last, and they systematically misreport the current political attitudes of their nuclear family, we must doubly query the status of answers to questions on the partisanship of long dead parents in the family home during the respondent's long past adolescence. Information type questions always tell us something about the informant, but should seldom be taken as objective truth about the informee.

3.4 Variations in data structure: panels, contexts, relationships (SN9)

The norm is atomistic: most questions in most surveys ask the respondents to tell us something about themselves—not least because their reports about other people tend to be inaccurate. And they also focus on the present, because respondents' memories are so unreliable. That produces an atomistic data structure: each person is divided off from the rest of the data set, divided off even from his or her own previous life history.

But even without relying on fallible memories and inaccurate reports, other less atomistic data structures are possible. Repeated interviews with the same set of respondents produce *panels* which set the individual in the context of his or her own development. Objective measures or even perceptions of the immediate spatial, social and political environment set the respondent in contemporary *contexts* and permit analyses of interpersonal *relationships*.

Incorporating a time dimension into a survey may mean no more than repeating the survey at intervals in order to establish time trends. The best known example of this is the monthly Gallup Poll which has, for decades, charted the electorate's voting intentions, the popularity of political leaders, and the salience of different political issues. A massive literature has accumulated which uses statistical time series methods to relate such monthly poll data to monthly war casualties or monthly economic statistics published by government agencies (early examples are Mueller 1970; Goodhart and Bhansali 1970; W. L. Miller and Mackie 1973; recent examples include Alt 1979). But often these series appear to respond to discrete, contingent political events such as the 1978–79 'winter of discontent', during which the British Prime Minister's popularity fell by 21 per cent in only three months. The timing of such short sharp changes can help to identify the causes of change (W. L. Miller 1981a: 248–9; Crewe 1981a: 265).

Another way of incorporating time is to reinterview the same panel of respondents in a sequence of surveys. This is called a *multi-wave panel*, and the term *wave* is used to denote one round of interviews. A panel can be used to estimate trends which are relatively free from the corrupting influence of sampling error. If, for example, one sample showed 52 per cent support for the government and another, a month later, shows only 48 per cent, we cannot be sure that any real change has occurred: samples are always more or less inaccurate reflections of the population sampled and even on purely statistical sampling grounds there is more than a one-in-twenty chance of two samples of size 2,000 differing by over 4 per cent. Since there are more sources of variation and error than those included in statistical calculations of sampling error, even a decline from 52 per cent to 42 per cent might not be entirely convincing evidence of a trend when the figures were based on different samples of respondents. But a panel shows *real* change—at least amongst its own respondents. A panel which showed 52 per cent government support one month and only 48 per cent the next could do so only because at least 4 per cent of its members changed their individual attitudes from support to opposition. In a more typical case we should find perhaps 10 per cent of individuals swinging away from the government and 6 per cent simultaneously swinging towards it. And these groups of swinging electors would not be statistical constructs, mere percentages. They would consist of identifiable individuals. The change would be real.

Not quite as real as it appears, however. While the change *within the panel* would be real, it would also be true that *within other panels* of respondents the changes might, on sampling grounds alone, be somewhat different. The two waves of the panel could be regarded as a sample of a population that includes constants, swingers towards, and swingers against the government. And like any sample, it would be more or less inaccurate. Sampling error would therefore not be entirely eliminated, but luckily the sampling error of the difference between the two small percentages of swingers (pro and anti) in the one sample is smaller than the sampling error of the difference between the two larger percentages representing government support in two separate samples. Hence using a panel survey to chart trends greatly reduces, even if it does not entirely eliminate, sampling error. Panel surveys have been used for three main purposes in political studies. First, as a means of estimating trends more accurately (Worcester 1980). Second, as a means of revealing volatility distinct from net change: revealing, that is, the extent to which there are cross-currents of change. (Butler and Stokes 1974: 281–2; Converse 1964). Third, as an aid to causal analysis. Since panels allow us to identify individuals who are changing, we can look to see what it is that distinguishes the changers from the constant. When individuals have, initially, several politically contradictory attributes, we can look at the way they resolve those contradictions. Do left-wing readers of the right-wing press change their political attitudes, their paper, both, or neither (W. L. Miller et al. 1982)?

Panels vary in the number of waves and the length of time between them. The earliest academic surveys of American presidential elections used a multi-wave panel of up to seven waves spread over the short period of the election campaign and, with fewer waves, this was the model for British academic surveys from 1950 to 1964 (see Chapters 7 and 8 below). Since 1964 it has been less popular with academics, but has found favour with the media. Regular campaign panels have been done for publication in the press or on television, or merely as an aid to improved election prediction, by NOP, ORC, Harris, and MORI, among others.

Analysts at Michigan University, later followed by Butler and Stokes in Britain, made extensive use of inter-election panels with one wave of interviews at each successive election (A. Campbell et al. 1966). Campaign panels could reveal political change only in so far as change took place within the short campaign period; they could not reveal the full change that occurred between one election and the next. Butler and Stokes maintained a long-term panel over the seven year period 1963–70, incorporating inter-election panels for 1964–1966 and 1966–1970. Similarly the Conservative Party's Research Department ran an eight-year panel between 1966 and 1974. But the only very long-term British political panel of which I am aware is Himmelweit and Bond's 1951–70 panel of London school children, which they used to study political socialisation.

A panel approach solves some difficulties but creates others. Panels appear to raise the political participation of panel members, though they have less severe effects on partisan bias (Särlvik et al. 1976; Butler and Kavanagh 1980: 269; MORI 1979). Conversely, over a period of time they suffer *panel mortality* as panel members literally die, move away, or refuse to continue to give interviews. For example, in MORI's 1979 campaign panel for the *Sunday Times*, 1,087 respondents were interviewed in the first week in April 1979. Only a month later, the panel was down to 883, that is only 81 per cent of its original size. Similarly, Butler and Stokes' original panel of 1,982 respondents in 1963 was down to only 718, that is only 36 per cent of the original panel, by 1970. Himmelweit and Bond also lost almost two-thirds of their original sample and ended up with only 246 respondents. Needless to say, the surviving panel members tend to be the less mobile, the more interested, the more informed, and the more middle class. Only death itself reduces the panel with biasing it with respect to the electorate. Panels also fail to take account of new entrants to the electorate, though they can, of course, be supplemented from time to time to bring them back into line with the current electorate. After a time, it may be wise to drop respondents who have been in the panel so long that their responses have been influenced by repeated questioning. A panel with regular expulsions and new entrants is called a *rolling panel*.

Another important category of measurement used in surveys, though not necessarily obtained from the interviews themselves, is *contextual*: measures which tell us something about the environment, the milieu, the conditions, restrictions, and opportunities that surround the respondent. Examples are the voter registration requirements in American states, or the pattern of party competition in the area (W. E. Miller 1956), or the social mix in the area (W. L. Miller 1978). Such variables can be critically important for a proper interpretation of the interview results. No matter how inclined an elector may be towards voting Liberal, he cannot do so without a Liberal candidate in his constituency. Similarly, though less obviously, the absence of working class neighbours greatly reduces an elector's probability of voting Labour, whatever his own personal class.

Introducing *relationships* between respondents produces just as radical a transformation of the survey norm as introducing a time dimension. At its simplest, this may involve nothing more than parallel surveys at different levels, and straight comparisons between them. Thus the political attitudes of children have been compared with those of their parents and teachers, and the political attitudes of party supporters in the mass electorate have been compared with those of the party activists, local councillors, parliamentary candidates, and MPs. Though this may provide interesting enough substantive results, methodologically it is as disappointing an under-utilisation of the relational technique as the use of panel surveys merely to improve trend estimates. The analysis is particularly disappointing when it consists of no more than aggregate comparisons of, for example, the percentages of Labour MPs and Labour voters who support some policy like nationalisation or high levels of public expenditure. Indeed, that sort of comparison can be taken from parallel but unconnected surveys: it is a comparison between simple surveys rather than a more complex survey design (R. Rose 1974a: 283–90).

However, on some occasions the respondents have been connected more closely. Miller and Stokes asked Congressmen for their perceptions of political attitudes in their own constituencies. They also questioned the constituents themselves. Thus Miller and Stokes were able to quantify the accuracy of the Congressmen's perceptions, and relate Congressmen's votes in Congress to their perceptions of constituency feeling and to the reality of constituency feeling.

Similarly, when children, parents, and teachers have been interviewed, or when husband and wife have been interviewed, they have sometimes been asked about each other as well as about themselves; and they have been compared not as aggregates, but each with the corresponding member of his own family. Such a design permits an analysis of interpersonal perceptions and interpersonal transmission of political attitudes. Certain attitudes, like generalised attachment to one party or another may be fairly well-perceived and well-transmitted, while more subtle attitudes like cynicism, or more specific attitudes relating to particular issues of the moment, may be both badly perceived and poorly transmitted (Jennings and Niemi 1968).

Although more usual, it is not strictly necessary for the respondents to be categorised into different groups or levels—élites and masses, or parents and children. Political surveys have on occasion used a *socio-metric* design in which all the respondents are at the same level and relationships may run in either or both directions between any pair of respondents. Fitton (1973) interviewed everyone residing in a particular neighbourhood, asking each person to name his or her friends in the area. Naturally there were cases where *A* named *B* and *B* named *A*, but others when *C* named *D*, yet *D* did not name *C*. This sort of socio-metric linkage was used to examine the influence of one person's partisanship on that of his friends. Socio-metric linkages can also be used to form socio-metric maps on which cliques or clusters of respondents may be revealed or the relative centrality of different individuals assessed (Budge *et al.* 1972). These are particularly interesting ways of analysing élites—a town council, a legislature, a party leadership.

If *saturation* sampling (interviewing everyone in a neighbourhood or in a legislature) is not possible, then it can perhaps be approximated with a *dense* sample using a high sampling proportion (Searing 1978). Saturation samples or dense samples are more like censuses than surveys, at least in their selection procedures. Another possibility is *snowball* sampling, which

Coleman *et al.* (1957) used to study the diffusion of medical ideas among doctors: each doctor interviewed was asked to name those other doctors whom he met frequently; then they were interviewed in turn. Though this method seems appropriate for a number of political inquiries, I am unaware of its being used in any political survey. (See also Coleman 1959.)

3.5 *Variations in analytic strategies*

The enormous quantity, variety, and complexity of survey data have been reflected in a wide variety of analytical techniques with associated computer packages to implement them. It would require another full-length book to specify even the more popular techniques in any detail. Instead of that, I intend to discuss just half a dozen ways in which broad analytic strategies may differ.

First, we may focus attention on *variables* or on *cases*. We may wish to say something about variables such as 'class', or 'voting', or 'social trust'. Most survey analyses do focus on variables. But as an alternative we may wish to state conclusions about people, or about places, that is about the *cases* in the data set. If our ultimate concern is about variables, then people and places serve only to provide us with data on the variation and covariation in levels of class, or wealth, or trust, or whatever. But if our ultimate concern lies with the people or the places, then variables become just a useful aid towards grouping or classifying the cases. Case-oriented analyses include routines for grouping cases into 'cliques' or 'clusters', displaying the 'network' of relationships between cases, or quantifying the 'diffusion' capability of the network. Thus, for example, members of the Parliamentary Labour Party (the MPs) can be subdivided into cliques with high levels of within-clique discussion and communication, or high levels of within-clique ideological similarity. Again, we could display the network of communications between MPs and identify certain individuals as central to the flow of communication and influence, while others would be revealed as more isolated and peripheral.

Such network and clustering analyses have not been widely used on samples of the mass electorate. Partly this is for the technical reason that the amount of computation involved tends to rise exponentially with the number of cases; so such methods are most appropriate to small data sets. But in addition, networks and clusters are interesting mainly when we recognise the people or places as individually significant. It may be intriguing to discover a discussion clique within the Parliamentary Labour Party, but it is much less interesting to locate a clique of nonentities in a mass sample. Moreover, the low density of sampling in mass surveys of large populations usually means that individuals can be clustered only in terms of their similarities, rather than in terms of their inter-communications.

The other broad category of analytical strategies focuses on concepts and variables instead of cases. Particular strategies differ according to the causal structure we assume between the observed variables. In the simplest analyses we assume *no causal structure*; in the set of methods known as 'causal modelling' we assume an *overt causal structure*, directly linking the observed variables; with another set of techniques known as 'dimensional analysis' we assume a *covert causal structure* in which the observed variables jointly depend upon some hidden causes and do not directly influence each other.

Thus the object of the simplest forms of analysis is merely to measure a level or describe a distribution: for example, the level of racial prejudice, the popularity of the government, or the inequality of income. While it is very easy to set these goals, it can be exceedingly difficult to achieve them. Marginal distributions are highly susceptible to sampling error, to question wording, and to the temporal context. It is far easier to quantify the relationship between social class and political partisanship than to quantify what fraction of society is working class. Instability can be reduced by combining several variables together, to form a multi-indicator scale of social class, or a multi-indicator scale of racial prejudice, but levels remain far harder to quantify than relationships.

In 'causal models' we postulate a pattern of cause and effect linking a number of observed variables. Then we observe how much a dependent variable changes in response to changes in its assumed causes. Ideally such analysis should be dynamic, based upon a panel survey spanning a period during which the postulated causal variables actually do change. But very often, lack of such data forces us to substitute a cross-sectional, statistical regression analysis for a dynamic, cross-temporal one. In certain limited circumstances a cross-sectional analysis will prove an adequate substitute, but more often it will not. Generally we should be extremely sceptical of an author whose tables are based on data collected at one point in time but whose text uses such language as 'trend', 'change', 'implications for the future', 'new', or the like. The more affluent may vote more heavily for the Conservatives: that does *not* imply that increasing affluence will generate increasing votes for the Conservative Party. Cross-sectional data form a poor basis for dynamic conclusions.

What is worse, we need at least a sequence of repeated surveys (if not a true panel) before we can even make very firm statements about cross-sectional differences. A difference between British and German political culture *in 1959* is not the same as a difference between British and

German political culture (without a temporal qualification). Yet if our only data source is a set of surveys taken in 1959, we may find it very difficult to avoid the claim that our data show inherent national differences.

In constructing a multivariate causal model, we often start by observing a *correlation* between one dependent variable and one presumed cause. Then we check for *spuriousness*: is the correlation merely the result of both variables' joint dependence upon some other observed variable—do the respondent's class and partisanship merely reflect the social circumstances of his upbringing? Then we can search for *antecedent* variables (which cause the cause without directly causing the effect) and *intervening* variables (which interpret or explain the original causal link). For example, to an initial model which postulated respondent's class as a cause of his partisanship, we might add an antecedent cause—parental class causing respondent's own class, and an intervening variable which would depend upon his class but then, in turn, influence his partisanship—his attitude to council-house rent levels, perhaps.

The class variable could be replaced by a set of *component* variables—occupation, income, education, house tenure, and class consciousness, for example. We could look for *conjoint* influences that simultaneously influenced partisanship (e.g. region, or religion); we could test for *interactive* or *conditional* relationships between these various conjoint influences on partisanship—does class have a greater influence in the more traditional North of England and a smaller effect in the more modern South? Or does religion structure political behaviour in the middle class, but not in the working class?

In this way we can quickly build up a multivariate pattern of causal influence. But it is very sensitive to assumptions about the direction of causal influence, and there are no very convincing methods of statistically testing these *directional* assumptions. Techniques for analysing simultaneous two-way causal influences, or determining the direction of influence, do exist but they work better in theory than in practice. Often they require more difficult or more unlikely assumptions about the data than the assumption of causal direction itself. So the statistical cure is worse than the disease.

If, but only if, we have made the correct assumptions about causal directions, multiple regression analysis can be used to quantify the relative weight or power of the various influences in the causal model. If the dependent variable itself has multiple aspects—like partisanship in a multi-party system—'canonical' regression analysis may be useful. A canonical analysis of socio-political alignments, for example, will automatically determine which aspect of partisanship is most predictable from social variables. In British politics the most predictable aspect of partisanship might be the Labour vote (contrasted with all other choices), or it might be the choice between Labour and Conservative, or the choice between Conservative and non-Conservative voting. Multi-party systems cannot always be reduced to a single ideological dimension for analytical convenience: in Scotland, the SNP is a centre party between Labour and Conservative in social class terms, but Labour is the centre party between the SNP and the Conservatives in Scottish nationalist terms. W. L. Miller (1981b) outlines a number of regression techniques specially suited to the analysis of multiple partisanship.

Analysis may involve only a *single level* of data: it may be restricted to individual level characteristics, or to collective or aggregate level characteristics (such as parliamentary constituency data). Alternatively it may combine both kinds of data in a *multi-level* analysis, treating the collective and aggregate data as measures of the environment or milieu which surrounds the individual (W. L. Miller 1978).

Finally there is a very important distinction between *gross* and *net* effects in causal models, that is between analyses aimed at scientific generalisations and analyses aimed at historical explanations. The difference is a simple one, but easily overlooked. Suppose there are roughly equal numbers of ideological liberals and ideological conservatives in a society. Then if party choice polarised strongly along ideological lines, ideology could contribute a great deal to the structure of political choice; it could predict the behaviour of individuals very well, yet none the less have no net effect on the electoral outcome, because equal numbers of liberals and conservatives would be driven in opposite partisan directions. By contrast, suppose that two-thirds of the electorate prefer the personal image of one presidential candidate, while only one-third prefer the other. Then even if candidate attraction has only a very weak influence on the structuring of party choice, even if it does *not* predict the behaviour of individuals very well, it may still have a significant *net* effect on the electoral outcome, because what little effect it does have is heavily biased towards the party with the more popular candidate.

Paradoxically the variables that best predict individual choice may not be the variables that best explain the election victory (W. E. Miller and Shanks 1982). If our aim is scientific generalisation, we should focus on explaining the gross structure of political choice. If it is historical description, we should modify the structural analysis by taking account of the bias in the distributions of the causal influences as well as their ability to determine political choice.

Dimensional analyses—'factor analysis', 'smallest space analysis', 'multi-dimensional scaling'—in all their many variants are based on the assumption of a covert causal structure. Thus attitudes on a hundred different political issues might simply reflect a respondent's position on a single underlying ideological dimension; just as a respondent's scores in a hundred different IQ tests might simply reflect his or her general intelligence. These are extreme possibilities. More realistically, a multitude of attitudes might reflect his or her position on a *few* (not just one) underlying dimensions—a left/right dimension and a metropolitan/decentralist dimension in politics, for example (see Inglehart and Sidjanski 1976). Similarly a respondent's IQ scores might reflect both verbal and mathematical dimensions to intelligence.

Usually when we seek to uncover underlying dimensions, we seek only a very few powerfully predictive dimensions—half a dozen at most, two or even one if possible. Thus Verba, Nie, and Kim (1971, 1978) set out to show that despite a wide variety of specific possibilities for acts of political participation, people could be adequately described by their positions on a mere four or five dimensions of political activity—voting, electoral campaigning, community activity, personal interest lobbying, and protest activities.

Such an information reduction, from a myriad of specific measures to a few underlying dimensions, may be an end in itself: it helps us understand what is going on, it reduces the analyst's (and the readers') 'information overload'. There is less to talk about; so it is easier to understand what is being said. But dimensional analysis is also very important as a first step in causal modelling. By replacing many specific variables with a few more general scales or dimensions, the number of elements in the causal model can be greatly reduced and its structure greatly simplified, yet without a great loss in explanatory power. The stability of parameter estimates will be improved and the model will become much easier to describe and communicate.

PART II
ARGUMENTS FOR AND AGAINST SURVEYS

Part II sets out both the claims made by survey researchers for their method and the counter arguments of their critics. Chapter 4 describes the principles and ambitions of the behaviouralists, and the growing acceptability of behaviouralist ideas and Survey Methods.

Both critics and proponents of surveys are agreed that the Survey Method was one of the main engines of the 'behavioural revolution'—for good or ill. Surveys were not the only tools of the behaviouralists, but they were probably the most powerful. Chapter 5 looks at the Survey Method's contribution to the wider behaviouralist movement and judges survey practice by the standards of behavioural principle.

Truth and falsehood, knowledge and ignorance characterise the scientific criteria for evaluating survey research. But surveys can also be judged on a moral dimension: what contribution do they make to democracy? Surveys have been praised or attacked for giving the people more control over their rulers. They have been attacked, and less openly praised, for giving governments more control over the people. Chapter 6 considers both these arguments. It also looks at attempts by pressure groups to misrepresent citizens to their government and, more insidiously, to misrepresent citizens to themselves.

4   The behavioural revolution

The growth of survey research in political science has been closely bound up with what was known in America as the 'behavioural revolution'. The phrase itself is misleading, but it is the conventional term for a set of changes in method and orientation which were hardly revolutionary in their timing nor, in the case of political surveys, specially focused on behaviour (see Eulau 1963, 1969; Barbrook 1975).

4.1 *Principles, ambitions, and faults of behaviouralism*

Writing at the turn of the century, Graham Wallas argued that

> the efficacy of political science, its power of forecasting the results of political causes, is likely to increase . . . [because] modern psychology offers us a conception of human nature much truer though more complex than that which is associated with the traditional English political philosophy . . . [and] under the influence and example of the natural sciences, political thinkers are already beginning to use . . . quantitative rather than merely qualitative words and methods, and are able therefore both to state their problems more fully and to answer them with a greater approximation to accuracy. [Wallas 1908.]

Half a century later, Michigan University survey analysts restated their faith in Wallas's dream when they declared: 'Deep-seated *laws* of social behaviour we presume to exist and with proper phrasing they should not only outlast reversals of voting patterns but should predict them' (A. Campbell *et al.* 1960: 37). They also followed Wallas in seeking to express such laws in psychological terms. However, my quotation from Wallas has three elements, all of which were essential features of the behavioural movement in politics. There was the goal of predictive laws similar to those of the natural sciences; there was the strategy of seeking psychological explanations; and by no means least there was what Ions calls 'a preoccupation with questions of method which at times has seemed almost a neurosis' (Ions 1977: 149)—specifically an emphasis on quantification.

Sometimes behaviouralist ambitions were stated in a less extreme form: the aim was merely to produce systematic explanations by empirical methods, and to strive towards as much generality in the conclusions as might be possible. Thus in another part of *The American Voter* the Michigan team declared that while their 'primary aim . . . is to understand the voting decisions of the national electorate in a manner that transcends some of the specific elements of historical circumstance . . . much of this volume serves a descriptive as well as a theoretical purpose' (A. Campbell *et al.* 1960: 8).

Even a modest, purely descriptive, historical objective could have important implications. In a celebrated *Public Opinion Quarterly* article Lazarsfeld reviewed some of the findings of wartime surveys into military morale. He listed a set of apparently obvious findings and then continued, 'every one of these statements is the direct opposite of what was actually found. Since every kind of human reaction is conceivable it is of great importance to know which reactions actually occur most frequently and under what conditions: only then will a more advanced social science develop' (Lazarsfeld 1949: 380). Most survey analysts must have had similar experiences of shattered preconceptions. It was 'no longer sufficient for a theory or explanation to be persuasive, elegant, aesthetic, interesting or brilliant: it must be valid' (McClosky 1969: 9). It had to be scientifically convincing, in the sense that the research report should reveal the structure of the research design and the strength of the findings. As a discipline, political science required procedures for discovering and correcting its own errors by checking theories against new data and being prepared to abandon the theory when faced with conflicting evidence.

This behavioural approach went with a change of subject matter. Wallas had complained that 'nearly all students of politics analyse institutions and avoid the analysis of man'. Behaviouralism implied a shift of focus away from legal and structural descriptions of institutions, away from purely narrative history, and away from normative and prescriptive essays—not because any of these were unimportant, but because they were not all-important. Instead of law and structure, behaviouralists stressed group, personality, ideology, recruitment, socialisation, stratification, mobility, élites and masses. But they did not confine themselves in any way to behaviour: the typical political survey contained very few questions about behaviour, and far more about attitude, opinion, and ideology. Nor did they restrict themselves to the analysis of people.

Indeed, the change in subject matter was a major feature of behaviouralism—but not its essence. In the words of the critic, Edmund Ions: 'Behavioural science is now a house of many mansions, characterised by its methods more than by its subject matter'. Traditional methods of political inquiry included philosophic reflection on moral concerns, reading documents, perhaps going out into the field to make personal but unsystematic observations, collecting anecdotes, giving attention to individual phenomena and unique events, and bringing it all together with an individual and subjective interpretation. The behaviouralists, on the other hand, emphasised the search for regularities, systematic observations and comparisons, objective measurements, and even in theoretical work they emphasised brutally clear and precise definition. Techniques included laboratory experiments, mathematical models, computer simulations, content analysis, and statistical analysis of aggregate data like census tabulations and official voting returns; but it was the use of sample surveys which marked the greatest break with traditional methods, and specifically surveys of *mass* attitudes and behaviour (Butler 1958: 103). Many features of mass behaviour were simply not perceptible by older methods.

This approach was not without its critics, and by 1969 David Easton could claim that American political science had entered a 'post-behavioural' phase (Easton 1969), characterised by the view that substance must precede technique: whereas the behaviouralists had felt it better to be wrong than vague, the post-behaviouralists felt it better to be vague than irrelevant. Behaviouralists, in this view, had lost touch with reality in their search for abstractions and generalisations. Their urge to cut themselves off from intuition and personal experience, to view the world through the medium of data sets collected by others, and to derive theories from data processing instead of human inspiration was fundamentally wrong: 'when we quantify, then process and interpret the human act . . . the result is depersonalisation' (Ions 1977, see his introduction and chapter 2 especially).

4.2 *Growth of government surveys*

Though British government developed a strong interest in statistics during the nineteenth century, it was slow to adopt what I have defined as the survey norm. Like most other social investigators in Britain, it stuck to ennumerative, census-type methods long after the statisticians had developed the ideas and formulae for random sampling. Eventually, in 1923 the government took three samples of the unemployed: a 1 in 3 sample in January, a 1 in 10 in October, and, very daringly, a 1 in 100 sample in November. (Bowley had recommended a mere 1 in 1,000 sample.) For the first sample, information was taken from record cards, but in the later samples each person selected was interviewed in the local Employment Exchanges by the manager. Refusal should not have been a problem! Comparison of the results from these three surveys convinced government departments that there was some truth in the statisticians' claims: relatively sparse samples could provide information almost as accurately as the census, and a good deal less expensively (Jones 1948, Chapter 7). Today we should probably regard a 1 in 10 or even a 1 in 100 sample as much more of a census than a survey, but at the time even those without access to government funds were still sampling by taking high proportions of small areas. In 1936, Rowntree sent interviewers to *every* working class household in York. Between 1929 and 1934, Liverpool University researchers visited every thirteenth house in Merseyside. Late in 1936, interviewers from the Pilgrim Trust visited a 1 in 25 sample of the unemployed in six towns, varying the sampling proportion inversely according to the size of the town—1 in 35 in Liverpool, 1 in 5 in Leicester, every unemployed man in Deptford (Pilgrim Trust 1938).

But after the triumph of small sample polls in the 1936 presidential election ideas were changing, and when the need for wartime information prompted the British government to set up the *Wartime Social Survey* it operated with a sample of between 2,500 and 3,000, sharply different from a census of any sort. The sample was national in scope, at least in the sense that it covered the whole of England and Wales (leaving the Scots and Northern Irish to make their own arrangements); and the sample design was a multi-stage, stratified random sample with clustering in rural areas. So the Wartime Social Survey conformed very closely to my survey norm (Jones 1948, Chapter 14). It researched topics like food supplies, cooking practices, clothing, housing, and health. For a while it also investigated civilian morale until it was denounced as a team of government spies and snoopers, 'Cooper's Snoopers' as they were called after Churchill's Minister of Information, Duff Cooper. And in a sense they were government spies, since they reported to the government and not to the people at large. Their data, unlike that of their American counterparts, were covered by the Official Secrets Act. After the war the Wartime Social Survey was renamed the Government Social Survey and ultimately became part of the Office of Population Censuses and Surveys. Until the mid-fifties it was in perpetual danger of being closed down for offending powerful politicians. Too close a link with one government would have provoked retaliation under the next. But it successfully avoided contentious political subjects and is now firmly established, producing an enormous output of *ad hoc* surveys in addition to continuous and regular surveys like the General Household Survey (GHS), the Family Expenditure Survey (FES), the Labour Force Survey (LFS), the National Food Survey (NFS), and the Workplace Industrial Relations Survey (WIRS). The NFS and FES began in the forties and fifties as single purpose surveys designed to monitor diet and prices. The GHS is a more recent development, started in the late sixties as a multi-purpose survey, a general carrier which provides a survey facility to a large number of government departments but does not have a single or fixed purpose. At about the same time, the FES was converted into a second multi-purpose survey facility (Hakim 1982b). Sample sizes are substantial. The GHS covered 30,000 individuals in 12,000 households during its first year, but it was still clearly a survey and not a mini-census.

4.3 Growth of media surveys

After a slow start, the British press has come to accept political surveys with enthusiasm, particularly in the years since Harold Macmillan's premiership. From 1937 onwards Gallup poll findings have been published regularly, first in the *News Chronicle* and later in the *Daily Telegraph*. At times they also appeared regularly in the *Scotsman*. Gallup's questions have become increasingly detailed over the years and it has maintained some very long-running series questions on political attitudes which provide valuable information on trends. By the late forties the *Daily Express* was organising its own in-house poll. Although it performed as well as any other poll at election forecasting, it collected relatively little information and the *Express* never accorded its findings much status. In 1969 the *Express* joined with American pollster Louis Harris and the (British) Opinion Research Centre to set up the Harris poll and discontinued its own. The *Express* later sold its shares in Harris, and since 1972 has published a variety of different polls.

Until the late fifties however, relatively few polls appeared in the British press. Gallup was published exclusively in the *News Chronicle* and the Express poll in the *Express*, but before 1959 the only other paper to carry a poll-based election forecast was the *Daily Graphic* (later renamed the *Daily Sketch*) which used Research Services (RSL) polls in 1951.

The proprietors of the *Daily Mail* set up National Opinion Polls (NOP) in 1957 and published regular findings in the *Daily Mail*. In 1965 the Conservative Central Office encouraged two of its former employees to set up Opinion Research Centre (ORC) which published regular monthly polls from 1967 to 1976 in various evening papers. Marplan, like Research Services, began as a subsidiary of an advertising agency. In 1968, it began political polling with quarterly polls for *The Times*. Finally, Market and Opinion Research International (MORI) began political polling in 1968 and although most of its early work was for private clients, it has published fairly regular monthly polls since 1977 in a variety of newspapers, starting with the *Daily Express*.

The growing number of commercial agencies publishing political polls reflected the media's ever-increasing interest. Most papers, eventually even the *Guardian* (but not *Daily Mirror*) commissioned their own polls and in 1970 they abandoned the convention of exclusive publication, reprinting and commenting on each other's polls in addition to their own. One index of press interest is the number of final election forecasts commissioned by the national press. There was only one in 1945, and two in 1950 and 1955; three in 1951 and 1959, four in 1964 and 1966, five in 1970 and six in February and October 1974, dropping back to five in 1979. However, partly because the 1979 campaign extended over the Easter period and also because media polls did not confine themselves to final forecasts, there were more polls published during the 1979 campaign than ever before. In Scotland, the *Scotsman* and *Glasgow Herald* have commissioned special Scots election-forecasting polls since 1974 and the *Express* since 1979. Scots media have published at least one Scottish poll per month since the middle of 1974 and frequently more than one a month. Twenty Scots polls were published in the first four months of 1979 during the run up to the devolution referendum and the general election. A particularly impressive series of polls by ORC investigated attitudes towards Scots devolution and independence throughout the years of the devolution debate. They were published in the *Scotsman* (W. L. Miller 1981a). Since 1979 the *Scotsman* has published regular quarterly polls by MORI.

In 1970, for the first time, stories about opinion polls dominated British media coverage of a dull campaign: eight of the twenty-three issues of *The Times* in the month before election day headlined poll results as the main front page story. By an unlucky coincidence the polls' forecasts in 1970 were outstandingly bad, but that failed to discourage media interest in polling at subsequent elections. In 1979 poll stories appeared in the press almost daily throughout the campaign. Lead stories in the popular press included the usual mixture of sex, violence, and non-election news as well as election material. However, on election day the *Guardian*, *Telegraph*, *Express*, *Mail*, *Daily Star*, and *Financial Times* all led with a polling story, leaving only the *Sun* and the *Mirror* to lead with exhortations on how to vote. And in the last fortnight of the campaign, twenty-two of the sixty election-oriented lead stories in national daily and Sunday papers took opinion poll findings as their theme (Bilton and Himelfarb 1980: 254).

4.4 *Private surveys for politicians and parties*

Political surveys have also proved popular with British political parties, but, unlike the media, the parties' enthusiasm for polls has fluctuated up and down. In part, this is because an increasing quantity of survey findings in the media make private polls less necessary, but it also reflects the financial plight of the parties, and a certain amount of ideological opposition to surveys. There are those, in all parties, who feel that it is the function of politicians to give a lead, to *create* a political climate or a political fact. They object to polls which show lack of popular support for their policies. How can real political debate exist, they argue, if it is to be dominated by a technical approach to ascertaining what the electorate wants? It would be as wrong for politicians to degenerate into political scientists as for political scientists to degenerate into politicians. This view has long been associated with the left wing of the Labour Party, and as the left has gained influence, so support for party expenditure on political surveys has declined.

By the early sixties, it was reckoned that two-thirds of American senate candidates and most congressmen used private polls. Kennedy used Louis Harris as a private pollster during his 1958 senatorial campaign and did so again in the 1960 presidential primaries and in the presidential campaign itself. Later presidential hopefuls used political polling even more intensively than Kennedy. But in Britain candidates, even party leaders, are far less significant than parties. There has been little incentive for private polls to aid the *candidates* in British elections: they stand or fall with their party.

For a long time neither British party showed any interest in political polling, other than the occasional attack upon it as a corrupt practice. The Conservatives discredited all sorts of market research techniques in the eyes of Labour activists when they hired the advertising firm of Coleman, Prentis and Varley to mount advertising campaigns in 1950 and 1951. However, the Conservatives themselves did not adopt Survey Methods. Though its advertising firms were interested in market research, the Conservative Party itself was interested only in advertising.

Defeat, or the prospect of defeat, made both parties more anxious to discover what was going on inside the minds of the voters, and made the party rank and file accept the need to compromise with the electorate if elections were to be won. Labour was the first to use surveys. With the support of their new leader, Gaitskell, backed by a couple of highly placed party advisers with survey research backgrounds, the party commissioned two small surveys in 1956 and 1957. It had suffered two defeats and three adverse swings in successive general elections. However, by 1958 the Conservative government had suffered a number of serious by-election reverses and, while the left-winger Bevan vetoed any more Labour party polls, the Conservative party conducted its first survey study at the Rochdale by-election. The Conservatives continued with a very small market research budget in 1958 and 1959.

Labour suffered yet another general election defeat and a further adverse swing in 1959. This, coupled with a number of personnel changes, cleared the way for Labour's first major exercise in survey research which began in 1962 with an RSL survey of 1,250 electors in marginal seats, and continued in 1963 and 1964 with postal surveys to several panels of respondents.

After its 1964 victory however, Labour paid less attention to surveys and it was not until the end of 1968, following numerous by-election defeats, that the party showed renewed interest. After a false start with the American, Conrad Jameson, it went to MORI (run by another American, Bob Worcester) in the spring of 1970. MORI had time for only two polls before the election in June (Teer and Spence 1973; Worcester 1980).

The Conservative party used NOP for a series of surveys during the 1959–64 parliament, including a post-mortem in Orpington where it lost the by-election to a Liberal, and a national 10,000 respondent survey of potential defectors. After general election defeats in 1964 and 1966, they began a more substantial survey programme which included a 4,500 respondent panel, 700 of whom were reinterviewed every seven months by British Market Research Bureau (BMRB). In addition, Thomson and Taylor, who had both worked at Conservative Central Office and in NOP, were encouraged to found ORC, which carried out medium- and short-term surveys for the party. Throughout the 1966 to 1970 parliament the Conservatives reportedly spent £30,000 per annum on survey research and the BMRB panel, begun at this time, was maintained right through until 1974. Private polls are credited with reconciling the party to comprehensive schooling but persuading the party to take the offensive on the issue of selling council houses.

For two years after its 1970 defeat, Labour did no polling. Then it hired MORI to undertake a large-scale panel study begun in 1973 and supplemented by a number of one-off polls, including one in Scotland on devolution. ORC continued its work for Conservatives. Thus, February 1974 was the first election when both parties used what Worcester calls 'extensive multivariate analysis of large-scale panel data' plus daily 'tracking polls' during the campaign and various ad hoc surveys. Labour had not won an overall majority in February and both parties anticipated another election within a few months. Starting in June 1974, Labour had MORI carry out a series of fortnightly 2,000-respondent tracking polls plus two 1,000-respondent surveys in Scotland, where seven Scottish Nationalists had been elected in February; and there was another recall of the 1973 panel. According to Butler and Kavanagh, Labour and the Conservatives probably spent about £30,000 each on their private polls between June and November of 1974 (Butler and Kavanagh 1975).

Labour discontinued polling after 1974, though Wilson privately funded some MORI work on the EEC referendum. However, in 1978 Labour once again turned to MORI and spent £87,000 on MORI polls during 1978 and 1979. Thanks, however, to massive inflation, that represented a cut-back compared to 1974. Hence though MORI ran a 1,000-respondent panel interviewed in April 1978, August 1978, and again in January 1979, there were only ten 'quickie' polls during the 1979 campaign, as against seventeen in October 1974. The Conservatives were more consistent in sponsoring polls. They scarcely cut their polling budget in 1975, and wound up their long-running BMRB panel mainly for technical reasons. In 1979 they spent more on polls than Labour and tied them very closely into their advertising strategy. In the campaign itself they mounted four 'state of battle' surveys restricted to England and Wales, supplemented by six 'quickie' surveys, plus special surveys on Liberal chances in two types of English constituency, and special surveys in three types of Scottish constituency (Butler and Kavanagh 1980, Chapter 13).

Minor parties have always been so short of funds that they have been totally unable to match Conservative or Labour polling exercises, though they have sporadically commissioned surveys. Private pressure groups and government agencies have much larger purses. It has become almost standard practice for Royal Commissions to fund surveys, and pressure groups use surveys to inform themselves, influence decision makers, and influence the general public. A notable early example was the 1964 NOP survey of 3,600 respondents for Aims of Industry, which focused on the issue of nationalisation. Abortion law reformers, pro-Europeans and anti-devolutionists are among other groups which have made recent use of private surveys. Quite apart from circulation or audience surveys, the media themselves have used political polls for essentially private purposes. Independent Television News has used surveys to inform its new reporters and interpreters, as well as to provide material for direct broadcasting. In 1979 ITN used its own ORC political surveys as a basis for determining the content and presentation of non-survey material. For example, the ORC survey determined which five issues were of most concern to the electorate, and ITN's political correspondent then examined each party's treatment of those issues in some detail.

Despite all the continuing expressions of scepticism—often well justified —the use of polls and surveys is now accepted as natural. Indeed, we now feel dangerously exposed and uninformed if we do not have access to surveys, preferably surveys we have designed and commissioned ourselves. Government, politicians, the media, pressure groups all very evidently feel that way. So should academics.

4.5 *The growth of behaviouralism in the universities*

Despite fierce criticisms, the behavioural approach prospered in America to such an extent that Bernard Crick could title his attack on it: *The American Science of Politics* (Crick 1959). At the end of the sixties Richard Jensen calculated that 'since world war two the space filled by behavioural articles in the *American Political Science Review* has rocketed from 16 per cent to 59 per cent' (Jensen 1969: 226).

Yet as late as 1962 David Butler could write 'I know of no British student of politics who would describe himself as a political behaviour specialist' (Butler 1962: 209). As Butler noted: 'the structure of British academic life (up to the sixties at least) has not produced the men or the money to develop behavioural research on a larger scale, nor have British students of politics been impelled in this direction by the incursions of those in neighbouring disciplines'. The British contribution to political science, he said, had been philosophical, descriptive, historical, and reflective. It lacked all scientific rigour and depended upon the perceptiveness and judgement of the writer. The distinctive British contribution to political studies was the Nuffield series, studies of electioneering rather than electoral responses, whose founder, R. B. McCallum, expressed strong opposition to attempts at probing the secrets of the elector's mind. Writing in the 1955 volume of *Parliamentary Affairs* he said: 'I would hope that success (in probing voters' motivations) will not be achieved. In the long run there is the secrecy of the ballot, the pencilled cross in the secluded polling booth, the great eleusian mystery of the democratic state. It must be respected as an article of faith' (McCallum 1955: 509). The world would be better off without a knowledge of voters' motivations as, perhaps, it might be better off without a knowledge of nuclear weaponry.

While Butler was denying the existence of any British behaviouralists, he himself was collaborating with Donald Stokes to prepare a large-scale application of Survey Methods to British politics. None the less, over a decade later, Richard Rose could still introduce his 1974 edition of *Politics in England Today* with the claim that 'the bulk of writings about English politics since the second world war have concentrated upon describing the formal institutions of government. Studies end without generalisation: description is valued as a thing in itself. Many (British) students of politics have argued against the possibility or desirability of generalising about the premises of political action' (R. Rose 1974a: 19).

Crick denounced the *American Science of Politics* as more American than scientific: the 'presuppositions outweighed the propositions' and 'the great concern of (the American) Lasswell to reduce politics to a series of statistical techniques' degenerated into 'mere fact-gathering, shapelessness or triviality'. Over-technical and lacking relevance, 'too many books by (American) political scientists are now addressed neither to problems nor to public'. Crick's attack on Americans reflected the greater success of behaviouralism in America, but he could equally well have attacked the nineteenth century Englishman Booth as the twentieth century American Lasswell. Booth after all had been determined to reduce poverty to a 'numerical relation'.

Butler also denounced books 'containing meticulously compiled tables which reveal nothing useful and which stand as monuments to the author's industry or even to his intellectual ingenuity but not to his common sense' (Butler 1958: 71–2).

Yet even some of the most severe critics of behaviouralism had to admit to a sneaking respect for *electoral* surveys. Quoting American examples and ignoring a variety of British electoral surveys, Crick admitted that they had produced 'some well-grounded, if hardly surprising, generalisations' and he had to content himself with the grumble that 'however worthy and fascinating such studies, the vote is, after all, but a small part of the political process. There is a very real danger that the importance of voting can be exaggerated at the expense of the more important problems of party responsibility, influence and internal structure' (Crick 1959: 230-1). Similarly, a few pages after denouncing books which testified to their authors' industry rather than common sense, and after declaring that it was more important to study government rather than the governed, Butler described sample surveys as 'the most notable technical break-through in the study of politics in this century' (Butler 1958: 103).

In Britain, the war produced a great advance in the application of Survey Methods, through the founding of the Wartime Social Survey. But because of the secretive and centralised nature of British government, this encouraged survey work within the government machine but not outside it. Moreover, the government had taken over the British Broadcasting Company (renaming it while retaining the letters BBC). British broadcasting was a monopoly, controlled by an élite, and politically timid. The contrasts with America are very sharp. In the USA, the government's wartime morale surveys were handed over to independent academics, along with large foundation grants to provide funds for analysis. *The American Soldier*, a study by Stouffer *et al.*, appeared in 1949. British social scientists had neither the access nor the funds to do comparable work—even if they could have acquired the motivation and expertise.

The second point of contrast concerns radio broadcasting. Radio was a new and, it was thought, a powerful medium: the medium of Hitler's and

and Churchill's speeches, of Baldwin's successful appeal against the 1926 General Strike, and of Roosevelt's fireside chats. The early years of radio were potentially much more revolutionary and exciting than the subsequent switch from radio to television. American radio was commercial and competitive, which may not have improved its quality but certainly stimulated non-governmental research on its audience and radio's influence upon them. The BBC began using surveys in 1936 for standard audience-research purposes, but the BBC was too much part of the government machine to generate such wide-ranging studies of sensitive media topics as those carried out by Lazarsfeld's Office of Radio Research with the encouragement of the Columbia Broadcasting System (and funds from the Rockefeller Foundation).

Various American academics had organised political surveys in the twenties and thirties, but the first of major importance was a mere by-product of inquiries into the influence of radio on *all* forms of social activity—purchasing choices, leisure pursuits, response to public information campaigns and, almost incidentally, political attitudes and behaviour. Lazarsfeld, Berelson and Gaudet interviewed inhabitants of Erie County, Ohio during the run up to the 1940 presidential election. Their study, published in 1944 as *The People's Choice*, inspired many subsequent academic studies of election campaigns. The National Opinion Research Centre carried out a national survey in 1944. Berelson, Lazarsfeld and McPhee took their own work further with a 1948 survey of Elmira, New York. Michigan University began its long-running series of national election surveys with a pilot study in 1948 and a major investigation in 1952.

British academics were most influenced by the 1940 and 1948 studies by Lazarsfeld and Berelson. Half a dozen British academic surveys on the 1950 and 1951 elections produced three significant books—on politics in Greenwich, Glossop, and Bristol—as well as a number of journal articles. The Bristol team repeated their 1951 survey in 1955, but none of these early British surveys led to the establishment of a group or institution with a continuing commitment to political surveys, and the total quantity of academic survey work done in Britain during the fifties remained small, at a time when Michigan was developing its biennial national panel surveys.

A second burst of academic polling followed the 1959 election, including surveys in Newcastle-under-Lyme, London, and Glasgow, two more broadly scattered surveys of working class Tories, a survey on the influence of political television in Leeds, and another on the political reactions of the newly affluent working class in Luton. Most significant of all, Butler and Stokes began their work on a national inter-election panel survey. With appropriate modifications to British conditions, this panel replicated the format of Michigan panel surveys of the American electorate during the fifties. Altogether at least ten important books were based on British academic surveys done between 1959 and 1964. The Centre for Television Research at Leeds retained a continuing interest in media-oriented political surveys, and though Butler and Stokes did not establish any group with a permanent involvement in national election surveys, their work itself has inspired enough interest for others to continue their surveys until 1979, after which the British SSRC withdrew the financial support it had given since its foundation in 1965.

Academic journal articles on the 1950 and 1951 elections appeared primarily in the new *British Journal of Sociology*, partly because their content was more sociological than later British political survey work, and partly also because specifically political journals like *Political Studies* and the *British Journal of Political Science* had not yet been established.

Political Studies began in 1953. Though the very first editorial committed the journal to behaviouralism, the proportion of space given over to survey-based articles was small. It is particularly difficult to draw the line between survey and non-survey articles in early issues of *Political Studies*. Interviews with thirty-five ward secretaries in Manchester, or with sixty community leaders in Birkenhead, for example, produced interesting articles, but hardly constituted surveys in the strict sense of the term. Such studies were a long way from that large number of cases, randomly or quasi-randomly selected from a very much larger population, which is the essence of the Survey Method. Let me set a reasonable minimal requirement: I will count an article as survey-based if it reported an original survey, or presented an original re-analysis of a survey, but not if it merely made passing reference to some published poll. In addition I will require that the survey reported be based on at least one hundred respondents and the information presented be sufficiently rich as to require two tables *or* any more complex statistical technique for its analysis—regression or factor analysis, for example.

By that criterion, *Political Studies* never gave much space to survey reports. It published very few, kept them short, and often set them in specially small type. None the less survey articles have become more available or more acceptable to the journal's editors of late. Up to 1966 the average space allocation to survey articles in *Political Studies* was only 1 per cent; thereafter it averaged about 8 per cent.

From 1971 onwards the *British Journal of Political Science* provided a new outlet for behavioural work generally, and survey articles in particular. On average it has given 26 per cent of its space to articles based on surveys. This represents a considerable increase in British academic publication of survey-based articles in the seventies, compared to the fifties and sixties. But there is no indication of an increase in the availability or acceptability of survey-based journal articles during the seventies, merely a quantum jump at the start of the decade. It seems likely that the new British journal, *Electoral Studies*, which started publication in 1982, will produce another quantum jump in survey articles during the eighties.

Harrop (1980a) has analysed the content of two other journals—the *British Journal of Sociology* and the British Sociological Association's *Sociology*. Between 1968 and 1978, 24 per cent of their articles were based on surveys, but surveys of lamentably poor quality. Not one of them was based on a sample of the adult British population, and other samples were generally used for convenience rather than for good theoretical reasons. Almost a third of the survey reports were based on studies conducted outside Britain—which Harrop interpreted as due to British lack of interest and competence rather than as evidence of internationalism.

Behavioural principles have made some progress in Britain, though never so much as in America. And the spread of behavioural practice in Britain, especially in its universities, has lagged even further behind.

5 The scientific value of surveys

'Variability is the most constant feature of electoral behaviour' wrote Pomper in his survey-based review of a mere two decades of American voting (Pomper 1975: 186). Political studies 'cannot be, now or in the foreseeable future, a rigorous science. Its aim can only be to produce explanations of human conduct which, like all historical explanations, may account for particular phenomena at a particular time and place and which may perhaps be less exactly paralleled in other periods and countries' (Butler 1955: 98). 'Almost all discoveries about man's behaviour relate to a particular time and locality and cannot be made the basis of absolute or universal laws' (Butler 1958: 19).

The subject matter of political science is certainly far more variable and unpredictable than the subject matter of mechanics, or perhaps even psychology. Universally valid statements about political attitudes and behaviour might not be very interesting even if they could be formulated. But does that mean the study of politics cannot be a 'rigorous science'?

5.1 *Surveys have encouraged a scientific posture*

One of the common meanings of *science* is a body of generally applicable laws. But equally common, and more appropriate here, is the definition which focuses on the way in which knowledge is acquired, rather than on the content of the knowledge itself. Knowledge acquired by rigorous, quantified observation; propositions derived inductively from a study of observed data, or tested against it, can quite properly be termed scientific. The scope of the generalisations may be limited, but it would be absurd to require universal applicability before using the term 'science'. Where some of the extreme exponents of behaviouralism fell into error was in suggesting that universal political laws might be discoverable. The dichotomy presented by this is false. There are alternatives to ignorance on the one hand and universal laws on the other. When Ions claims: 'I have been unable to locate any important new idea or any new theorem or paradigm that throws fresh light on our condition. Least of all does one encounter findings that could be termed scientific, if by that we mean theories or theorems which have been firmly established and which may be applied to groups within society or generalised to society itself' (Ions 1977: 153–4), he is simply wrong. Recurrent political patterns do exist. Lazarsfeld and

Berelson's 1940 study of Erie County in Ohio is still relevant to British political behaviour in the nineteen eighties, precisely because important patterns of political behaviour have generalised widely across both space and time.

But it would be equally wrong to see the development of political science since the forties as a steady accumulation of universally valid, quantitatively expressed propositions. Instead we have seen a steadily deepening understanding of the influences at work on political behaviour and a steadily lengthening period of more accurately described political history. New developments in the future will come from both sources. The scientific aspect of political science should be viewed as a kit bag of tools —some more technical, others more theoretical—for observing and interpreting that future. Let us suppose that we wish to determine public attitudes on some political question: a new proposal to nationalise the banks, for example. On the basis of previous surveys we should be inclined to guess that the British electorate would be opposed to that policy, but we should not know that fact in the way that we know a certain design of bridge will carry a ten-ton lorry. The scientific contribution of old surveys in forecasting future attitudes may well be limited. However, on the basis of past surveys and past survey analysis, we know how to mount a survey to measure attitudes to the nationalisation of banking, we know that these should take some account of whether people care about the issue, and we know that even people who are strongly opposed to the policy may still vote for the party that proposes it. In short, we know how to collect relevant data and we know the sorts of models we need to fit to that data. We do not know in advance how well those models will, in fact, fit, nor what the values of their parameters will be.

Alternatives to a scientific approach based on a survey include watching the press for letters or, worse, editorials on bank-nationalisation; noting any violent demonstrations reported in the media; inferring nationalisation attitudes from election results; substituting the recorded views of elected representatives for those of their electorates; or retreating into pure guess-work and blind assertion. A glance at almost any history book dealing with the period up to the last war will show these alternative methods in application. It is a measure of the scientific success of surveys that we know just how misleading every one of these alternatives can be.

There is an important element of uniqueness about every political pattern, yet only an element. Political surveys cannot ever give final answers—any pattern may change, and most political patterns are, to a greater or lesser degree, in a state of flux. Yet it would be absurd to suggest that only final answers are answers, that changing patterns are unimportant or uninteresting, that science can study only an unchanging world, or that its rigour is determined by its subject matter rather than by its methodology.

Surveys exerted a major influence in encouraging the adoption of a scientific posture in political studies. While it is true that a 'handful of large scale voting studies have in three decades taught us more about the act of voting than was learned in all previous history' (McClosky 1967: 71), the influence of election surveys has extended beyond elections and beyond surveys. They have emphasised the value of quantification, the value of searching for such regularities and uniformities as may exist, the value of rigorous, empirical techniques, the value of well-defined concepts, well-specified relationships, and systematic observation. Surveys advertised and popularised these behaviouralist beliefs. Survey research stimulated the development of empirical theorising, analytical techniques, computer packages, and machine-readable data banks—the whole infrastructure for a scientific approach to politics.

More specifically, surveys have produced an unlimited quantity and richness of political data, an enormous volume of facts which are often interesting in themselves but are even more important as an environment in which theories can be generated and tested. Often perhaps, as the critics never tire of complaining, these facts may be obvious. Indeed the truth may be obvious; but the obvious is not always true. The complaint that findings are obvious frequently testifies to nothing more than a lack of imagination, or a failure to understand the significance of quantification. Speculation may or may not be true in fact; evidence helps us to decide whether it is convincing or not.

Some findings, however, are neither obvious nor even anticipated. Current British survey evidence for example, shows declining class polarisation at a time when constituency election results indicate steady or increasing class polarisation. Neither polarisation nor depolarisation can thus be 'obvious'.

5.2 *Surveys cover a broad range of specific topics*

Votes are an ideal unit of account, because they are relatively easy to quantify and compare across space and time; they represent political behaviour rather than belief or attitude; and they are the most significant political activity of the majority of citizens in liberal democracies. But even voting surveys are not limited to voting. They have been used to study political culture, the party system, the conditions of attitude change, the nature of group identity, the role of personality, the use and effects of the media, social-ecological structure, the significance of the family, the nature and impact of ideology, the interpretation of voting behaviour for the political system (e.g. mandate theory) and for the individuals within it (e.g. distinguishing instrumental from expressive motivations).

As an indication of the sheer quantity of information produced, *Voting*, by Berelson *et al.*, published in 1954, listed in an appendix 209 'propositions' arising from early academic political surveys. A decade later, Berelson and Steiner's *Inventory of Scientific Findings* (1964) ran to 712 pages, fifty of them devoted to politics. McClosky (1969) presents a masterly summary which emphasises the range of substantive findings in political surveys. Even a selection from his list is impressive. He grouped findings under nine headings—public opinion, participation, voting, *élites*. ideology, socialisation, psychology, institutions, and comparative. To demonstrate the sheer breadth and range of topics covered in political surveys, let alone other social science surveys, I cannot do better than quote a few of McClosky's examples.

Surveys of *public opinion* have looked at party preferences, candidate preferences, the popularity of presidents and prime ministers, and public attitudes on issues—including policy preferences, issue salience, knowledge of the issue, and perceptions of party policy. The first major, survey-based article in the British journal *Political Studies* was an analysis by Polsby (1960) of McCarthyism, based on a re-analysis of Gallup polls. Public opinion analyses of commercial and academic polls have been used to show that there is a variety of publics interested in different issues; that only a few electors could be described as ideologues with highly organised attitude systems; that attitudes on issues tend to be volatile, especially among the less informed, the less interested, and the less self-consciously partisan; that social categories tend to be only very loosely tied to opinion categories, especially if there is no direct logical link like that between Roman Catholicism and Catholic schooling; and that the causal direction between party support and opinion outlook is in doubt and probably varies from issue to issue and person to person. An outstanding piece of multi-level survey research by W. E. Miller and D. Stokes has shown how American congressmen perceive and respond to political attitudes in their constituencies and how their response varies between, for example, foreign and domestic issues.

Surveys on *political participation* have been used to study the influence on voting turnout of demography and life-style, a personal sense of political effectiveness, ideology, party affiliation, and attitudes towards American presidential candidates or British party leaders. There have been numerous special or comparative studies of all kinds of activists from party élites down to those who merely canvass for the party or who are active in non-party or anti-party ways like writing letters to the press or demonstrating in the street.

Surveys of *voting* have been used to interpret the election result by relating voting choice to issue attitudes. They have shown how far voting choices have been shaped by a sense of attachment or belonging to one or other party; and how far this sense of partisanship has, in turn, been shaped by interactions with family, friends, workmates, or peer-groups; by group membership and group identification; by social or geographic location; by social or geographic mobility; by age, sex, and generation. Two grand surprises which invalidated a great deal of pre-empirical theorising were the discovery that the media did *not* have the dominating influence so often attributed to them, and that those electors who determined the outcome of elections by changing their voting choice or switching to and from abstention, were *not* uncommitted, unpartisan, unbiased, rational judges of current party manifestos, but rather uncommitted, unpartisan, but (alas) ignorant, indifferent, and cross-pressured electors marginal to politics in its entirety as well as marginal between the parties. Survey-based analyses of voting patterns have also been used to classify elections as maintaining, deviating, reinstating, or realigning.

Surveys of *élites* have revealed their social origins, political participation, ideological sophistication; and in the case of political élites, their pattern of recruitment, their ideological differentiation, their attitudes towards the 'rules of the game', their tolerance of opposition, and responsiveness to mass opinion. Surveys have studied conference delegates, local councillors, MPs and Congressmen, lawyers, doctors, teachers, university staff, university students, military men, business élites, civil servants, negro élites, trades union élites and local élites. Though the format of élite surveys often differs from the standard formal questionnaire format used in the typical mass survey, élite groups have also proved willing to submit to the formal style of interview used in mass surveys. When élite studies fail to meet the minimum requirements of a sample survey, it is often because they include only a small number of respondents and a non-systematically selected subset of the particular élite population.

Surveys on *ideology* have shown how little constraint exists at times in mass attitudes: taking one side on a particular issue does not necessarily make respondents' views on other issues very predictable. Over time, surveys have documented trends in the level of ideology and issue constraint.

Surveys on *political socialisation* have charted the development of party affiliation as young adults mature; they have measured the influence of family, of peer groups, and of objective circumstances. Studies of *personal psychology* have used surveys to show the relationship between deep inner personality factors and political tolerance, authoritarianism, classic non-economic liberalism, American isolationism, membership of extreme political groups, and choice of political leaders.

Though surveys would be an inappropriate method for studying many aspects of political *systems and institutions*, they have been used to relate the structure of mass attitudes to aspects of the party system, including its fragmentation, stability, and coalition formation. Surveys have investigated the accuracy of the electoral register and the effect of electoral procedures on registration and turnout. Elite level surveys have been used to study the behaviour, as distinct from the legal formalities or the organisational structure, of institutions like parliaments, parties, trade unions, and the civil service. And multi-level surveys have been used to study the inter-relationships between mass attitudes and institutional responses.

Finally, in the decade since McClosky wrote, there has been a growing number of *comparative studies*: cross-national surveys comparing among other things political participation, political values, political culture, attitudes towards the EEC and attitudes towards protest and direct action in different nations; and cross-temporal studies looking at changing voting patterns, changing attitudes towards government, and political responses to changing economic and political circumstances.

Surveys have not merely contributed a mountain of facts on these topics. Surveys and the process of survey research have also contributed to the development of *theory*. Political theories come in two kinds: theories about what is, and about what should be—explanatory theories and normative or moral theories. When critics claim that surveys have contributed very little to political theory, they need to specify which kind of theory concerns them. We might reasonably expect data-gathering exercises like surveys to contribute more to explanatory theory than moral theory.

Surveys have been criticised as inherently amoral and conservative. It is said that they neglect the whole question of proper standards of knowledge, conduct, and behaviour by individuals and institutions; that they over-emphasise superficial description of the status quo and are irrelevant to questions of what the world should be like; that they are indeed value-free in recording the status quo without criticising it (Easton 1969).

In terms of explanatory theory, survey studies have been criticised for being insufficiently causal and excessively descriptive, amassing facts without increasing understanding; or for explaining trivial political phenomena. It is in this sense of theory that Fielder (1959) characterised statistical analyses of surveys as a triumph of an anti-theoretical drift in political studies. *Straight Flight*, based on a survey in Bristol was, he said, the worst offender: 'no idea contaminates the purity of its research'. Leiserson was only a little more generous when he attacked the 'quantitative analysis of miniscular problems of uncertain relevance to the sweeping institutional complexes of politics' (Leiserson 1958: 371). Surveys over-simplified political concepts and elevated technique at the expense of substance and theory.

Yet pure theory, even pure moral theory, in political science is a self-contradiction. In so far as theory is meant to apply to politics instead of remaining an exercise in mathematical reasoning or in intellectual gymnastics, its 'architecture is suspect and its exposition unconvincing' unless it is anchored in factual knowledge of the real world of politics. There is no logical opposition between fact-grubbing and political theorising. Verification is essential to explanatory theories, and moral theories need to be grounded in realistic postulates about political psychology and behaviour. If surveys sometimes encourage over-simplification of concepts for statistical analysis, they also expose the shallowness of theoretical discussions whose terms are figures of speech, rather than concepts imbued with deep meaning. Even when surveys are not used directly to test theories, the example set by surveys has encouraged greater precision in the definition of concepts. And (dare one say it) sophisticated fact-gathering tools like surveys have helped to relax one of the constraints that has for centuries tied political theorists to *moral* theorising for want of other outlets for their talents.

Inevitably, the richness of factual data gathered by surveys has produced a myriad of highly complex, detailed explanatory theories of middle range phenomena. The contribution to grand moral theories has been more diffuse, operating through the provision of a vast array of factual data and a deeper understanding of political psychology and political processes. But surveys have made significant contributions to grand moral theories. They are not, in my view, inherently conservative, if only because the aspects of the status quo that they reveal so often include a great deal of disaffection and desire for change.

Surveys have confronted democratic theory with democratic practice. From their beginnings in the forties, academic election surveys have been used to compare the realities of mass opinion and behaviour with theoretical pre-conditions for a well-functioning democracy, with the doctrine of the mandate to govern, with the liberal ideal of rational and independent electors. All of this has a direct and immediate bearing on important moral theories. The survey contribution is not purely explanatory and these topics are in no sense minutiae. Crick is simply wrong when he claims that voting and elections are 'but a small part of the political process'. A part, yes; a small part, no.

Elections and the Political Order (A. Campbell *et al.* 1966) was one outstanding attempt by survey analysts to interact with broad theory. Within the one volume, the Michigan team presented a theory of the 'normal vote' and an associated classification of elections, they extended their theory of party identification to France in order to explain the chronic instability of the party system there, they revealed the critical role of the least informed members of the electorate in deciding the alternation of governments, they questioned the postulates of Antony Downs' *Economic Theory of Democracy*, and they tested the behaviour of Congressmen against three theories of representation—constituency delegation, party delegation, and Burkean representation. Of these five important contributions, three were to explanatory theory, two to moral theory. All five were relevant to institutions, though the data were gathered in mass surveys: three focused on the party system, one on the electoral system, one on the interplay between the internal and external aspects of Congressional processes.

5.3 *Principles versus practice*

Yet this roll-call of topics studied by means of surveys would not convince the critics that surveys have, in fact, contributed much to our understanding of politics. 'Cautious empiricists,' says Ions, 'have come to be as wary of claims to prediction as they are of claims to uncover general laws' (Ions 1977: 33). They show a 'reluctance to cast final results in precise or even recognisable statements of probability and earlier claims to precision evaporate in the conclusions'. 'The appearance of mathematical rigour in the main body of the study obscures the blending of platitude with subjective presumption in the initial research design, not to mention the inconclusive or trivial nature of the conclusions at the end of the study' (Ions 1977: 33). In short, such critics would claim that there is a world of different between studying politics by means of surveys, and actually finding anything out. The kinder critics would claim that surveys have produced a 'bulging inventory of facts with no relation to comprehensive theory' (Kirkpatrick 1962), while the more severe would dispute the existence of a 'bulging inventory of facts'. Sometimes, even the exponents of survey analysis have apparently come close to this view. In Blumler's second survey-based book on the political influence of British television he wrote:

until 1964 *only one affirmative proposition* could be placed firmly in the category of research-supported generalisations about the political

> impact of British television. Television had helped to increase the store of political information available to voters at the general election of 1959; a phenomenon which was confirmed by the results of the 1964 survey. In a sense, the later enquiry *doubled* our stock of tenable propositions, for it showed that television had also helped to boost the popularity of the Liberal Party at the general election of 1964. [Blumler and McQuail 1968: 263.]

though he went on to note that the Liberals had also enjoyed campaign boosts of popularity before widespread television penetration. Similarly, shortly after the appearance of Berelson's *Voting* with its 209 listed propositions from British and American academic surveys, Butler could conclude that 'the main discouragement to such studies has been the paucity of results' (Butler 1955: 100).

Yet when we look at these criticisms in more detail, they fall short of a convincing dismissal of the Survey Method. Sometimes they confuse a negative finding with the lack of any finding at all. Thus, I have been somewhat unfair in my selected quotation from Blumler, since the outstanding and largely unexpected finding of early media studies was that so many of the apparently obvious propositions about the political influence of the media, which were widely believed before the survey studies, simply failed to fit the facts uncovered by surveys and had to be abandoned. Secondly, when the critics flesh out their grand denunciations, their criticism is often reduced to a list of detailed errors committed by incompetent, inexperienced, or under-financed survey researchers; and the detailed criticisms may even contain within themselves the seeds of their own amelioration. Christie's attack on Eysenck's survey study of the personality of communists in which a 'plausible conclusion turns out to be based upon errors of computation, uniquely biased samples which forbid any generalisations, scales with built-in biases which do not measure what they purport to measure, unexplained inconsistencies within the data, misinterpretations and contradictions of the relevant research of others and unjustifiable manipulations of the data'—is not a criticism of survey methodology, but of bad practice which future survey researchers would do well to avoid (Christie 1956).

Let me present some of the more frequently voiced objections-of-detail. I shall relate them to the sequence of features which I used to define the survey norm.

Scope and timing (SN1–SN3): As Harrop (1980a) stressed, surveys should be aimed to represent a population of some kind. The nature of the research may dictate what population is appropriate. It need not be the national electorate at election time, but all too often samples have been drawn which did not represent any well-defined population—convenience alone seemed to determine the sample. Sometimes the geographical scope (SN1) was wrong: local studies used samples that may well have been well-defined samples of their localities, yet the intellectual concern went far beyond the locality and the fit between intellectual objective and chosen sample was obscure. Lazarsfeld and Berelson's classic studies of Erie County and Elvira were criticised for this, and only the fall-back to claims of universal findings could give them adequate justification. Similarly, it is not enough to do a study of Glossop and title the book *Small-town Politics*. The study itself provides no grounds for believing that Glossop politics typify small-town politics.

Even within a properly defined geographic area, the wrong population may be sampled (SN2). *The Authoritarian Personality* by Adorno *et al.* suffered from a fault common to many research projects in psychology, in that it used samples of students and the mentally unbalanced rather than the general population (Adorno *et al.* 1950; see also Adorno 1969 for an apologia). The sample studied by Goldthorpe *et al.* for *The Affluent Worker* was intended as a critical case which admittedly forbade generalisation, but it was selected by such peculiar criteria that it would have been extremely difficult to draw any firm conclusions from it at all—even if the sample had been large enough to eliminate problems of sampling errors.

Time-scope errors (SN3) are the least obvious, but not the least dangerous. Since attitudes, opinions, perceptions, and even supposedly enduring values change, sometimes very rapidly, a sample taken at the wrong time misrepresents its population. And in politics the wrong time may be only a day or two away from the right time. Indeed, with conventional survey techniques, the minimum period necessary to carry out a survey may be longer than the difference between the wrong time and the right time. Let me give just a few examples of what is a very frequent failing. Party identification, that generalised feeling of attachment or belonging to a party is often treated in analyses as one influence on voting choice—and in American studies it is often the major influence. Now some academic surveys have consisted of a single wave of interviews taken after the election. Since the samples were random and the interviews so lengthy that it was necessary to fix convenient times for interviews, the interviewers had to call back at selected addresses for several weeks or even months until they had obtained sufficient interviews. No doubt the time lag was not too long to prevent respondents recalling their election voting choice accurately enough, but their sense of party identification was measured as of the time of the interview—memories would be far too unreliable for any other strategy. Consequently, when we come to analyse these data, using measures of party identification to predict and explain measures of voting choice, we are predicting *backwards* in time, which makes nonsense of the usual causal interpretations of such predictions. While media survey data are often criticised for containing prior attitudes but only voting intentions, rather than actual votes, academic surveys often contain good measures of actual voting behaviour, but all the motivational factors have been measured after the behaviour, and not before it.

Another example of a time fault concerns proper measurement, rather than problems of causal inference. Moser and Kalton quote, approvingly, a National Opinion Research Center survey of the immediate public reaction to President Kennedy's assassination (Moser and Kalton 1971: 135) which took only ten days. But public reactions to such traumatic events as Kennedy's assassination, or the unfolding events in the Watergate Affair, or (for Britain) the Argentinian invasion of the Falkland Islands can go through several different phases in the course of ten days. As Prime Minister Harold Wilson noted: 'a week is a long time in politics'. A measurement spread over ten days measures nothing at all in times of crisis; it is merely a hotchpotch of half a dozen different reactions on different days. It was their recognition of this problem during the Watergate Affair that spurred the American television networks to develop better technology for high-speed surveys.

A recurrent cause of time-scope errors is the media's motivation for commissioning surveys.. They tend to sponsor surveys on special issues when some recent event has made the issue unusually topical, and automatically made the time inappropriate for a proper evaluation of public attitudes. Academic freeriders then acquire the media poll data and compound the error. Examples include polls on mass attitudes to parties keyed to major party conferences; or polls on mass attitudes to immigrants just after a speech by Enoch Powell in the late sixties, or after Mrs Thatcher's famous 1978 television interview in which she referred to fears that Britain would be 'swamped' by immigrants.

Size and Sampling (SN4–SN5): Sampling has sometimes been shoddy. Samples of British ethnic minorities and of élites—both somewhat difficult to reach—have degenerated into attempts to interview whoever happened to be available. High rates of non-contact or refusal have raised more general questions about the adequacy of the samples actually interviewed in contrast to the samples of names originally selected.

But the most pervasive problem of all has been the rather dull but important problem of sample size—not just the size of sample interviewed, but the size of sample available at the point of analysis. This explains why Ions is right to complain about the lack of precision and quantification in findings. Campbell, Donnison and Potter (1952) were almost uniquely self-depreciatory when they concluded their report on a survey of 545 respondents in Droylesden with the statement that all their findings about social influences on voting choice were statistically insignificant. In his statistical appendix to the Market Research Society's investigation of the polls' disastrous forecasts in the 1970 election, Alan Stuart noted: 'the fact that must be faced is that the very quantity that everybody wants to know about, the change in the inter-party gap (between Conservative and Labour) is the most vulnerable to sampling error' with a sampling error approximately three times as large as the sampling error of a single party percentage in a single poll. But for most academic and analytic purposes, the situation Stuart highlighted as the worst is, in fact, the best. Almost the least complex academic analysis consists of a contrast between the party gap in one subsection of the electorate and the party gap in another. Each subsection of the electorate is represented by a subsection of the sample, and it would be very unusual to find that these subsections were exhaustive and of equal size. Thus the typical minimal analysis—a measure of class polarisation, for example—would require an estimate of the difference between the party gaps within two subsets of the sample, one subset comprising perhaps half the respondents, and the other perhaps only a quarter. And having made such an estimate of class polarisation, we should then want to compare it with estimates taken from surveys in other places or at other times to see whether class polarisation in Britain was increasing or decreasing, whether it was greater than or less than class polarisation in Europe, America, or the old dominions. With initial samples of say, 2,000 respondents, we should quickly find that even apparently large differences or trends in class polarisation would have to be rated statistically insignificant. Even if the difference between the Labour lead over the Conservatives in the middle and working classes narrowed by say 20 per cent over a sequence of surveys, the change would not be significant according to conventional significance tests: it would not provide conclusive evidence that any real change was occurring in the electorate.

Even this is a minimal example. Any moderately imaginative researchers will soon find themselves testing propositions which are based on very much smaller subsets of their original sample. Rokkan (1967) bases percentages on twenty respondents; Himmelweit and Bond (1974) contrast the characteristics of twenty-seven panel respondents moving to the

Conservatives with those of the ten moving to Labour; the study by A. Campbell *et al.* (1960) of agrarian political behaviour uses percentage breakdowns of as few as nine respondents (yes, the nine are broken down into further sub-categories!), while, Converse and Dupeux (1962) in their study of French electors split five respondents into five categories and percentaged them. The Luton study by Goldthorpe *et al.* was based on only 229 respondents to start with, and soon progressed to a constrast between the voting intentions of seven slum dwellers and ten 'other private' house dwellers; or between the voting intentions of the fifteen council tenants with extensive white-collar affiliations and the eighteen respondents who lived in middle class areas as well as enjoying extensive white-collar affiliations. One of the most interesting sections of Butler and Stokes' *Political Change in Britain* concerns the political effect of changing house. Moving house may involve a change of tenure, of social milieu, of neither or of both. Though their study began with 2,009 respondents interviewed, only 718 were interviewed throughout the 1963–1970 panel, of whom 610 remained in the same type of housing and the other 108 changed tenure in six different ways. Only about twenty switched from council tenancy to owner-occupation. If we wished to distinguish the political effects of tenure change *per se*, from the effect of a change of social milieu, we should need to further subdivide those twenty respondents. Butler and Stokes did not take their analysis so far, but they did contrast political trends amongst the approximately 200 respondents who remained as council tenants throughout the decade, with trends amongst the twenty or so who switched from council tenancy to owner-occupation. And this analysis is far from atypical: Butler and Stokes' treatment of party preferences amongst middle class non-conformists in the pre–1918 cohort is based on similarly small numbers of respondents.

Data Collection Procedures (SN6–SN9): Critics often suggest that survey information has been gathered in an unreal or irrelevant context (SN6). Ions quotes the example of soldiers who were interviewed in camp after the war about their reactions to combat stress. Again, we know private opinions are very different from social action. The difference has two components. First, opinion, attitude, perception, and belief do not translate automatically into action. There are plenty of electors who will attack the policies and personalities of a party and then vote for it; or who will approve of direct action without stirring themselves to take part in it; or who will disapprove of strikes for high wage claims but will take part in them. Second, politics is social: political behaviour is a social activity and, less obviously, political attitudes and opinions also have a social dimension.

Too often, it is claimed, surveys atomise their sample: respondent's views are sought in the quiet of their home and the isolation of the one-to-one interviewer–interviewee setting. The normal everyday habit of arriving at political views after reading the press, watching television, discussing matters with family, friends, workmates, and chance acquaintances is excluded by the standard survey interview format. Even the unit of analysis can be criticised. Instead of individuals, they should perhaps be groups, communities, inter-person interactions, or conversations. In a moderate version of this criticism, Goldthorpe *et al.* noted that media surveys 'tend to concentrate on individual characteristics such as age, sex, level of income and education—and fail to take into account the properties of social structures in which the individuals in question are located, for example those of work organisations and local communities'.

While true of some survey work, this is certainly not true of Goldthorpe *et al.*'s own study, nor of Butler and Stokes, nor of W. L. Miller (1977a, 1978), nor the classic studies by Lazarsfeld and Berelson. Indeed, academic surveys generally have shown considerable sensitivity to electors' reactions to their social and geographic context. We know that it is dangerous to view respondents as isolated, independent, political units just because so much survey work has been done on this theme. So it is frankly anachronistic that Ions should include such criticism in an otherwise well-informed book published as late as 1977. The error lies, I think, in confusing the unit of data collection with the unit of analysis. Data may well be obtained from individuals in isolation at the time of the data collection, but their views on the issues and content of the interview should have already been formed in a social context, and their responses may well be analysed in a social context, using measures of social and political milieux derived from perceptions reported during the interview, from parallel interviews, or from census and other official sources.

Next, critics attack the procedure of pre-set questions and answers. Answers are obtained, not volunteered. The interviewer determines the topic and it may be in some sense the wrong one. Surveys may take a picture of the electorate, but they certainly do not have a wide-angle lens: the view is narrow and the lens may be pointing at an unimportant part of the scene. However, survey analysts are well aware of this defect, and standard advice to those drawing up questionnaires is to take as broad a view of the subject as may be possible. Some surveys no doubt answer the intellectual questions they were intended to answer, perhaps even with the anticipated answer. But others do not. Lazarsfeld's 1940 election survey was intended to show the power of the media: instead it revealed the power of social networks. Not only the answer, but the topic itself was changed by the survey. Still, the danger of seeing only what surveys look for remains; and it is particularly acute when one researcher bases his or her work on a re-analysis of surveys done by other researchers interested in subtly different topics. Inappropriate questions bend and distort the analysis.

All manner of things may be wrong with the questions. There may be bias in their wording or their sequence; they may be too technical; fail to include all the options, or include too many suggested alternative answers; fail to sensitise respondents to the implications of various answers; trigger stereotype responses; or be too inclusive, bracketing heterogeneous stimuli together by, for example, soliciting attitudes towards 'trades unions' when respondents have different attitudes to different unions, or to different aspects of unions. Criticisms of this type apply to particular surveys or indeed to particular questions in particular surveys. However valid they may be in specific instances, they are no criticism of the method as such. (See Hoinville and Jowell 1977 for the practicalities of good survey technique.)

Some broader criticisms of survey questions are more fundamental. First the whole technique of asking respondents to choose from a pre-specified set of possible answers may at best restrict the respondents' freedom of thought and, at worst, prompt thoughts they would not other-wise have had at all; so that the survey analyst ends up analysing responses which are in essence the products of his or her own imagination. Second, no matter how attitudes on issues are solicited and measured, they may have no real significance. Converse in America, Butler and Stokes in Britain, have tried to show that on many, perhaps most, issues, opinion is highly volatile down at the level of individuals, even when it is stable in the aggregate. Moreover, Converse suggested that the pattern of opinion change on some issues could be simulated by a model in which the only change was random switching of opinion in the bulk of the electorate, coupled with total immobility of opinion among a small minority— perhaps a fifth of the electorate.

One solution to the problem of putting ideas into the heads of respondents is to use open-ended questions. A standard Michigan procedure was to open the interview with four questions asking simply what the respondents liked and disliked about the Democratic and Republican parties and their presidential candidates. The only prompting was a recurrent 'and what else?'. Respondents' unstructured responses were recorded in detail and later subjected to a variety of ingenious classifications and codings. Yet this is not a perfect solution. The attempt to study ideology and issues by analysis of answers to questions about party likes and dislikes has been criticised for imposing as much bias as a study of partisanship based on answers to questions about ideology. Open-ended questions are expensive to process, the categorisation of responses cannot be referred back to the respondent, nor to the reader of the final survey report, for their approval. A less extreme solution is to use open-ended questioning of a few respondents as a pilot stage when pre-set answers to closed-ended questions are being formulated. In addition, interviewers can be briefed to note down any spontaneous comments by respondents, or answers other than those on the pre-set list.

Converse's famous article on issue volatility has misled as much as it has informed (Converse 1964). It was not, in fact, his intention to claim that all issue change was random, still less that most electors' preferences on all issues were meaningless. His random change model was intended as a limiting case, and a warning against pushing issue analysis too far. As long ago as 1948 Gallup had recognised the problem and devised a five-stage issue-question sequence to overcome it. Respondents were questioned first about their awareness of the issue; then asked an open-ended preference question; then a closed-ended pre-set choice of answers question; then an open-ended probe to get at the reasons for their opinions; and finally Gallup measured the intensity of their attitude on the issue. The sequence was too cumbersome and expensive and was later abandoned, but it shows how the problem of meaningless opinion responses can be tackled if and when there are doubts about the depth of public feeling on an issue.

Moreover, there is some positive value in pre-set questions which remind the respondent of the possible range of answers. In a short, fast-moving interview the inarticulate and slow-witted may well find a check list useful; and in so far as the set of possible answers simulates political debate and discussion it may improve the realism of the interview. Obviously, the pattern of responses will be a function of the range of alternatives offered, and good survey reports state the questions in the text—not in the appendix. For example, the choice between Scottish self-government or the status quo produces a rather different percentage opting for independence than a multiple choice between self-government, federalism, devolution, and the status quo. Answers must necessarily be interpreted along with the question and not treated as absolutes. There is no perfect question and it would be waste of time to search for it. We need to treat question and answer as a dyad, but in practice that is neither difficult nor unusual.

A rather different problem is that of faulty answers, rather than faulty questions: answers which are, in some sense, false. At its simplest, respondents may tell lies. They may claim to be poorer than they are. They may claim to have voted when they did not. They may deny voting for socially unacceptable parties like the Communist Party or the National Front. They may find it prudent to deny participation in various illegal forms of direct action. Some foresight may allow the survey researcher to avoid this problem by shifting the study towards an analysis of expressed sympathy for these activities, rather than admitted involvement in them. Sometimes, to correct for bias in the whole sample, we can weight more heavily those respondents who do admit to such deviant behaviour; but that covers up the problem, rather than solving it. Weighting has no effect at all on contrast between those who claim they have and those who claim they have not behaved deviantly, and it fails to alter the fact that some respondents have misclassified themselves.

Direct, self-conscious lies may not be a widespread problem in British or American political surveys—though as deviant political behaviour grows, it may become one—but wherever respondents are asked to report on other people, other times, or both, their reports are likely to be inaccurate. Niemi (1973) showed, by interviewing students and their parents separately, that the students had a fairly inaccurate view of their parents' current vote preference, a still less accurate view of their parents' turnout to vote, an inaccurate view of their parents' sense of partisanship, and an appallingly inaccurate view of their parents' level of political interest. Almost every panel study has shown respondents unable to give an accurate account of their own voting behaviour at the preceding election some four or five years prior to the interview. For example, the Scottish Election Panel found that almost half the respondents who had claimed a Scottish National Party vote when interviewed in 1974 recalled voting for other parties in 1974 when they were re-interviewed in 1979. And this despite the fact that the SNP had won almost a third of the vote in 1974, was socially acceptable, and very clearly differentiated from the other parties in leaders and policy. Such findings must call into question all those analyses which use respondents' reports of their neighbourhood milieu, the partisanship and class of their childhood home, and the partisanship of their parents, spouse, friends, and workmates. All of these may grossly over-estimate consistency and homogeneity, since memories and perceptions are not only inaccurate, they are typically biased towards respondents' current socio-political characteristics.

Perceptions by interviewers cannot always be trusted either. Golembiewski *et al.* (1969) report findings on the consistency with which interviewers assigned respondents to socio-economic status grades. Intra-interviewers assignments correlated only moderately, while inter-interviewer assignments correlated remarkably weakly.

Another recurrent criticism is that despite all the rhetoric of behaviouralism, the dynamic and causal element in survey research is comparatively small (Truman 1969; Ions 1977, chapter 1). Though surveys often extend the range and improve the quality of descriptions, purely descriptive accounts were the very object of the behaviouralist attack. In their report on the 1948 Elmira study, Berleson, Lazarsfeld and McPhee criticised survey research for using too many single wave studies and not enough panel studies. They argued that single-wave cross-sectional surveys could be used only for description, rather than analysis, and could study only conditions, rather than processes. Ions makes the same criticism without showing the same awareness of a solution when he claims that cross-sectional surveys provide a weak basis for analysing dynamic processes. He also claims that political variables are, in general, inter-dependent and cannot reasonably be divided into dependent and independent. Let us take, for example, partisanship and attitudes towards nationalisation. A cross-sectional survey will show a correlation between support for nationalisation and support for the Labour Party. It is an elementary, but none the less troublesome rule of statistics that the correlation itself cannot tell us whether the issue attitude causes partisanship, or vice versa, or whether both attitudes arise from some common cause like social class location. Statistical analysis of a cross-sectional survey can provide some test of this third possibility, but cannot easily distinguish between the first and second.

It would be wrong to claim that surveys are useless for testing and quantifying relationships of interdependence. Using advanced statistical methods even cross-sectional data can, in fact, be used to quantify relationships of interdependence, even quantifying the relative influence of each variable on the other. But while these methods are satisfactory in principle, in practice they require combinations of variables which are difficult to obtain in political surveys. In my example, we could analyse the interdependence between nationalisation attitude and partisanship using a cross-sectional survey if we could find two further variables in the survey, one of which directly influenced nationalisation attitudes but not (directly) partisanship, and the other of which directly influenced partisanship but not (directly) nationalisation attitudes: a difficult but not necessarily impossible task. However, relationships of interdependence can be analysed much more easily in a panel survey. For example, we can look at those respondents whose partisanship and nationalisation attitudes are initially in conflict to see how, in later waves of the panel, that conflict is resolved. Panels will not help, however, if respondents change both attitudes—for example, from a pro-Labour, pro-nationalisation position to an anti-Labour, anti-nationalisation position.

Most academic surveys of British politics, and an increasing number of the media surveys also, have used a panel format for collecting the data. But they have not made full use of the panel format for causal analysis. Analysts have lacked statistical sophistication, many of the panels have been over periods of only a few weeks, and the numbers of respondents changing attitudes and partisanship have sometimes been small. So panel surveys have not always produced work which could be described as panel analysis. Once again we need to distinguish between the characteristics of the data set and the characteristics of the analysis.

If we are really serious about studying causal relationships, why not abandon surveys altogether and imitate the natural scientists with their experimental approach? Perhaps the best analogy is with those brilliant scientists who developed coal briquettes which burned so well in the laboratory and so badly in the hearth. Political behaviour is so very much conditioned by environment that it is exceedingly dangerous to study it in anything but the best achievable approximation to the natural environment. Cohen notes that experimental methods suggest that communications have a large effect on attitudes, while Survey Methods suggest they do not, and he goes on to explain why, in this example, experimental methods prove so very misleading (Cohen 1964: 129–32). In experiments there was no self-selection of communications, no possibility of avoidance; the experiments measured effects shortly after the communication and before decay had set in; experiments gave no chance for respondents to discuss the communication with friends and neighbours; the nature of an experiment gave the communicators an aura of authority greater than real political communicators enjoy; and experimenters tended to pick issues on which movement of opinion was possible and likely while political issues, if they are important, get deeply rooted in the socio-political fabric. In general, therefore, an experimental approach would not be any improvement over Survey Methods. What surveys lack in terms of control over causal stimuli they more than compensate for by wider generality and a more realistic environment for data gathering. Yet the methods could be combined by targeting surveys on groups of respondents who are at the receiving end of some great social change or experiment. A study of the unemployed, the affluent workers, the purchasers of council houses, the newly married, or new recruits to the armed forces would not necessarily meet the requirements of a quasi-experiment. We need to observe the object of the experiment before as well as after the stimulus. However, a panel study of those who were about to become unemployed, become affluent, purchase a council house, get married, or get their call-up papers would indeed come close to the ideal of a quasi-experiment in a natural setting. By chance, the decision to switch printing of the *Scottish Daily Express* to Manchester and the subsequent loss of half its Scottish circulation during the period of the 1974–79 Scottish Election Panel provided one such quasi-experiment (W. L. Miller *et al.* 1982).

Survey researchers have been criticised for failing to give enough attention to problems of meaning—answering the question 'what?' without giving a convincing answer to the question 'why?' Even causal analyses may answer 'what?' better than 'why?' Statistical analysis may show that even when we control for the influence of other social variables correlated with Catholicism, Roman Catholics are specially likely to vote Democrat. In once sense it is then correct to say that, to a degree, Catholicism causes Democratic voting. But that is somehow insufficient. It still makes sense to ask 'why do Catholics tend towards the Democrats?'. Once the question is posed explicitly, then we are on the way to discovering something about motivations. For example, the Michigan analysts asked whether Catholics, in their political responses were (1) a self-conscious group or (2) a set of people with similar life experiences or (3) a social group only in the sense that being a Catholic made contact with other Catholics much more likely, leading to a degree of group consensus, yet unconscious group consensus. We could expand this list of facets of Catholicism. Is the Catholic response based on community or on doctrine? Is it the spontaneous reaction of rank and file Catholics, or is it stimulated by the demands of the Church hierarchy, or the appeals of politicians at the hustings? What aspect of Catholicism is the target for politicians' appeals—the interests of their church, the tenets of their faith, their moral principles, or Catholic people as a social community?

Once such questions are posed, surveys can attempt to answer them by disaggregating the question 'Are you a Catholic?' into component questions about the respondent's relationship to Catholicism and about his or her perceptions of the relationship between Catholicism and politics. It is even possible to ask respondents about their motivations directly, provided we treat the answers as perceptions rather than truths.

5.4 *Cost effectiveness*

Even when critics accept that surveys can add to our knowledge and understanding, they may still complain that the cost is too high in terms of research funds, in terms of scarce academic time, and in terms of scarce computing resources. Critics assert that the bureaucratic organisation of surveys leads to arid specialisation and provides jobs for hordes of mediocrities. Even those who commission surveys sometimes seem to begrudge the cost. A relatively cheap newspaper poll might cost £3,000 and for that sum, the editor will tell you, the paper could send a special correspondent to Latin America for a month, or commission a series of perhaps half a dozen articles by well known 'names'. An academic survey with 2,000 respondents might cost £50,000 in fieldwork and associated costs which could otherwise pay for a year's work by five junior research assistants. Labour Party surveys in the year or so before the 1979 election cost it £87,000. The party had only seventy full-time agents in the constituencies and they were paid just over £3,000 per annum at the time. So the polling budget could have paid for a very significant percentage increase in agents in the field.

But these figures need to be put into context. Labour spent 2.5 million in the last five weeks of the 1979 campaign on central advertising and local candidates' expenses (Pinto-Dushinsky 1981). Labour spending on surveys and other opinion research came to under 3 per cent of total campaign expenditure, excluding subsidies, and to only 1.5 per cent of total expenditure if subsidies are included in the calculation. The other parties spent even smaller proportions of their budget on surveys. Media expenditure on polls is also low when taken as a percentage of their total budget, and the same is true of academia. Taking a full five-year period, 1975–80, only a third of the research grant expenditure and only one fifteenth of total expenditure on projects approved by the British SSRC's Politics Committee went on survey-based studies: and that during a parliament in which the unusual circumstances of referendums in 1975 and 1979 temporarily increased the quantity of electoral behaviour available for study.

One significant difference between the media, the parties, and academia, however, is the way in which expenditure is divided up. Academic surveys have been relatively few in number and relatively expensive. The parties and the media have spent their survey funds on a much larger number of less expensive studies. Typically they have formed an enduring link with a particular survey organisation but commissioned a series or even a programme of surveys, always spread over time, sometimes distributed over a variety of places and/or employing a variety of survey techniques. Spending available funds for academic surveys on a few large grants has tended to produce something of a 'closed-shop' in academic survey research and militated against a wide diffusion and continuity of practical survey experience.

A second significant difference between academic surveys and others is that in one important sense, surveys cost academics less than they cost the media or the parties, even when the price tag is the same. Both media and parties are primarily interested in the present and the immediate future.

Once used, their surveys are of relatively little interest to them. Their surveys are essentially throw-away, disposable commodities whose full utility is extracted immediately; academic surveys are a more re-usable commodity, because academics are interested in the past no less than the present, and interested also in relatively timeless features of socio-political patterns. In a meaningful sense academic survey data accumulate: the return outlasts the expenditure by many years. Numerous academic studies now use a full set of American electoral surveys since 1952 or British electoral surveys since 1963 as the basis for their analyses. Survey data are extremely transportable and easily exchanged through data banks. So the cost of major academic surveys per eventual academic user, or per eventual academic inquiry is low and declines steadily as more students and researchers reanalyse the data. The Michigan team can quote hundreds of doctoral theses and dozens of books based on their election survey series. No comprehensive list of work derived from British academic election surveys exists, and the quantity of reanalysis is probably very much less than for the American surveys. But in addition to two dozen publications by the survey directors themselves, the 1974 British election survey is known to have formed the basis for research by other academics at over twenty universities in Britain, Canada, Australia, and America; it provides a valuable data base for a variety of taught courses in sociology and politics, and for numerous student papers, dissertations, and theses.

All surveys are not equally suitable for a wealth of reanalysis. The most suitable are those which are most general, both in terms of the geographic spread of the sample and the number and conceptual range of the variables measured. The number of possible bivariate relations that can be explored rises exponentially with the number of variables included in the same survey: ten variables correspond to forty-five bivariate relationships, 100 variables to 4,950 bivariate relationships. And, of course, three-way and four-way relationships are often interesting as well. I would not want to argue that a typical academic survey with a hundred variables in it really does provide almost five thousand significant possibilities for analysis. Some conceptual duplication occurs and some relationships are uninteresting, but this crude arithmetical calculation does indicate why it is that the original investigators usually leave ample scope for interesting and important reanalyses. Despite the fact that several variables may all get at roughly the same concept, despite the fact that there is nothing to be discovered by looking at the bivariate relationships between many pairs of variables, a hundred or so variables still leave a great many more potentially interesting relationships than the original investigators have time to study.

Political science is a relatively inexpensive discipline, especially in terms of the marginal cost of its tools. Libraries already exist, principal researchers are already in post as members of teaching departments. Much research can be done for the cost of a modest travel budget and a little research assistance. So political surveys look expensive because they occur in the context of an extremely low-cost discipline, many of whose costs are not only low but hidden in routine university expenditure. Survey costs would arouse neither interest nor comment if set against the background of research expenditures in science, engineering, or medicine; especially since the real equivalent of a political survey in these other disciplines is not a single research project, but a research facility to be used by many researchers on many projects spread over many years.

6 The democratic value of surveys

According to Rokkan (1962: 47) the growth of survey research was closely related to the extension of the suffrage which made mass views important. If market research provided the method, and behaviouralism the academic imperative, the extension of the franchise provided a political imperative. No one today could, like Dicey in 1914, title a book *Law and Public Opinion in England* without giving some attention to *mass* opinion. It is, of course, quite wrong to assume that masses are only important in democracies. Victorian social reformers were interested in the poor long before the poor gained access to the franchise and, for not entirely dissimilar reasons, totalitarian regimes today use political surveys to gain an understanding of the masses they attempt to control. For any government, democratic or not, surveys provide an 'invaluable part of the feedback system between politicians and public—at least as valuable as pressure groups, lobbyists, constituency letters and views collected by MPs from their friends' (Taylor 1970).

None the less, surveys have been used to further what Crick calls the 'old Progressive and Populist illusions' that a head-count of mass opinion should influence, if not determine, public policy. Recent evidence suggests that surveys even provide a better guide to public opinion than the formal referendums advocated by classic American populists (Wright 1978: 160; W. L. Miller 1981a: 250–2). In the seventies, British government agencies as diverse as the Royal Commission on the Constitution (Kilbrandon Commission) and the Advisory, Conciliation, and Arbitration Service (ACAS) used polls and surveys in an explicitly referendum mode.

6.1 *Populism versus democracy*

The insidious penetration of populist ideas can be seen in the way British and American pollsters have constructed their national samples. Their sampling procedures are designed to produce a representative sample of the whole electorate or, worse, the full adult population whether on the register or not, with every individual having the same equal chance of appearing in the sample. Why should they construct such a sample unless motivated by populist instincts? The British electoral system recognises only constituency electorates, not a single undifferentiated British electorate. An elector living in Glasgow Central in 1979 had a vote worth over five times as much as an elector who lived in Midlothian, because five times as many electors lived in the Midlothian constituency. Generally, Scots electors had one and a quarter times the representation in parliament of an equivalent number of English electors. Any analysis of the electorate which weights electors equally, instead of weighting them in accordance with the electoral system, reveals its populist bias.

But in other, more significant ways public opinion may have to be distinguished from a head-count of mass opinion. Studies by Converse *et al.* (1965) and again by Verba and Brody (1970) have shown how American letter writers and demonstrators in the sixties were more polarised than the general public, with letter-writers biased towards the right and demonstrators towards the left. None the less, in interpreting public opinion prudent governments may need to pay more attention to the active and intense than to mere head-counts.

The populist view of public opinion has three elements: first, that public opinion can be measured adequately by a head count; second, that government should respond to public opinion; third, that elected representatives, and institutions like trades unions, parties, and parliaments, merely get in the way of proper implementation of the people's wishes. Parliamentarians refute these claims. In their view politicians have to take account of political realities like small but powerful veto groups, they have to consider the full implications of political action and, not least, they have to take full personal responsibility for their own actions. Thus Edward Boyle in his 1969 speech on hanging could 'see no inconsistency in saying that we should be responsive to concern felt by public opinion over a particular social problem, and that at the same time we are determined not to vote [in the House of Commons] for something we feel with all our being to be wrong'.

Public opinion, particularly as measured by media opinion polls on current issues, but also as measured in academic surveys, may reflect the view of the unaffected, the inexpert, the uninterested, or the irresponsible, and may merely echo the output of the media. The views of those whose homes may be destroyed by a new London airport or a Highland oil-rig construction site may be very different from those of the general, unaffected public questioned in a national poll. The general public may simply lack interest and information on particular policies, or lack understanding of the full implications. In an opinion poll they may happily reject all political leaders and parties currently on offer, in contrast to an election in which they must necessarily offer a constructive vote of no confidence by voting *for* one candidate in order to *defeat* another. And in a poll they may feel free to answer without the worry that their answer may have consequences. Lastly, their views, particularly on political leaders or the importance of various issues may reflect no more than media coverage or lack of it. Questions about popular choices for party leader tend to produce selections from among the handful of politicians currently catching the media's eye and questions about the 'most important issues' usually select topics from the week's television news. On many matters opinions measured by polls are highly derivative. Many present-day politicians might echo the claim made by Sir Robert Peel in 1841 that 'it is dangerous to admit to any other recognised organ of public opinion than the House of Commons'. A populist regime in which top politicians communicate to the masses by television and gauge mass responses by sample surveys, relegating intermediate organisations like parties and parliament to an insignificant role, might be a highly defective democracy. In Britain, employers have increasingly adopted a populist stance with respect to their workers, rejecting the legitimacy of trades unions, and relying on surveys and advertising as twin channels of communication with the workforce.

None the less, polls and surveys do give the mass electorate a voice, whether or not it has anything worthwhile to say, whether or not its voice should be heeded, whether or not the electorate itself wishes its voice to dominate. Politicians, interest groups, political scientists, and historians are always in the business of attempting to state or interpret the public mood, and in the absence of survey information they place too much weight on élite memoires, letters and editorials in the press, riots and demonstrations in the street, simplistic interpretations of election results, or simple unsupported assertion. While some of these phenomena are politically significant in their own right, they are poor measures of mass opinion. When parliament defeated the first Scotland and Wales Bill on devolution, various politicians and commentators drew attention to the lack of any consequent riots and used this as evidence that Scots did not want devolution. Yet a government which only responded to violence in the streets would be substituting mob rule for democracy. The mob and the mass have different political attitudes and priorities. At the least, polls and surveys allow governments and politicians access to the view of the unorganised, inarticulate, quiescent masses, which they can weigh against the advice coming from organised interest groups, political activists, and the civil service.

If the views of the mass electorate are to be incorporated into the governing process, polls and surveys may be a better way of measuring them than formal referendums. The referendum is an inflexible device. It does not cope very well with changing moods, nor with different ways of looking at the issue. It assumes so much authority that the organised groups the populists sought to keep out of politics actually invade and corrupt the referendum process. The issue on the ballot escapes. When the voters in de Gaulle's 1969 referendum on constitutional reform were asked *why* they voted for or against the proposals, the vast majority on both sides said it was to support or oppose the government of the day—few were motivated by the issue printed on the ballot paper. Similarly, as the date of the 1979 Scotland Act referendum approached, the voting intentions of Conservative and Labour partisans diverged sharply. The parties tried to make the vote a test of party loyalty. Within the last four weeks before voting day, surveys show that the difference between Conservative and Labour support for a vote in favour of the Scotland Act shot up from a 20 per cent gap to a 50 per cent gap. Meanwhile, the same Labour and Conservative partisans, in the same surveys, never differed by even as much as 20 per cent on the general principle of devolution. In short, the Scotland Act, which was the Labour Government's proposed scheme for devolution, came to be associated more with the Party than with the policy. Paradoxically, the referendum vote was not an issue vote in Scotland any more than it had been ten years earlier in France.

While some critics have attacked polls and surveys for misleading politicians, others have attacked them for misleading political scientists, whose attention may be unduly distracted away from proper consideration of élites and institutions. These critics allege that polls increase the attention paid to the masses by observers of the political process far more than they increase the respect paid to the masses by élite participants in the process. I must say that I find this criticism excessive. It is a question of balance, and in Britain the balance of observers' interest and attention is still tilted towards élites and institutions. In principle they might be ignored and neglected, in practice they are not.

Alderman (1978) has argued that polls enhance mass feeling of involvement and so help to legitimate the government, the electoral process, and the whole democratic system. It may be hard to see how American election forecasting polls in 1948 or British ones in 1970 or 1974 could legitimate the election process when they almost unanimously picked the 'wrong' party as the eventual winner. Over the whole run of surveys since the war, governments have, on average, lagged behind the opposition in the monthly opinion polls. The 1979–83 government's lead, for example, did not last beyond the high summer of 1979. Again it may be difficult to see how such monthly polls can do anything but undermine the legitimacy of governments and of the system which produces them. But that is too narrow a view. Before the advent of monthly Gallup polls, a run of by-election defeats tested the nerve of Lloyd George and his partners in the 1918–22 Coalition to breaking point. What polls and surveys have done is not to provide proof that governments are unpopular in the mid-term—the evidence for that was clear enough already—but to provide new interpretations of mid-term unpopularity which actually increase the legitimacy of governments. By asking a variety of vote intention questions, Gallup, BMRB and others have been able to show that people distinguish between their *by-election* behaviour on the one hand and their party identification or future general election voting intention on the other. So the polls have reduced the authority of by-election defeats, rather than the legitimacy of governments.

Polls have also shown how quickly and how strongly support can rally to the government when faced with an external crisis. During the Falklands affair, support for the British government went up by 20 per cent in the polls, long before there was any prospect of military victory. The crisis broke when unemployment had reached unprecedented levels and the Conservative government had just lost a by-election in a constituency which had never before elected anyone but a Conservative. So the huge surge of support in the polls provided much-needed evidence of a popular mandate, less colourful but more impressive than the crowds in front of the Casa Rosada in Buenos Aires.

Fears have been expressed that academic and private political surveys could damage democracy by providing governments and parties with the tools for manipulating the electorate. Hence McCallum's desire to preserve the 'great eleusian mystery of the democratic state'. The Government Social Survey owed its origins in part to war-time attempts to gauge civilian morale, and the ever-present fear that it might be used for totalitarian ends has kept it well away from topics related to party preferences and political psychology in general.

Hodder-Williams (1970) lists four effects which surveys are alleged to have had on British parties. First, monthly media opinion polls, supplemented by private party polls, have strengthened the Prime Minister's power to choose his or her own time for a general election: the PM acquired the prerogative from the monarch before the days of surveys, but surveys now give him or her the necessary information to use it effectively. We might be even more convinced by this argument if the polls in 1970 and 1974 had not proved so misleading. Still more recently, Callaghan decided against a 1978 general election at a time when private Labour Party polls were showing Labour doing specially badly in marginal seats, and trailing on issues as well as voting preferences; but for a Prime Minister considering when to call an election, that is yet another unhappy precedent for relying on polls, for the 1978–79 'winter of discontent' forced him into an election at an even more unfavourable time.

Second, Hodder-Williams thinks polls have enhanced the status of party leaders. Private polls, particularly the early Abrams polls for the Labour Party showed that Britain was not a nation of ideologues, and that the way to win elections was to show the politically amorphous middle ground that the party had a better team of economic managers than its opponent. Hence the need to invest heavily in glamorising the leader—which had important consequences within the parties as well as outside. Again, the experience of 1970 and 1979 when the more popular leaders lost the elections—we might add 1945 to the list—must weigh against too much concern for personalities. In so far as polls have any real effect on leader's status within their parties, the polls must have reduced rather than enhanced the status of every Conservative Prime Minister since Macmillan.

Third, says Hodder-Williams, surveys have provided support for government against well-organised pressure groups on issues like seat belts and breathalyser tests, income policies, devolution, and abortion. That does not mean surveys always support the government position, but when the authority of an elected government is coupled with the authority of mass attitudes expressed in surveys, pressure groups find it particularly difficult to advance alternative views.

Lastly, Hodder-Williams suggests that political surveys have influenced the parties' electoral strategies. The parties' private pollsters get quite schizophrenic about this. To maintain good relations with their party sponsors, they wish to claim that they do no more than show the party how to present its case to best advantage. To maintain good relations with the wider public, they wish to claim that they have manipulated the parties as much as the public, encouraging them to adopt popular policies and generally head for the middle ground. In some measure, they have done both. Early Labour party surveys were indeed part of an exercise designed to move the party towards its public on questions like nationalisation. Similarly, Conservative party surveys are said to have encouraged the party to accept comprehensive eductation despite its activists' love of grammar schools and fee-paying schools. The 1966 wage freeze came soon after an ORC/Sunday Times poll in its favour, and Wilson's application to join the EEC came after a series of polls showing popular support for membership. Recent Labour Party polls have been used to point out to party spokesmen how little support there is for nationalisation and how much of the party's mass support lives in owner-occupied houses: with the implication that further nationalisation should not be advocated nor owner-occupiers attacked. Similarly, private Labour polls in 1974 were used to convince the doubters within the party that Scottish devolution would be an electorally rewarding issue.

However, party polls have sometimes shown that the party can move towards the policies favoured by its activists without any loss of electoral appeal. Thus the Conservatives were encouraged by polls to advocate the sale of council houses, a cut in taxation, and a reduction in public expenditure. Since their surveys showed that certain types of public expenditure, notably on health, were relatively popular, the party was at pains to exclude certain areas from proposed cuts and its 1979 manifesto specifically pledged no reduction in National Health Service spending. On the Labour side, the private polls largely determined Crosland's response to Thatcher's 1974 pledge of cheap mortgages. They convinced him, perhaps wrongly, that the pledge only damaged the Conservatives' credibility.

My impression of the parties' use of survey research is that the democratic or populist influence of surveys, driving the parties towards the public, is a mark of incompetence and inexperience. What the parties want from surveys is not just to find a way of winning elections, but a way of winning elections on their own terms. As they get more professional in their use of surveys, the emphasis does indeed turn to manipulating the public rather than the parties. Their survey work focuses on identifying the most volatile elements of the electorate and their sources of information, identifying the party's own most popular policies and its opponents' most unpopular ones, and finding the best way of presenting party policy and creating a party image. It is tied in closely with party leaders' speech themes, with party election broadcasts, and with press and poster advertising. Austin Mitchell, a political academic and MP, put it this way in a recent Fabian pamphlet: 'polls bring knowledge of which subjects to tackle head on, which chords to strike, which issues to push home and which to avoid, which policies will sell and which won't. Labour is as much in the merchandising business as the makers of biological Ariel. There is little point in confusing bad merchandising with high principle' (quoted by Worcester, the Labour Party's private pollster: Worcester 1980).

6.2 *Manipulation and corruption*

Pressure groups suffer no moral doubts. They are in the business of getting their own way, not representing the people. The same goes for commercial enterprises which formulate political objectives. Sometimes they use surveys to discover how successful they have been in putting their case to the public. Sometimes they use surveys as evidence of popular opinion which they can use as part of the case they put to government. But on other occasions they put surveys to a more sinister use.

For the electorate themselves, polls can serve a democratic purpose. It is difficult to form political views without some guide to what others are thinking, since the essence of democratic control is that large numbers have to be agreed before any decision can be reached. Surveys provide for the general public that *sense of the meeting* which can only be experienced directly in relatively small-group situations such as committees. There is evidence that increasing numbers of electors, perhaps a majority, are now aware of poll findings at critical times. The danger is that instead of deriving an ersatz sense of the meeting, they derive an ersatz *sense of the crowd*. An NOP poll in Orpington shortly before the 1962 by-election showed the Liberals had a chance of victory and the poll itself is credited with turning that possibility into a reality. Something similar occurred at the Bermondsey by-election in 1983.

But in general, Liberal surges in national monthly opinion polls seem to have followed by-election successes, rather than caused them, and polls published during general election campaigns seem to have contributed to those anti-bandwagon effects which have frequently produced trends away from the leading party and towards the second and third parties. American findings are similar: Beniger (1976) has shown that during the campaign season, American primaries seem to influence candidates' popularity in the opinion polls, rather than vice versa, echoing the pattern of British by-elections and opinion polls. America is divided into a number of time-zones. So when voting has finished in the East, and the television networks have begun their election results programmes, the people in California still have another five hours in which to make up their minds and cast their votes. There is no evidence that they are influenced by the early results from the East (Tuchman and Coffin 1971).

Incidentally, the only convincing method of testing for these bandwagon effects is to use a panel survey, like Tuchman and Coffin, and compare the late swing of voting intention among those who have not heard the early results from the East, with the swing among those who have. Until 1918, British parliamentary elections did not take place simultaneously in all constituencies. They were spread over a period of three weeks, and candidates in the later-voting constituencies used the early results as part of their propaganda. Day after day the press headlined results from the most recent constituency elections. The general election was, in one important respect, very far from being 'general' (see Blewett 1972, Chapter 7). But because there were no sample surveys at the time, these three-week elections cannot be used to test for bandwagon effects. Roughly speaking, the boroughs voted in the first week, the counties in the second, the universities in the third. But different swings in borough and county constituencies cannot be viewed as evidence for bandwagon or anti-bandwagon effects, because the areas were socially and politically different: and they behave differently even today, though elections now take place simultaneously.

However, although there is no evidence in Britain or America for bandwagon effects on voting intentions during a short campaign or on election day itself, other kinds of political bandwagons may operate, perhaps too slowly to be detected easily. Beniger showed that in the longer term, American opinion polls did influence the nomination process. Noelle-Neuman (1974) has put forward a 'spiral of silence' theory and backed it with some data from German surveys. Her idea is that people who perceive themselves to be in a minority on a political issue may become less willing to talk about it, and by doing so they further reduce real support for their side of the issue, as well as deepening the impression that they are in a minority. The process may be slow, especially where partisanship is the issue, because partisanship is so explicit and so well supported by the family and political system that it is highly resistant to outside influence. But positions on issues and attitudes towards political objects other than parties are much less well protected.

There can be no doubt that the power of conversation over political attitudes, even partisanship, is immense *in the long run*. It forms the basis for well documented and widely accepted models of ecological or environmental influence. Without it, we could not explain the patterns of class voting in English constituencies, for example (W. L. Miller 1977a, 1978). These models do not require the notion of a 'spiral of silence': it is sufficient that a minority will naturally fail to dominate inter-person contacts and conversations. If minorities perceive themselves to be minorities, a spiral of silence will only intensify a natural process that would occur anyway.

Noelle-Neuman, however, was drawing attention to the possibility of corruption if perceptions of minority status were wrong and especially if they had been deliberately manipulated by outside agents. I said at the start of this section that polls could contribute to democracy by giving electors an ersatz 'sense of the meeting'. Pressure groups purposefully try to manipulate their public meetings with 'planted' speakers from the floor. Chris Hall's very practical handbook, *How to Run a Pressure Group*, describes standard methods for manipulating the sense of the local meeting in the church or village hall (Hall 1975: 13–16). On a grand scale, pressure groups with access to large funds have used surveys in a similar way to manipulate the entire electorate's sense of its own opinion.

In 1958 and 1959, the Colin Hurry Organisation spent what was then the enormous sum of £475,000 on a British Market Research Bureau poll of 1,948,314 electors in marginal constituencies using a questionnaire designed to produce prejudiced answers on nationalisation (Editorial, *Political Quarterly*, 1959). Two decades later, in 1978–79, T. F. Thomson, former head of ORC, used his old polling company to do another series of nationalisation polls in marginal constituencies. These showed nothing new, but because they were newly-taken polls in specific localities, they were widely reported in the local press. The idea was to reinforce majority opposition to nationalisation, in both quantity and intensity, by 'playing majority views back to the public' (Butler and Kavanagh 1980: 269). When Thomson proposed another round of surveys, this time on trade union power, widespread protests forced his sponsors, Lord Plowden's 'Committee for Research into Public Attitudes' to delay till after the election. But these activities operate, necessarily, on a long time scale. The polls on trade union power duly appeared at the end of 1980.

The most reputable of polling organisations provide no guarantee against biased questions and distorting surveys designed to influence rather than report public opinion. I have, myself, carried out polls for British newspapers and television. In my very limited experience my sponsors exerted no pressure at all as to what questions I should ask, nor how they should be framed. Indeed, I tried hard to get them to suggest questions, but without success. They were busy with other concerns and they trusted my political and journalistic judgement. But pressure groups have clearer political objectives than the media and explicitly, or probably implicitly, they define the questions to be asked, the way they must be framed, and the way they must be analysed and interpreted.

MORI does much of its work for the Labour Party, but when it appeared in a union-versus-employers court case, on the employers' side, the High Court Judge criticised MORI's interpretation of the facts (see *Guardian*, 20 April 1979; also Worcester and Stubbs 1978, 1980). Marsh (1982) quotes the example of two surveys in 1980 on attitudes towards abortion, one done for the pro-abortion lobby, the other for the anti-abortionists. Both surveys were done by Gallup. One survey asked whether female respondents would seek an abortion 'after being raped', the other asked whether abortion should be available 'on demand'. Even when the two surveys asked similar questions, the qualifying phrases which introduced the questions were sharply different.

I could quote far worse examples than these. My reason for referring to

BMRB, ORC, MORI, and Gallup is that these are among the best in the business. They have the highest levels of expertise and integrity amongst British pollsters. Yet the realities of commercial life have not allowed even them to stand aside from the battle between pressure groups.

PART III

THEORY AND METHOD—CONTINUITY AND CUMULATION

Politics can be discussed without reference to data of any sort, provided we restrict our attention to abstract principles, be they moral or mechanical. However, when we wish to move on from the ideal and the abstract to the real and concrete, data of some kind are essential. But data alone are not enough. In the words of Henry Mayhew introducing the fourth volume of his *London Labour and the London Poor* in 1861,

> Facts are merely the elements of truths and not the truths themselves: of all matters there are none so utterly useless by themselves as your mere matters of fact . . . we must compare them with some other . . . we must generalise them, that is to say, we must contemplate them in connection with other facts and so discover their agreements and differences, their antecedents, concomitants and consequences. It is true we may frame erroneous and defective theories . . . nevertheless, if theory may occasionally teach us wrongly, facts without theory or generalisation cannot teach us at all. [Mayhew 1861: 1–2.]

In place of abstract theories about ideal worlds, we seek to construct empirical theories about real worlds: theories about the way society and politics operate, at least in some well-defined times and places.

Data contribute to theory in three ways. They can be used to *test* whether or not some theory adequately describes reality. They can be used to quantify the parameters of a theory, to *measure* the extent or degree of relationships, for example. Last, we can simply *confront* our theories with relevant data and see what thoughts are prompted by that confrontation. Sometimes the data appear to be consistent with our theories; at others we conclude that the data disprove the theory; at others we are led to suspect the validity of the data, or driven to look for errors in our computer programming; but at its most exciting, the data confrontation may suggest new and better theories.

Ultimately the contribution that surveys make to political science depends upon this confrontation of theory and data, not on a mere accumulation of data. Data themselves, however valid, are only the raw material for the confrontation. Does the kind of data produced by surveys prompt or confront important political theories, or is it irrelevant to all but the least significant? How sharp is the confrontation? Even if the data are relevant to the theory, how close are they to the essence of the theory? How well, how decisively, do the data test the theory? How accurately, how precisely, do the data quantify the theory's parameters? How many details of the theory can be tested against the data? Are there lines of cumulation, or do later surveys merely corroborate or reverse the findings from earlier work? Does the *process* of survey research generate and build significant theory?

Chapters 7, 8, and 9 trace the development of political theory through a sequence of related surveys. Questions of cumulation, of the interaction between theory and method, of the development of theory, cannot be answered by looking at one survey in isolation from others, nor even at a selection of unrelated examples.

Chapter 7 centres around a sequence of American presidential election surveys, beginning with Columbia University's classic studies of the 1940 and 1948 elections, and continuing with Michigan University's series which covers every election from 1948 to 1980. The Columbia studies developed sociological explanations of voting behaviour, Michigan emphasised social-psychological factors such as party identification as well as attitudes towards ideology, issues, and candidates. One important feature of this series of studies is its length: so many recent analyses almost inevitably focus on cross-temporal comparisons and trends.

Throughout the fifties, Columbia's classic presidential election surveys served as the model for British surveys. Indeed, British and American traditions diverged largely because the British stuck to the Columbia model, while Michigan was developing a very different approach in America. In the sixties, Donald Stokes of Michigan collaborated with David Butler of Oxford to produce *Political Change in Britain*, the most impressive piece of survey research into British politics. But although Butler and Stokes adopted many of the outward forms of Michigan surveys, their study still remained very much in the Columbia tradition. It was not until the seventies that there was any serious attempt to apply the Michigan model to Britain. In Chapter 8 I trace the development of British survey research, looking particularly at the extent and the causes of its divergence from American trends.

Chapter 9 focuses on a sequence of multi-national surveys and a topic which is particularly suited to cross-national comparison: political partici-pation. The classic text is Almond and Verba's *Civic Culture* study of Germany, Italy, Britain, the USA, and Mexico with a follow-up study fifteen years later in Austria, India, Japan, the Netherlands, Nigeria, Yugoslavia, and the USA. These studies emphasised questions about *conventional* participation: voting, taking part in election campaign activities, contacting officials, joining political parties or community organisations. More recently other multi-national surveys in EEC countries and again in Germany, the Netherlands, Austria, Britain, Finland, Switzerland, Italy, and the USA have studied *unconventional* participation: demonstrations, sit-ins, tax strikes, disruption, and violence—what is often termed 'direct action'. Despite their multi-national methodology and their focus on participation, these studies are closely connected with some of those described in earlier chapters: the *Civic Culture* study influenced the British survey tradition, while cross-national studies of direct action grew out of earlier British work on political violence in Wales, and have been extended by recent work in Scotland and Wales.

Chapters 7, 8, and 9 are not intended to provide comprehensive coverage of all areas of survey research in politics, nor of all the surveys in their respective areas. But they cover a substantial number of important surveys spread over four decades and a wide variety of countries. They show how ideas developed, findings cumulated, and techniques evolved in three important traditions of survey work. I could have selected other examples of survey research traditions, but not better examples. These are amongst the best. They allow a fair and realistic test of the Survey Method's contribution to the development of theory.

7 Presidential election surveys since 1940

If the 1936 presidential election produced the first great success for small-sample surveys as a means of forecasting election results, 1940 produced its first great success in contributing to political science, though the report on it, *The People's Choice* (Lazarsfeld, Berelson and Gaudet 1944), did not appear until four years later. Paul Lazarsfeld, who was director of the Office of Radio Research at Columbia University, drew up plans for a seven-wave panel survey of audience reactions to a sequence of radio broadcasts. Originally he proposed to carry out this study of media influence by analysing reactions to a sequence of broadcasts by the U. S. Department of Agriculture. Somewhere in the process of obtaining research funds, the focus got switched from agriculture to a presidential election campaign (Lazarsfeld 1969: 330). Lazarsfeld persuaded the Rockerfeller Foundation and Time Incorporated to fund a panel survey of the 1940 presidential election, but still with the intention of using it to show how political advertising on the radio influenced political consumer choices on election day (see Rossi 1959).

7.1 *The Columbia tradition*

Lazarsfeld's consumption-based model assumed that voting was an individualistic act, mainly in response to the voter's personality characteristics and exposure to the mass media. This was reflected in the full title of his report—*The People's Choice: How the Voter Makes up his Mind in a Presidential Campaign*. Yet when he and his associates came to analyse the survey responses, they found that none of their personality measures carried much weight; that there were few late deciders and even fewer late changers —only 54 respondents changed their political preferences; and the major function of the mass media seemed to be to reinforce existing preferences through selective exposure. In the language of market research the consumer showed an entirely unanticipated level of brand loyalty.

Moreover, in a society which prided itself on being the land of opportunity, free from the European disease of class divisions, the great social melting pot, the survey showed up surprisingly strong social influences on voting choice. At the level of primary group contacts, party preference appeared remarkably homogeneous within the family; those few respondents who changed preferences frequently mentioned personal contacts as the reason for their political change; and personal communication generally appeared more important then media communications. Socio-economic groups voted in distinctive ways, and Catholic/Protestant voting differences appeared particularly striking since sectarian divisions had only a remote connection with the 1940 campaign.

Lazarsfeld, Berelson and Gaudet devised an *Index of Political Predisposition* based on religious sect, occupational class, and urban/rural residence. Those whose social characteristics very strongly indicated a Republican or Democratic preference were more likely to decide early, more likely to turn out to vote on the day, and more likely to vote in accordance with their socially-predicted disposition. Late deciders and changers had none of the characteristics of a rational independent judge. They were people with low interest in politics, a low level of exposure to political communication, cross-pressured by combinations of social characteristics predisposing them towards both parties.

Two features of the survey design should be noted, one good, one bad. The survey was restricted to Erie County in Ohio. Since Erie County itself was not specially interesting—the people of Erie Country were not the 'People' referred to in the title—it was difficult to generalise from a sample in Erie County to the population of interest: the American electorate. In the event this may not have mattered, since we know from more extensive, later studies that the main findings could, in fact, be generalised to America as a whole, and even beyond.

Conversely the very best feature of the survey design failed to realise its full potential: that was the seven-wave panel design. An original sample of 3,000 was interviewed in May 1940. Thereafter one group of 600 was interviewed every month right through until after the election in November. The rest of the 3,000 were divided into other groups of 600, each of which was re-interviewed only once, one group in July, another in August, and so on, to check against the corrupting influence of too much re-interviewing. This was a superb tool for examining change during the last six months of the campaign. Unfortunately very little change occurred.

Berelson, Lazarsfeld, and McPhee (1954) used a variant of this methodology for their study of the 1948 election. This time a panel starting with only 1,029 respondents was interviewed in June, and re-interviewed in August and October. Each time over fifty questions were put to respondents. After the election in November a mail questionnaire was used to find out how respondents actually voted. All those whose behaviour in November differed from their intention as expressed during the pre-election interviews were then contacted by telephone or in person and asked another eleven questions. Like other panels it suffered some attrition, and only 746 respondents were contacted in all four waves. But in this one study as long ago as 1948, they used a four-wave panel, they put close on 200 questions to respondents, and they combined personal, postal, and telephone interviewing. It was a *tour de force* which still arouses admiration.

Though their sample was confined to the small town of Elmira in New York State, their title *Voting: A Study of Opinion Formation in a Presidential Campaign* indicated a concern with findings that would not be purely local to Elmira. 'This is *not* an anthropological or sociological investigation of a community', they wrote. 'Nor is this a current-history survey.' 'We are, instead, interested in just what the title of the volume states, namely *voting*, and we seek to identify, formulate, and test some generalisations on that subject.' 'National samples . . . gain in generality at the cost of blurring specifics. For example, the degree of social differentiation in politics is blurred by nation-wide averaging of data representing quite different patterns of cleavage, e.g. sectional, with ethnic and class.' 'Generalisations in the future will depend heavily on replication and comparison in different times and places, and it is an ultimate advantage to pin down each study to a distinct—and not necessarily typical—context.' Though this strategy had intellectual merits and minimised the cost of the study, haphazard replication could be very expensive in aggregate and could easily fail to provide the combination of times and places necessary for generalisation. Multi-locality, as distinct from national, surveys can certainly be justified, but they need to be planned as an integrated whole, not left to the vagaries of replication.

The authors of *Voting* were enormously impressed by the influence of context and environment on individual voting choices. So they described Elmira's social conditions, its historical development, its institutions, and the events of the 1948 campaign in Elmira. It was, for example, such a strongly Republican area that neither the AFL nor the CIO, as national organisations, made much effort locally; and amongst local union leaders there were more registered Republicans than Democrats. This small point illustrates the difficulty of generalising from Elmira to the USA. Yet despite the drawback of a local survey which at times threatened to force them into just that sort of community study they wished to avoid, they did succeed in finding out a great deal about truly general patterns of electoral behaviour—not patterns which were universally applicable, but patterns which were very generally applicable.

Most reviewers would agree that the Columbia tradition enshrined in *The People's Choice* and *Voting* served as the model for almost all British political survey research until the mid-sixties. Some might argue that

Butler and Stoke's *Political Change in Britain* (1969) represented the first important departure from the Columbia tradition in Britain. I would not. Despite many differences, even Butler and Stokes's work seems to me to flow from the ideas set out in *Voting*, and it is only in the seventies that radically different models have been used.

Voting claimed to be a psychological as well as a purely social study, covering topics like the authoritarian personality (which however failed to distinguish Democrats and Republicans); perceptions of group voting traditions or candidates' stands on the issues; class consciousness; interest in politics; and the process of interpersonal transmission of political ideas. It also covered institutional matters like the socio-political polarising effect of the campaign, the behaviour patterns necessary for a healthy democracy, and the effect of local party activity, canvassing, and the like.

Janowitz and Miller (1952) criticised the use of the Index of Political Predisposition on the grounds that it was insufficiently predictive. For one reason or another, little more than half of the Erie County respondents had been assigned an IPP score and, amongst those who had, only 61 per cent voted in accordance with their IPP score. So IPP prediction was little better than a random 50:50 division of respondents into Republicans and Democrats. In *The Voter Decides*, the Michigan team sharpened their criticism as follows: 'Many a political prognosticator has been led into difficulties by the confident assumption that the major population classes will vote in the next election as they have voted in the recent past' (Campbell, Gurin and Miller 1954). This criticism grossly misrepresented Columbia findings on IPP. It was inappropriate to use some crude statistic of 'voting in accord with IPP' when the IPP model stated that those with intermediate scores on IPP should vacillate more during the campaign and split their votes equally between the parties in so far as they voted at all. In addition, there had been no suggestion that social group voting was invariant over time. Indeed, the Columbia team did not see social categories as important in themselves: 'clearly the bulk of our data relate either to primary groups or to clusters of them in social strata with the latter data taken in fact as indicators of present and past primary contacts' (Bereleson *et al.* 1954: 301). This stress on family, workmates, friends, and neighbours—the so-called primary groups—was repeated in several British studies and used to very good effect by Butler and Stokes.

Similarly Berelson *et al.* noted how respondents more closely approximated the dominant partisanship of a social, religious, or trade union group the more they interacted with it, or the more closely they self-consciously identified with it. All of this was a long way from a crude social analysis which merely showed different voting patterns in different social categories. It was, in fact, at least as psychological as social, and Columbia's explicit aim was a unified social science which could not be described as either sociology or psychology.

Though the Michigan team were later to achieve some distinction by centering their analyses around the concept of 'party identification', both the concept and the measure later used by Michigan first appeared in the Columbia survey where the authors of *Voting* asked their respondents: 'Regardless of how you may vote in the coming election how have you *usually* thought of yourself—as a Republican, Democrat, Socialist, or what?' They also, like Michigan later, asked a question about intensity of partisanship, though they measured intensity in connection with voting intention, rather than with party identification. None the less it was the Columbia group who first anlysed voting and voting intentions in terms of the consistency or conflict between party identification and issue attitudes, and Columbia who analysed issue positions and political interest in terms of the direction and strength of partisanship, using a five point scale running from 'strong Republican' through to 'strong Democrat'. However, the Columbia group did not make very extensive use of party identification, stressing instead the concept and measures of previous vote or previous vote intention, dividing panel respondents into 'constants, crystallisers, disintegrators and converters'.

Columbia's model of voting had essentially three elements: 'the probability of a person's vote . . . is affected by his position in the social structure, by his former party allegiance and by the specific appeals of the campaign'. The structure of their surveys as a seven-wave panel in 1940, and four-wave panel in 1948, particularly suited such an analysis. Whereas party identification can be used in a single wave, non-panel survey to show the tension between habitual party loyalty and candidate, or issue attraction as influences on voting, a similar analysis using previous vote instead of current party identification requires either too much reliance on systematically warped memories or it requires a panel survey design.

The concept of long-standing partisanship was also implicit in the Columbia team's analysis of inter-generational partisan transmission. They found that children tended to follow the partisan inclinations of their parents at least through their twenties and into their thirties, but noted 'the relationship between children and parents *within* homogeneous (social) groups is *not* very high . . . as one takes more heterogeneous groupings and eventually the community, there is a quite marked correlation of parents' and children's votes, more because they share the same social locations than because through life the father has determined the child's vote. . . . the tendency is for people's votes in time to become independent of parents' preferences in the individual case but to remain closely proportionate to aggregate parents' preferences as a social group . . . a political tradition is a class and religious, i.e. a social, heritage as well as a purely family inheritance' (Berelson *et al*. p. 137).

Such a quotation typifies the sophistication of their analysis, but perhaps also illustrates the claims of some critics that their analysis went far beyond what the data could support. The study never ascertained the partisanship of parents, co-workers, friends, or whatever. The data base for this quotation about the influence of family partisanship was the question 'As you remember it, for which party did your father usually vote in Presidential elections when you were too young to vote?' It is not difficult to think of several reasons why answers to that question should correlate less well with the current partisanship of older respondents—less accurate memories over longer periods is only one plausible alternative to the explanation set out in *Voting*. Indeed the authors had a general tendency to treat perceptions as factual reports or psychological fictions according to the argument they wished to make at the time. Thus a response about parental partisanship long ago was treated as a factual report, but responses about candidates' policy positions in the current election were treated as subjective perceptions of candidates' policies, and even questions about respondents' own current social class were treated as subjective 'class consciousness'.

The conclusion that 'when we follow voters through six months of a political campaign we focus in a general way on decision making, but what psychological mechanisms will come into play depends to a considerable extent upon the nature of the campaign: and this can be known surely only after the fact' showed that even if the authors of *Voting* did not wish to do a current history study, there was a place for such studies; elections and election campaigns had their specific, even unique, elements which could be of great importance. In the 1948 campaign the authors characterised the most important psychological mechanism as 'reactivation of a previous tendency' as intending deviants come back into line with their social milieu.

This finding is clearly a product of their particular survey design, as well as the particular election circumstances of 1948. Change is nothing more than the difference between two positions, a starting point and a finishing point. It has no meaning except in terms of these points. Conversely its meaning varies according to the points between which change is measured. In electoral studies the finishing point is usually the vote itself, but there is no obvious starting point. At least four base lines for change may be used. First there is the change measured by *Voting*, the change from the cool of the mid-term to the heat of election day, in which reactivation may be specially significant. Second, there is the change between one election and the next. If we focus on that sort of change, reactivation will simply not be visible either in 1948 or at any other time. Third, there is the change during the short period of intense campaigning shortly before election day. By then, much of the normal reactivation may have already occurred and a different sort of change may come to predominate. So for example, in British election campaigns, third parties have normally been squeezed in the months before the start of the short campaign proper, their support down to a fraction of its mid-term level as major-party dissidents return to the fold; but in the three weeks of the campaign proper, third party support has tended to rise under the influence of quite different mechanisms, including an excess of media coverage. Lastly, we might measure change as the deviation of actual voting from some hypothetical, timeless, 'normal' vote—a technique pioneered by the Michigan analysts.

What I want to stress, is that these different forms of change correspond to different survey designs. Or conversely, that different survey designs will reveal certain sorts of change but obscure other sorts. The survey design for *Voting* was well-suited to the investigation of only one of the four forms of change I have listed. It is easy to remember that the study was about the 1948 election, yet forget that it was equally about the situation six months prior to the election, and the changes over *that* period rather than over other periods.

The authors themselves were well aware that only certain limited types of change could be studied using their survey. But within its limits, their treatment of change was impressive. They noted, for example, that roughly constant but very unequal levels of Republican and Democratic voting over the years meant that the rate of defection must necessarily be higher amongst the minority party—a logical point which was still being 're-discovered' by British political scientists thirty years later—and they explained this paradox in terms of their contact-breeds-consensus theory.

Although *Voting* used a four-wave panel, relatively few variables were measured in more than one wave: so in some ways it was a single interview in four parts, rather than a true panel. Berelson, Lazarsfeld, and McPhee advocated the use of '16-fold tables' to analyse 'interactions'. The terms 'two-way causation', 'mutual causation', or 'interdependence' might be more appropriate than their less specific term 'interaction'. Three examples were: (1) liking Truman and rating class issues as important; (2) being interested in the campaign and being exposed to media coverage of it; (3) expecting one party to win and preferring that party to win. Within each of these pairs we might plausibly expect that each variable would act positively on the other. Being interested in the campaign would encourage the respondent to read about it in the press and listen to relevant radio programmes; and conversely exposure to media coverage would increase his or her interest. By classifying respondents into high interest versus low interest, and high exposure versus low exposure in each of two waves of the panel, we get a 16-fold table, from which we can determine whether exposure comes into line with interest or interest into line with exposure, or both. But as the authors of *Voting* admitted 'it is unfortunate that, because of limitations in the 1948 data and editorial requirements of a volume of this type, we could not use such analyses more often in this report'. Kessler and Greenberg (1981) also point out that the 16-fold table technique allows two-way causation with a time lag, but assumes no instantaneous two-way influences.

Yet whatever the criticisms of these pioneering studies, *The People's Choice* and *Voting* set high standards in sample design and in intellectually sophisticated, but non-technical analysis. They also set themes which proved of continuing interest: media influence, social networks as distinct from mere social categories, personality effects, the distinction between position issues and style (later called valence) issues, partisanship as an influence on voting, the sharp contrast between the Demos of democratic theory and the reality of the American electorate, the gateway theory of issues, and the campaign behaviour of political parties.

7.2 *The Michigan tradition*

Lazarsfeld and Berelson's pioneering studies of the 1940 and 1948 presidential elections were followed by a wave of academic political surveys on both sides of the Atlantic. But whereas British analysts followed the Columbia model so closely that they produced almost carbon copies of *Voting*, American analysts at Michigan University adopted a survey model which differed from Columbia's in both survey design and political substance. Moreover, they stressed these differences to the point of exaggeration: so that the differences received more attention than the similarities. The British, by contrast, were self-conscious imitators of Columbia.

Michigan studies differed from *Voting* in three important ways. First, Michigan claimed their studies were social psychological. So, of course, did Columbia. But Michigan focused very heavily indeed on individualistic psychological mediating variables between social structure and voting, principally 'party identification'. Second, although Michigan's primary aim was the same as Columbia's—to search out broad generalisations whose validity transcended restrictions of space and time—Michigan tilted towards 'current-history' surveys, whereas Columbia had tilted towards a 'community study'. Thus Michigan analysts employed a nation-wide sample and repeated their study at each succeeding election, using many of the same variables each time. Third, Michigan stressed the importance of institutions, both as forces conditioning mass political behaviour, and as important parts of the political system in their own right; but the one institution they did not give much attention was the election campaign itself which had so fascinated Columbia analysts.

The Michigan group did not deny the importance of social structure. They noted in *The American Voter* that 'the stability of mass perceptions depends on how well they are bound into the social fabric' and they investigated the political influence of age, sex, education, industrial sector, and class, concluding: 'class is clearly one of the underlying dimensions of party affiliation in the USA' (Campbell, Converse, Miller and Stokes 1960). Eulau (1962) used Michigan surveys for his *Class and Party in the Eisenhower Years*. But Michigan also found: 'it (class) does not have the overriding importance that it has in the party systems of many Western European democracies where the parties tend to be more closely identified with specific economic ideologies'. Appropriately enough this comment appeared in the book entitled *The American Voter*, a title which denotes a very different objective from the one encapsulated in Chicago's title, *Voting*. Although members of the Michigan team later co-operated in a number of important non-American surveys, they were remarkably diffident about exporting their basic political model in an unmodified form. Paradoxically, Michigan's much more widely spread sample went with a much more geographically restricted conceptual model than Columbia's, especially in the early years.

Michigan's Survey Research Centre was formed after the war by ex-members of the US Department of Agriculture Programme Surveys Division, mostly without any background in political science. Shortly before the 1948 election they tacked some political questions on to a survey for a government agency and, following the media pollsters' disastrous forecasts of the 1948 result, they went back and re-interviewed their respondents partly to help in the SSRC post-mortem. They asked very few questions, though they relied heavily on open-ended questions with subsequent classification of the answers. Their report was also very short, but came out commendably quickly as a mimeo in April 1949— less than six months after the election—and later in printed form as *The People Elect a President* (Campbell and Kahn 1952).

Michigans's 1948 sample comprised only 577 respondents, spread right across the United States. The analysis was routine and sociological and gave little clue to the direction Michigan surveys would take from 1952 onwards, though the fifth of six suggestions for future research was to analyse the nature and correlates of party identification, including its origins in the family. However, Michigan's own 1948 study did not use either the concept or the measure of party identification in the text.

In the interval between 1948 and 1952 Janowitz and Miller criticised Chicago's Index of Political Predisposition, but their article itself still looked forward to refining rather than abandoning the Index. Belknap and Campbell (1951), however, published an article titled 'Political party identification and attitudes towards foreign policy'. Despite its title, this article still made no use of any explicit measure for party identification. It was based on hypothetical voting preferences. But it did stress the concept, if not the measure, of identification.

Belknap and Campbell had noticed that, in their 1948 survey, party preference correlated with attitudes to domestic issues but not with attitudes to foreign policy issues. However, when the bipartisan foreign policy in Congress ended in 1951, media surveys began to show intending Democrats and Republicans differing on foreign policy as well as on domestic policy. Moreover, foreign policy differences were most marked on issues that came closest to implying open approval or disapproval of President Truman. Not for the last time, newspaper published polls proved critically important for academic theorising.

We could explain this change between 1948 and 1951 by a rise in the salience of foreign affairs, coupled with better differentiated party policies on foreign matters. (See Nie, Verba and Petrocik 1976: 100–101 for Gallup trends in foreign policy issue salience.) But the change prompted Belknap and Campbell to suggest another plausible explanation, namely that 'for many people Democratic or Republican attitudes regarding foreign policy result from conscious or unconscious adherence to a perceived party line, rather than from influences independent of party identification'. As Campbell, Gurin and Miller (1954) put it later: 'Identification with a political party undoubtedly varies from a superficial preference for one or the other party to a strong sense of association with the symbols of the party, a feeling of group-belonging, and a high degree of involvement with party activities.' At one end of the continuum, partisanship might well depend upon issue attitudes, but at the other, partisanship might be so strongly rooted in the individual that it would act as an independent, causative force, influencing his or her other political attitudes. Recent analysis of the tension between partisanship and attitudes towards devolution in Scotland (W. L. Miller 1983) illustrates just such a pattern of varying causal dominance.

This line of thinking was first expounded at length in *The Voter Decides*, Michigan's analysis of its 1952 presidential election survey. In this, Campbell and his associates admitted social influences were strong—58 per cent of the managerial classes voted Republican, compared with 38 per cent of other white-collar groups, 15 per cent of skilled and semi-skilled workers and only 12 per cent of the unskilled, according to Michigan figures. However, the focus of their interest was not on 'ultimate causes' but on 'intervening variables', the psychological influences motivating voting choice and immediately prior to it. Michigan found six of these influenced voting in the broad sense of turnout and party choice: personal identification with one of the parties, concern with issues, personal attraction to presidential candidates, conformity to group standards of associates, a sense of political efficacy, and a sense of civic obligation. The first three were prime determinants of the party choice component of voting behaviour, the others were more relevant to turnout than party choice. Of the first three, party identification represented a relatively stable long-term influence, while issue and candidate attractions represented relatively short-term influences specific to a particular election campaign. Party identification was measured by a variant of Berelson and Lazarsfeld's question: 'Generally speaking, do you usually consider yourself a Republican, a Democrat, an Independent, or what?'

These motivational variables were close to the behaviour they sought to explain—some critics claimed they were too close to be interesting. After all, a finding that Democratic identifiers tend to vote Democratic if they vote at all is a bit like saying Catholic identifiers tend to attend Catholic rather than Protestant places of worship, if they attend any at all. No doubt identifications do explain behavioural choices, but the span of the explanation may be very limited.

Yet the significance of party identification as a concept rested, paradoxically, on its failure to predict voting. It was necessary for respondents to cast votes out-of-line with their party identification to establish the existence of identification, independent from voting. Campbell and his collaborators pointed to the 'tenacity with which most people hold to their party label even when they are crossing party lines to support the opposition (with their votes). We do not know how long it takes to convert any appreciable segment of the electorate from one party to the other, or under what conditions. Apparently such a phenomenon occurred during the Roosevelt era. It has not occurred thus far during the Eisenhower period'. In short, the function of party identification was not to explain the election of Eisenhower, but to explain why the natural governing party in America remained the Democrats, even though the electorate had elected and went on to re-elect the Republican candidate Eisenhower.

Michigan's stress on party identification seems to have grown out of theoretical attempts to explain various paradoxes in American political attitudes and out of the analytical need to cope with complex voting outcomes like split-ballots. Party identification, if not imposed on the data, certainly did not spring out of it. Michigan placed great emphasis on open-ended questions about respondents' likes and dislikes concerning the parties and the candidates. They categorised most electors as non-ideological when they did not respond to these likes and dislikes questions with answers rich in explicitly ideological terminology. But fewer than one respondent in six expressed his or her likes or dislikes about the parties in terms of conscious identification with them (see Nie, Verba, and Petrocik 1976: 21). Something like 40 per cent named party as the reason for liking or disliking a presidential candidate; but, since British parliamentary candidates are virtually unknown to their electors except in party terms, that figure might rise to near 100 per cent in Britain without proving the need for a concept of party identification distinct from party preference.

This theoretical concern with party identification as an independent variable constitutes the main point of interest in *The Voter Decides*. Although the sample was much bigger than Michigan's 1948 sample, this time up to just over 2,000 respondents spread nationally throughout the USA, the survey design introduced few innovations and the panel element was reduced to a mere two waves, one before the election, one after.

In some ways it was unfortunate that Michigan began by using party identification in the context of a presidential election. Eisenhower's election may have revealed the need for a concept of party identification, but it obscured the power of the concept. Perhaps it is obvious that when people vote for presidential candidates they are likely to be influenced to a substantial but less than total extent by their party colours as well as their smiling faces. Party is one, but only one, of a candidate's significant attributes. It is a good deal less obvious that party is one, but only one, of the significant attributes of a party itself. When a *party* contests an election it goes into the contest with all the loyalties, associations, affiliations, and identities built up by its past history. It also goes into the contest with current policies, and in a political climate influenced by current events and by tactical considerations. The Democratic identifier who voted for Eisenhower because he or she liked the man illustrates the concept of party identification less well than the Liberal identifier in Glasgow Central who votes Conservative because there is no Liberal candidate in that constituency, or the pro-EEC Labour identifier who votes Conservative because the issue temporarily takes precedence over his or her long-standing partisanship, or the extreme Labour identifier who votes Conservative in the hope that popular reactions against four years of right-wing government will lay the foundation for a Labour government with a mandate for a strongly socialist programme. Clearly an American presidential candidate is a person, something distinct from a party; but in my British examples, parties themselves are the objects of partisan influence. This surely is the purest example of party identification, where the voter votes against the very object with which he or she identifies, not against some closely associated object, yet still retains a meanful identification with it.

Naturally, it would not do if everyone voted against the party they identified with. The concept is useful if enough people vote at odds with their party identification to establish its reality, but not so many as to destroy its predictive power. In the fifties critics attacked Michigan for using a concept which was so close as to be almost indistinguishable from the voting it sought to explain. In the seventies critics attacked Michigan for devising a concept whose predictive power was visibly failing. Both sets of critics were wrong and their criticisms, taken together, constitute a resounding justification. But the concept is a subtle one and needs the most careful operationalisation and analytic treatment. For example, a single wave post-election survey which asks both vote and party identification is asking respondents to recall their recent vote and describe their current sense of party identification. David Hume would have been horrified by the temporal inversion implied by treating that measure of identification as a cause of that measure of vote. Party identification may be treated as a major influence on current and future voting but is itself partly dependent on past voting choices. It may be durable, but it is not invariant, and the time point at which it is measured is significant.

Michigan enlarged on its treatment of party identification in *The American Voter*, based on its 1956 survey. Party identification had its origins in early politicisation in the home and was later modified by personal forces—such as a change of milieu occasioned by intergenerational class mobility, geographic mobility, or marriage; or by social forces—such as national crises like the Civil War or the New Deal era. Class influenced party identification, but its influence varied systematically across the vast terrain of the USA. Class was most powerful in the West, while its influence was virtually non-existent in the South, where partisanship sprang from other factors. Similarly class effects were different in different age groups, reflecting the disruptive effects of the New Deal era.

In most of these analyses, where party identification was the dependent variable and class, region, age, etc. were treated as the independent causative variables, Michigan gained very little other than theoretical tidiness by using party identification instead of party preference. But in other analyses which looked at the causal flow beyond party identification, they were able to treat topics that would have been totally intractable otherwise. In particular, one section of *The American Voter* discussed the notoriously volatile American farm vote. Michigan analysts found that in rural areas the level and strength of party identification was low. They interpreted this finding as an indication that farmers had relatively little 'psychological anchor' in the existing structure of the traditional parties. While they discussed some of the reasons for this, they stressed the causes less than the consequences: without a strong sense of party identification, rural voters would be open to the appeals of new parties. From the systemic viewpoint low party identification provided the conditions for 'flash' parties—sudden flashes of voting support unrooted in deep commitment or careful consideration. They hypothesised a similar explanation for the rise of Nazi voting in the Weimar Republic. Later they applied this model to surveys of the French electorate and recently it has been applied to British politics.

The exciting possibility was that it might be applied predictively. That is, survey analysts might be able to warn of impending voting volatility by detecting a prior drop in the pervasiveness or the strength of party identification. The voting volatility of American farmers and the French had been observed before Michigan was able to measure their party identifications. So in these cases the explanations were *post hoc*. Declining party identification did not predict the increase in voting volatility in the sixties, either in Britain or America. In America the era of electoral landslides began as a response to the Goldwater candidacy in 1964 and party identification declined in the wake of voting volatility. Indeed, the percentage of strong partisans did not drop even in 1964. What happened in 1964 was that the predictive power of partisanship dropped. The drop in partisanship itself did not occur until 1966. (See Nie *et al.* 1976: 49 and 165.) Similarly in Britain, the drop in strong Labour and Conservative party identification did not occur until 1974, long after increasing voter volatility had become evident in swings at general elections, by-elections, and monthly opinion-poll party-preferences. So in this important respect, the concept of party identification has still to prove its predictive capability.

Between 1956 and 1960 Michigan continued to develop its own brand of political surveys. First the series begun in 1948 (or more realistically 1952) was extended by another four years. This feature of Michigan surveys is so obvious that it is easily overlooked. A major feature of the Michigan tradition is simply an emphasis on routine collection of series information over a very long period of time, now a third of a century. Secondly, in 1958 Michigan began regular surveys of the 'off-year' elections when Congressmen but not Presidents are elected. Since 1956 therefore, they have surveyed the electorate at two-year instead of four-year intervals. Thus their work has moved further away from the early attempts to seek out timeless generalisations about voting, and further towards a highly sophisticated brand of current history survey. In addition their 1956, 1958, and 1960 surveys constituted an inter-election panel in which the same respondents were re-interviewed over a period of four years, in contrast to the six-month campaign panels of the Columbia group and the three-week campaign panels of some early British surveys. This 1956–58–60 panel served as the model for Butler and Stokes's 1963–64–66–70 panel study of the British electorate.

Quite unconnected with their development of an inter-election panel, Michigan also made special efforts to show the relevance of mass surveys to institutions and to theories of the political system. Hence the title of their report: *Elections and the Political Order* (Campbell et al. 1966). Party identification was used to develop the concept of the 'normal vote', that is the party shares of the vote that could be expected in the electorate as a whole, or in any subgroup of it, given the levels of Democratic and Republican identifiers. It would be wrong to assume that the 'normal' number of Democratic votes would simply equal the number of Democratic identifiers. Many Independents would normally vote Democratic, as would some weak Republican identifiers and even a few strong Republican identifiers. Conversely, some Democratic identifiers would normally defect. But the rates of defection and gain could be estimated from past surveys.

Using this normal vote analysis, the Michigan analysts went on to classify elections as maintaining (1948), realigning (1928, 1932, 1936), deviating (1952, 1956), and reinstating (1960), depending upon whether presidential voters merely strayed away from the normal voting choices predicted by their partisanship, or changed that partisanship itself.

Party identification analyses were extended to the class-ridden Norwegian electorate and the highly volatile French electorate. Although Frenchmen who could recall their parents' partisanship themselves adopted some party affiliation as readily as Americans, most Frenchmen could not recall their parents' partisanship and were reluctant to associate themselves with any party. According to the Michigan analysis, this led to low levels of party identification in France and hence to an unstable party system.

In addition to these developments in party identification research, Michigan extended its treatment of institutions and theory in other ways. Miller and Stokes used a parallel survey of Congressmen's perceptions of their constituents, combined with mass survey data in a regression-based recursive causal model, to evaluate the representation model followed by Congressmen. On race issues Congressmen followed a delegate model, voting in accord with their perception of constituency attitudes; on social-welfare issues their votes reflected constituency attitudes, but mainly because the partisan election process had produced Congressmen whose views on these issues coincided with the dominant view in their constituencies; on foreign issues Congressmen's votes did not reflect constituency attitudes in any way, but responded to other influences.

In another attempt to integrate surveys with theory, this time empirical rather than normative theory, Stokes compared the premises of Antony Downs's *Economic Theory of Democracy* with Michigan survey findings about mass attitudes towards parties. When Ions called Downs an 'economic imperialist' describing an 'Alice-in-Wonderland World', he was essentially relying on the solid survey evidence produced by Stokes. If not, he was merely expressing the unhelpful view that Downs's intuition did not match Ions's.

The panel element of Michigan's 1956–58–60 survey was used most powerfully by Converse, but in a highly destructive way. Converse found that between elections it was the least informed and least involved who changed their party identification most and who deviated from it most easily in their voting. This essentially reiterated Columbia findings based on campaign panels. He also argued that mass political attitudes showed little evidence of constraint, either in the sense of coherence between attitudes on different issues or in the sense of stability over time.

A small team of senior researchers read through every questionnaire in the 1956 survey, paying special but not exclusive attention to the answers to open-ended questions. They classified respondents according to how much ideological content appeared in the answers. Only 2 per cent were classified as ideologues and a further 9 per cent as near ideologues. This method of classification was subjective, uncheckable, and highly expensive. It has not been repeated very often.

But Converse used other systems of measuring attitude constraint which have been repeated more frequently. First, he correlated attitudes towards different issues like guaranteed employment policies, federal aid to education and the like. Correlations between domestic issue attitudes were low, and correlations between domestic and foreign issue attitudes very low indeed. Correlations between policy attitudes and partisanship were also very low. The same procedure applied to élite samples produced rather higher correlations, typically two or three times as large as in the mass electorate. Thus in the electorate at large a knowledge of someone's attitude to one issue did not permit prediction of his or her attitudes to other issues. Hence logical, psychological, or even social constraints on issue attitudes were absent, said Converse, though his method would not have detected subgroups of the electorate with internally homogeneous attitude packages that differed from subgroup to subgroup.

Next he used the 1956–58–60 panel to show that attitudes were not constrained over time, that knowledge of a person's attitude to an issue in 1956 could not even be used to predict his or her attitude to the same issue in 1958 or 1960. Over the two-year interval 1958–60, party identification correlated with itself at 0.72; but a segregation attitude enshrined in agreement or rejection of the proposition: 'the government should stay out of whether white and coloured children go to the same school' correlated with itself at only 0.48; and attitudes on foreign aid, foreign military intervention, or government intervention in electricity supply and housing provision each correlated with themselves at only around 0.30. Thus, in a sea of unstable political attitudes, only party identification stood out as the solid rock of continuity and consistency. Converse did not stop there. By comparing correlations over the two short periods 1956–58 and 1958–60 with that over the longer period 1956–60, he raised doubts about the meaning of attitude changes. The argument is highly technical, but it hinges on the finding that correlations over the longer period were low, but no lower than over the shorter periods. This paradox can be explained by a number of mathematical models, including ones that postulate high levels of measurement error or 'homing' tendencies towards long-run consistency. But Converse pointed out that what he called a 'Black-White' model fitted some of his data. In this a few respondents, perhaps a fifth, have genuine attitudes on the issue. The rest merely say *yes* or *no* at random with, of course, no connection between their replies on one occasion and on another (Converse 1964). As Converse later stressed, his Black-White model was presented only as a limiting case and only as a possible explanation (Converse 1974). His analysis of the 1956–60 panel was a caution against giving too much weight to attitudes or 'non-attitudes' measured by opinion poll questions. Too many of those who read his article interpreted it as evidence that the public had no real opinions and would never acquire them. Then, as this view proved at odds with later data, the question arose whether Americans had always been genuinely concerned about issues or whether the US was experiencing a rising tide of issue voting and ideology.

A wide-ranging critique of the classic Michigan studies appeared in *Party Identification and Beyond* (Budge, Crewe, and Farlie 1976). Crewe, Thomassen, and Kaase, working respectively with British, Dutch, and German survey data, suggested that party identification was neither logically nor temporally prior to voting if, indeed, it was distinguishable from voting at all. Crewe pointed to the 'inability of the (Michigan) model to explain political change in Britain' since Labour and Conservative identification did not drop during the sixties, nor in 1970, despite increasing voting volatility. Nor was party identification durable: by the early seventies Converse and Dupeux's finding that France had a much lower level of party identification than America had been reversed (Inglehart and Hochstein 1972), suggesting that changes in party identification lag behind other more visible and ultimately more important political changes. Thomassen found in a 1970–72 panel survey of the Netherlands that respondents changed their party identification considerably more than they changed their party vote preference. Using partial correlation methods of causal modelling, he concluded that party identification in the Netherlands was not distinct from vote preference, that both were imperfect measures of the same thing, and that the only real indicator of long-term dispositions was the respondent's socio-religious background. Kaase used several German surveys to make the point that party identification in Germany was not truly distinguishable from vote preference, though changes in question wordings made his results less than decisive. In addition he was willing to dismiss the acknowledged fact that a sizeable number of SPD identifiers had cast their 'second vote' for the FDP as a strategic choice to preserve parliamentary representation for the SPD's coalition partner. Clearly this was a case of party identification distinct from voting choice, but Kaase remained unimpressed because these respondents' basic SPD adherence could be measured more directly by the direction of their 'first vote' without the need to employ psychological constructs like party identification. Again Kaase saw long-term political dispositions as rooted directly in social structure, and social rather than political identification.

As a corollary to their critique of party identification, contributors to *Party Identification and Beyond* did not dismiss the utility of ideology as an organising concept for political analysis. In the multi-party systems of continental Europe an ideology-based view of the parties, arrayed along a left–right spectrum of some sort, had a wonderfully simplifying effect upon political choice. Using feeling-thermometers to measure warmth of feeling towards each party, supplemented by measures of issue attitudes and analysed by the new dimensional techniques of multi-dimensional scaling, they attempted to infer the dimensional structure of mass belief systems—with some success. Correlations between issue attitudes and between issue and partisan attitudes might be low, but the relative sizes of the correlations exhibited a readily interpretable structure (Inglehart and Sidjanski 1976). Fully 83 per cent of a nine-nation European sample of 12,000 respondents were willing to place themselves on a left–right scale, and although this generally seemed to reflect party attachment more than issue attitudes or highly developed ideological thinking, this was not always so. For example, the survey finding that in the 1974 French presidential election the Socialist candidate won 87 per cent of the votes of Socialist Party identifiers but 97 per cent of the votes of Communist Party identifiers is more easily explicable in terms of ideology than party identity; as is the fact that Giscard won 90 per cent of the Gaullist vote after a bitter first ballot contest in which he had defeated the Gaullists' own candidate. Throughout the seventies, therefore, Michigan surveys have sought to measure ideological identification on a liberal–conservative scale, as well as purely party identification. (See Eijk and Niemoller 1983 for a recent restatement of the ideological identification theme.)

Michigan's 1980 presidential election study 'differed from its predecessors in many ways but most sharply in its deliberate attempt to capture the dynamic elements of change in individuals' political attitudes, beliefs and behaviour' by using a six-wave panel design collecting information at 'points in time ranging from just prior to the first primary election to the period immediately following the general election itself' (W. E. Miller and Shanks 1982). While that design differed from its Michigan predecessors, it was remarkably similar to the original Columbia panel studies of the 1940 and 1948 election campaigns, and Michigan rediscovered some old reactivation processes still operating in the run-up period. Between the early primaries and the national nominating conventions in the summer there was a sharp increase in ideological polarisation, but not party polarisation: that is, self-confessed 'liberals' began to see Carter as much closer to themselves on policy matters, while self-confessed 'conservatives' felt increasingly close to Reagan; but Democratic and Republic identifiers did not polarise in the same way. After the nominating conventions, however, with Carter and Reagan now representing their parties, there was a swift and even more extensive perceptual polarisation along party lines. Democratic identifiers now and only now saw Carter's policies as close to their own, while Republicans similarly perceived Reagan's position as close to theirs. Partisanship was clearly still a highly influential factor, a powerful cause of other political attitudes.

Miller and Shanks found no evidence of partisan realignment, partisan dealignment, or ideological realignment in 1980. But 'party identification was apparently not as dominant a determinant of the vote in 1980 as it had been a quarter of a century earlier. Even if the erosion of the sense of partisanship stopped in 1976 and was reversed in 1980, the consequences of having a party preference were less decisive in 1980 than they had been only four years earlier.' Party identification in 1980 remained the principal determinant of voters' choices between Carter and Reagan, but cross-party voting increased sharply and other factors exerted a major, if subordinate influence on presidential voting choice.

Michigan's perennial interest in institutions as well as individuals comes out very clearly in Miller and Shanks's analysis. The question they set out to answer was one with very important implications for the interpretation of democratic elections: namely, did Reagan's election constitute a mandate for ideological change or was it merely a by-product of the rejection of an incumbent president or even a by-product of persistent rejection of Washington government?

Before they could begin to answer this question, Miller and Shanks argued that explanatory models of voting behaviour were of two different kinds: either they explained polarisation—that is, they discovered the factors that made one person vote for Reagan and another for Carter; or they explained the plurality—that is, they discovered the factors that contributed to the overall majority for Reagan. Now some factors might have an enormous influence on polarisation but dispose as many electors towards Carter as towards Reagan and hence contribute nothing to the victory of one over the other. Conversely other factors might have relatively little influence on individuals, but that influence might be so biased in favour of one candidate that its net effect on who won might be highly significant.

In 1980, Miller and Shanks concluded that partisanship was by far the greatest influence on individual vote choices, but because of the balance in numbers between Democratic and Republican identifiers, it only contributed 10 per cent towards the margin of victory. And since there were more Democrats than Republicans, its contribution was to *reduce* Reagan's majority by 10 per cent. Ideological identification had a smaller effect, and in a pro-Reagan direction, since more Americans identified themselves as 'conservatives' than 'liberals'. Purely personal characteristics of the candidates had large effects on individual voters' choices, but influenced almost as many voters towards one candidate as the other and thus had a minimal net effect on the overall outcome.

But the central question had been whether Reagan's election owed more to repudiation of Carter's record or support for right-wing policy changes. Here Miller and Shanks found that both factors made a large net contribution to Reagan's majority. But while evaluations of Carter's performance had considerably more influence on individual voters' choices than did preferences for policy changes, attitudes on policy changes were so much less evenly balanced than evaluations of Carter's performance that preference for change had a considerably larger net effect on the overall outcome.

These conclusions about 1980 are still provisional, and other analysts would still dispute them. (See Williams 1982 for a review of alternative interpretations of the 1980 result.) Yet Miller and Shanks's basic conceptual distinction between 'explaining the vote' and 'explaining the outcome' is of fundamental importance. However clear and obvious it appears when stated explicitly, persistent failure to recognise and articulate the distinction has produced a lot of muddled thinking by other researchers. Michigan's focus on *elections* as distinct from *voters* represents a real advance over the Columbia studies.

The panel element of the 1980 study is to be commended. But it went only part of the way towards fulfilling the declared objective of 'monitoring the impact of campaign events and assessing their contribution to the final decision in November'. A six-wave panel spread over the election year was particularly suited to studying those reactivation processes that went on as politics was transformed from a 'mid-term' to an 'election' footing. But it was not well suited to studying the impact of the campaign proper —that is the period between nomination and election. The pre-election wave of interviews was 'spread fairly evenly throughout September and October' and was thus insufficiently time-specific. As Miller and Shanks admitted, 'the design simply does not provide data in finely enough spaced intervals to assess or interpret changes during that final weekend (before the election)—but something appears to have happened during that period'. One wave of interviews every two or three months, especially when a single wave takes two months of interviewing, provides a suitable base for studying general processes of reactivation but not for 'monitoring the impact of campaign events'.

7.3 *Comparative analyses*

From quite early on in the Michigan series of election studies it was apparent that an essential part of their approach was to survey, survey and survey again because they were writing electoral history and, indeed, more broadly conceived political history. Panels proved that respondents' memories were untrustworthy: so although Michigan used memories when nothing better was available, a major developing concern was to document changing political and electoral moods as they happened, for they could never be adequately documented again. During the seventies this approach matured and the series of Michigan electoral studies spanning two, then three, decades grew long enough for changes and trends to be distinguished from mere wobble. A feature of much recent work is its use of anything up to a dozen Michigan surveys. Harvard University Press has recently published two guides to the data amassed by Michigan: a *National Election Studies Data Sourcebook 1952–78* and a *Social Attitudes Data Sourcebook 1947–78* (Survey Research Centre, 1980a, 1980b). Though there are inevitable problems of comparability in such long time-series, Michigan's continuous oversight has produced far more possibilities for long term analyses than would have been likely if each survey had been the product of a different team of investigators, or worse: if the mounting of each survey had depended upon the chances of different teams of investigators sequentially concluding that their work required a national survey around the time of the next presidential election.

It has now become almost standard practice to analyse the whole sequence of Michigan surveys as a single time-structured data set. An interesting relationship found in one survey will be checked for generality and trend, using all the other surveys in the sequence. This research strategy has underlined the significance of Berelson and Lazarsfeld's early assertion that voting patterns depend, among other things, on the 'specific appeals of the campaign'. Surveys over time have not shown exogenous trends in mass political behaviour; they have brought political events and campaign appeals into the model. Mass political behaviour has clearly responded to changes in élite behaviour. V. O. Key's early complaint that surveys 'took the politics out of political science' was never a fair attack on Columbia work, but his attack could not even be made with any semblance of plausibility on recent studies of Michigan series data.

One example of this series approach is Wright's *Dissent of the Governed: Alienation and Democracy in America*, which traces the trends in respondents' sense of political efficacy and in their trust in government over the years 1956 to 1972. Still more typical are studies which have looked at the changing relationship between partisanship, narrow political issues, broader ideology, and voting choices—including Pomper's neutrally titled *Varieties of American Political Behaviour*, Nie, Verba, and Petrocik's *The Changing American Voter*, and W. E. Miller and Levitin's evocatively titled *Leadership and Change*. Nie and his associates used the full Michigan 1952–72 series. So did Pomper, though he concentrated attention on 1956, 1964, and 1972. Miller and Levitin used the series from 1952 to 1976, but concentrated on more recent years: 1970, 1972, 1974, and 1976.

Though these various studies attend to different aspects of American political attitudes and behaviour, several themes recur in them all. The classic Michigan work on the late fifties probably under-estimated the amount of ideology and issue-responsiveness in the American electorate at that time. Since then, however, there appear to have been real changes. The extent and power of party identification declined at least until 1972: fewer Americans identified with any party at all, and those that continued to do so were less bound by their party identification when voting. Class and ethnic political differences mostly declined, primarily as social group partisanship declined and the number of Independents increased, rather than through a more even party balance in within-group partisanship. Simultaneously there was a rise in issue constraint, in ideology, and in the power of issues to determine voting. The changes have been described as 'partisan dealignment' rather than 'realignment'.

But terms like 'rise' and 'growth' can be misleading. Two critical features of this so-called rise in ideology and issue voting were, first, the discontinuity in trends which occurred in 1964 and, second, the discontinuity in content between the new American ideology and the old. Curves depicting a growing correlation between different issue attitudes, or between issue attitudes and voting do not show a steady rise from the elections of the fifties to those of the seventies; they approximate to what mathematicians call a 'step-function', with a sharp discontinuity in 1964. Indeed, the curves often peak in 1964 and decline somewhat, after an explosive rise in 1964 itself. This suggests that the Goldwater candidacy of 1964, which self-consciously offered 'a choice, not an echo', had a major effect on structuring mass political attitudes and behaviour. And this view is supported by the relationship between campaign appeals and mass responses in subsequent elections. Carter's 1976 campaign, which deliberately avoided contentious issues or sharply delineated ideological appeals, produced an election in which party identification 're-emerged' as a determinant of the vote (A. H. Miller 1978) and 'the 1976 election was as much a party election as those elections from the 1950s or early 1960s in which party was acknowledged to be a major determinant of voters' decisions' (W. E. Miller and Levitin 1976: 211).

However, the progress of events also probably contributed to changes in attitude patterns. For example, Gallup data show a sudden eruption of popular concern over race issues in the summer of 1963, following the Birmingham (Alabama) riots. Unfortunately, the frequency of Michigan's survey series is insufficient to allow us to pin-point the exact time of changes, or the precise sequence. Surveys restricted to election times are unable to distinguish the impact of mid-term events from those of the campaign.

The second feature of the 'new' American politics was just that: it was *qualitatively new*, rather than merely quantitatively different from the old politics of Roosevelt's New Deal. If class differences declined, age or generational differences increased. And whereas the core of the old New Deal ideology had been support for or opposition to government intervention and welfare schemes, the new American ideological dimension centred round a different mix of issues: 'social' issues rather than economic issues. 'Social order' issues would perhaps be a better description. They concerned the role of the police, the civil liberties of dissenters, crime and violence, the morals and values of the young. Self-confessed 'liberals' and self-confessed 'conservatives' now switched positions when asked about their attitudes to big government. Liberals increasingly saw state intervention as the instrument of political oppression, rather than social liberation (see Nie *et al.* 1976: 127, for example).

Stimulating though these studies were, they were disappointingly weak on causal analysis. Trend analyses may be more informative, certainly more thought-provoking than single-wave cross-sectional studies. But if they merely comprise a sequence of cross-sectional surveys, instead of a panel re-interviewed at intervals, too many of the thoughts that are provoked remain nothing more than informed speculation. Causal priorities cannot be determined. Thus Nie and his associates lamented their inability to decide, without panel data, whether the increased correlation between issue attitudes and voting reflected an increased power of issues to determine voting choices, or whether it merely meant 'that citizens in 1964 felt greater necessity to adopt issue positions consistent with their favoured candidates or were more likely to rationalise their preference for a candidate in issue terms'. Similarly, they lamented their inability to 'test our sequential model of change in attitudes' concerning the causal relationship between declining trust in government and increasing ideological coherence, again quoting the lack of panel data as the reason for their inconclusive analysis. Likewise, Miller and Levitin had to admit that 'since the same people who were interviewed in the 1970 Michigan study were not re-interviewed again in the 1972 study, the descriptions and explanations of the 'who' and the 'why' of change must, perforce, be speculative'. Even in the 1980 study, which was at least a year-long campaign panel, the panel was used primarily for accurate trend analysis rather than truly dynamic analysis, and the final conclusions were drawn from a cross-sectional regression on the final pre-election wave.

8 Parliamentary election surveys since 1950

In America the most notable response to Columbia's early election studies was broad acceptance of the method, coupled with a change of focus from social to psychological influences on voting. But British academics either rejected the whole notion of mass surveys, or copied both Columbia's methods and Columbia's themes. Throughout the fifties, British election surveys drew samples from one or, at most, two constituencies and used a campaign panel-study format. Sample sizes were usually in the range 500 to 1,000 respondents. They focused on social alignments, the influence of the media, the electorate's qualifications for democratic participation, and on the peculiarities of the local environment in which the study was set. They also followed Columbia in neglecting the theme of party identification. All major British survey publications in the fifties referred explicitly to the Columbia studies, but Michigan got just one dismissive footnote.

Why so? The answer is probably that Columbia themes fitted well with pre-existing interests in British political science. Columbia's technique of a local survey, in a locality close to the base university, certainly fitted well with modest British academic budgets! Social alignments provided a natural organising principle, both for British politics itself and for British political analysis. Unlike America, one major party was explicitly and proudly a class party; and in contrast to continental Europe, all British parties were notoriously pragmatic and non-ideological. Labour was a class party first, and a socialist party second. So it was natural to expect that the dominant political alignment would be social, rather than ideological or even issue-based.

In 1950 British businessmen and university graduates had just lost their rights to multiple votes, women had enjoyed full voting rights for a mere two decades, and the process of decolonisation was in full swing. All these factors renewed interest in old debates about qualifications for democratic participation, and Columbia's theme of using surveys to 'confront democratic theory with democratic practice' was timely.

It is more difficult to explain the lack of attention given to Michigan style analysis of party identification. Certainly Britain lacked the institutional factors like multiple ballots, or primary elections, which help Americans understand the distinction between partisanship and voting choice; and the power and pervasiveness of the class alignment reduced the incentive to search for alternative organising principles for political analysis.

But any close reading of early British survey reports will reveal a clear need for an explicit conceptualisation of partisanship and a proper measuring instrument for it.

In 1963 Butler and Stokes began a series of surveys which set a new pattern for political surveys in Britain. It would be tempting to say they broke with the Columbia tradition, especially since Stokes was a leading member of the Michigan team. But they broke with Columbia more in method than in substance. They switched from a local to a national sample and from a campaign-panel to an inter-election panel. Furthermore, they conducted most of their analysis in terms of party identification. But the analysis did *not* conform to the Michigan model, because party identification was used primarily as a dependent variable, not as an independent influence upon voting choice. The tension between party identification and other influences on the vote was not explored. Butler and Stokes's *Political Change in Britain: The Evolution of Electoral Choice* represents a flowering of the Columbia/British tradition, more notable for its excellent development of old themes than for a switch to new ones.

Michigan concepts of party identification were first applied in the Michigan manner by Conservative party researchers working on a private survey in the late sixties. Their approach was later developed by Särlvik and Crewe at Essex University, who continued the Butler/Stokes national survey series throughout the seventies.

By then, however, British politics had become less British. Regional diversity was much more evident than in the fifties, and survey designs that had been appropriate to a two-party system in a homogeneous polity were no longer adequate. Locality now became important, for substantive rather than methodological or financial reasons. Whereas in the fifties the presumption that British politics was homogeneous made local surveys a cheap option, patent political heterogeneity in the seventies made local surveys an expensive necessity.

Ironically also, as soon as academics had agreed that significant political change occurred between elections rather than in the campaign, campaigns became obviously important in determining 'who governs'. For a month or so before the 1970 election campaign and throughout the campaign itself, Labour was ahead in the opinion polls, yet lost the election on the day. In the month before the February 1974 campaign and during the campaign itself, the Conservatives were ahead in the opinion polls, as indeed they were in the voting, though they lost i. terms of parliamentary seats. But during that campaign, Liberal support doubled and, in Scotland, SNP support went up by half. In October 1974 the Labour lead went down sharply during the campaign and in 1979 an early Conservative lead was whittled down during the campaign before increasing again at the end. Throughout the seventies it was simply not true that electoral outcomes were determined almost exclusively outside the campaign period. Sharp, politically significant changes occurred during the short campaign period.

Before I trace the development of these themes through three decades of electoral research, it may be helpful to fix the chronology of British election surveys. There was a burst of academic polling in connection with the 1950 and 1951 general elections, with surveys in Greenwich (Benney and Gleiss 1950; Benney, Gray, and Pear 1956); in Stretford (Birch and Campbell 1950); in Glossop (Birch *et al.* 1959); in Droylesden (P. Campbell, Donnison, and Potter 1952); in Bristol (Milne and Mackenzie 1954); and in Greenwich and Hertford (Martin 1952). In addition Bonham (1952, 1954) made extensive use of Gallup poll surveys of these elections. However, there was only one important study of the 1955 election (Milne and Mackenzie 1958).

A second wave of academic polling occurred at or between the elections of 1959 and 1964, including surveys in Newcastle (Bealey, Blondel, and McCann 1965); in Leeds (Trennaman and McQuail 1961); in Clapham (Sharpe 1962); in a selection of English towns (McKenzie and Silver 1968); in Luton (Goldthorpe *et al.* 1968); and in Glasgow (Budge and Urwin 1966). The Leeds study, focused primarily on media use and effects, was repeated in 1966, 1970 and 1974 (Blumler and McQuail 1968; Blumler *et al.* 1975, 1976).

Butler and Stokes started their British national panel series in 1963 (Butler and Stokes 1969 and 1974). It was continued through to 1979 by Särlvik and Crewe (1983). Regional surveys began with a 1968 survey of Northern Ireland (Rose 1971); followed by a 1974 survey of Scotland (W. L. Miller 1975, 1977b, 1981a) and Scots and Welsh surveys in 1979 (W. L. Miller 1983; Madgwick, Balsom, and van Mechelen 1983).

Regrettably, publication dates do not always give much guide to the date of the election being studied.

8.1 *The class alignment*

When academic surveys started at the beginning of the fifties, almost all the electorate voted, and almost all of them voted Labour or Conservative. In 1951 the two major parties took 97 per cent of the vote and 616 of the 625 seats in Parliament. Turnout, at 83 per cent, was close to the effective maximum that could be attained under the British system of registration. So the only topic for electoral analysis was the choice between Labour and Conservative, the reasons or the rationality behind it. Above all else, early

British surveys focused on the class alignment. Survey analysts sought to document the existence and power of the class alignment; they sought to determine its nature and quality; they measured the influence of social environments; and they went on to look at partisan variation within classes. Finally in an excess of enthusiasm for their findings about the power of class alignments, they began to treat partisan minorities within each class as deviants. Such was the power of the class alignment that they could not see it as one influence among many—in sharp contrast to American studies of class.

All the early studies found a very powerful structuring of votes by some measure of class. But at first there was no unanimity on what was meant by the class alignment. Obviously we can make any word mean whatever we like. The problem was not to define class in the abstract, but to discover empirically out of all the multitude of dimensions that are loosely associated with each other and encompassed in the general notion of class, which particular one was most closely associated with party choice.

Columbia studies had used a composite measure of socio-economic status (SES) incorporating breadwinner's occupational grade combined with education, and with the interviewer's subjective assessment of the respondent's economic level, which was based in part on ownership of common household utilities. At best this was a muddy, ill-defined composite; at worst it owed too much to the caprice of the interviewer.

But if class was to be represented in British political analysis by a single-concept measure, which should it be? Half a dozen surveys of voting patterns at the 1950 and 1951 general elections investigated this question. On the purely empirical grounds of which measure best predicted voting choice, they rejected the Hall–Jones scale of social prestige, and the Registrar General's scale of occupational skill in favour of occupational grade, dichotomised into manual versus non-manual occupations.

This same dichotomy could also be justified by an analysis of party propaganda. Bonham studied a 'large collection of articles and speeches . . . and party literature' to find out what 'class' meant in British political debate. Class was usually defined in terms of income and wealth, or in terms of 'industrial status', especially small business proprietors, or in terms of 'intellectual status', by which he meant non-manual occupations irrespective of the actual intellectual content of their work. Using cumulated Gallup surveys taken during the 1951 election campaign and totalling 9,225 respondents, he looked at the relationship between each of these and party preference. Bonham found that manual workers as a whole had low levels of Conservative preference, irrespective of income; and employers and managers as a whole had a high level of Conservative preference that was only slightly affected by income. He thus identified two social groups with a high degree of social and political coherence, and the defining characteristics were twofold—the distinction between manual workers and the rest, and the distinction between employers and managers and the rest. His findings were confirmed in other surveys with smaller samples, and these ways of defining politically relevant social classes were to recur in British political analysis.

Several studies also investigated the political impact of what may be variously described as 'self-assigned class', 'subjective class', or 'class identification': the respondents' own categorisations of themselves as middle class or working class.

Using a survey of Greenwich and Hertford, Martin found almost everyone was willing to allocate themselves to the 'middle' or 'working' class if pressed, though the middle class were more reluctant to admit the existence of class and class conflict. Both class and class identity powerfully structured vote preference, but with class somewhat more powerful than class identity. Milne and Mackenzie (1954) confirmed this finding in their survey of Bristol and noted that it reversed the conclusion in *The People's Choice* that for Americans 'the crucial factor was not so much a person's objective occupation, as his own opinion of his social status'. The survey of Glossop by Birch *et al*. revealed a more complex pattern: class identification had little effect upon voting behaviour in the extreme class categories—managers on the one side or manual workers on the other—but subjective class feelings had a large effect on the intermediate class groups who comprised lower or routine non-manual occupations. Benny and Gleiss found the same in Greenwich.

Somewhat as an exception amongst British analysts, Rose (1968) suggested that the various SES ingredients might be combined into the concept of an 'ideal-type' class measure. His ideal-type working class person would live in a council house, have minimum education, have a manual worker as head of household, feel working class, and belong to a trade union; while his ideal-type middle class person would lack all these characteristics. Rose noted that only about a fifth of the electorate fell into one or other of these ideal-class groups, and although there were more manual than non-manual workers, the ideal-type middle class was larger than the ideal-type working class.

Weber (1922) advocated the use of 'ideal-types', by which he meant that the 'choice is often between a terminology which is not clear at all and one which is clear but unrealistic and *ideal-typical*'. But the problem with piling up a heap of characteristics to produce a 'pure' or 'ideal' type definition is that there is no end to the list of class-associated characteristics.

Moreover, Weber's objective of conceptual clarity would be better achieved by multivariate analysis rather than confounding logically separate variables into muddy scores. For example, including class identification as part of an 'ideal type' class definition makes it impossible to answer simple but significant questions like 'Are people conscious of their class?'; or 'Are the working class more or less class-conscious than the middle class?'; or 'Why do some working class people describe themselves as middle class?'

Butler and Stokes's national survey confirmed many of these earlier findings from surveys of particular localities, but they extended the analysis of class voting by adding a time dimension. They saw party alignments as originating in mass responses to political appeals—the *primary* causes—and then being maintained, perhaps long after their original justification had withered away, by the *secondary* processes of personal contact and group influence. The *age* of an alignment might be defined in terms of its relative dependence on such primary or secondary causes. Butler and Stokes laid stress on the secondary process of intergenerational transmission of partisanship: 90 per cent of those from homes where both parents were agreed on their partisanship themselves started with the same partisanship and almost 80 per cent retained that partisanship at the time of the interview. However, amongst those whose parents supported the party which was not dominant in their class, only 70 per cent began holding their parents' partisanship, and only 58 per cent retained it till the date of interview. In Britain, moreover, 90 per cent of respondents who did *not* associate a party with their father none the less developed a partisan identification of their own (in sharp contrast, said Butler and Stokes, to America, France or Japan); and in 74 per cent of cases it was in accord with the respondent's class.

Alford (1963) had used nine British Gallup polls spread over the years 1943 to 1962 to chart the evolution of social alignments. He concluded that class was the only significant social alignment in Britain, but that its power was declining. Butler and Stokes replicated Alford's methodology, comparing the gross class alignments in successive waves of their study 1963–64–66–69–70. Like Alford, they detected a decline and subsequent surveys have detected a further decline, especially in 1979.

From the beginning, British election surveys tried to place individuals in context. Benney, Pear, and Gray's Greenwich study followed the Columbia model in stressing the influence of 'primary' groups and personal contacts: 'social classes, occupational strata, the trade union movement, the better educated and the less well educated are social groups *only in an indirect* sense'—only, that is, in so far as they structured personal contacts. Respondents who thought their family, friends, or co-workers intended to vote differently proved specially unstable in their political preferences during the three waves of the 1950 campaign panel. The analysis treated these reports of associates' voting intentions as indirect but factual reports on the world beyond the respondent, rather than as direct self-reports on his state of mind, and concluded: 'the political opinions of family, friends and associates at work have, then, a more powerful influence on how people vote than any of the factors we have so far examined'.

Since family and associates' own partisanship would again be most influenced by class, the influence of these primary groups could be interpreted as the influence of the 'class environment', though such an interpretation inverts the analytic perspective of the Columbia and Greenwich analysts.

Bealey, Blondel, and McCann designed their survey of Newcastle under Lyme as a set of twenty-one subsamples, each representing one ward in the constituency, and each with the same sample size, irrespective of the size of the ward's electorate. They showed that within-class support for Labour and Conservative parties varied systematically with social context. So also did the level of class identification within classes. Both middle and working class people thought themselves more middle class, and voted more Conservative if they lived in a more middle class area. Unfortunately, the presentation of their results obscured their findings. They were aware that even their unusually large sample of 1,516 respondents produced small numbers in the twenty-one subsamples, but they were excessively cautious in consequence.

Goldthorpe *et al.* also touched on the theme of environmental influence. Their sample was restricted entirely to working class respondents. Those workers who lived in middle class neighbourhoods tended to vote Labour less than those other workers who lived in working class areas. But the critical variable was the extent of contact with people in middle class occupations through parental family connections, spouse, or previous job-history. With a direct control for this family class contact, the social environment appeared to have little influence on voting. However, the table on which this conclusion was based contained only 153 respondents spread over six combinations of area and class-contact. Bealey *et al.* reached exactly the opposite conclusion, though the statistical details for their view were not set out at all.

Paradoxically, Butler and Stokes used national survey data to present by far the best treatment of local environmental influence ever attempted in Britain, though their own survey proved inadequate for this purpose.

They took cumulated NOP monthly opinion polls between 1963 and 1966, totalling over 120,000 respondents in 184 constituencies; then they broke this huge sample down into 184 constituency samples and produced scatter-plots relating within-class party preference to the class mix in the constituency. Building on Butler and Stokes's ideas, W. L. Miller (1978, 1979) showed that the overall class alignment amongst constituencies could be decomposed into an *individual level component*—representing the partisan difference between middle and working class individuals living in the same social environment—and an *environmental component* representing the effect of the constituency class milieu on the partisanship of individuals, irrespective of their own class. The two components could be quantified by comparing survey data on individuals and census data on constituencies. Quantitatively the results were startling: the influence of milieu contributed *more* than individual level class difference to the class polarisation of constituencies. Through the sixties and seventies the environmental component of class polarisation strengthened as the individual level component declined: so, despite survey evidence of a collapse in class polarisation amongst individuals, class remained as good a predictor of constituency partisanship as ever.

Predictively the best indicator of the social environment was not the level of non-manual workers in the locality, but the much smaller level of employers and managers. This led Miller to propose a revised ideal-type model of class alignment, incorporating some of the ideas of Bonham and Rose. Ideal classes would consist of occupations or roles, not people: managerial occupations on one side, militant opposition to them on the other. Very few people could be described as 'belonging to' either class, and most people would possess a multitude of links to both ideal classes. Their political response would depend not upon being 'in' a particular social stratum, but upon the balance between their links to the two ideal classes. Many occupations, and therefore many class links, would be relevant to each individual: a person's current occupation, previous occupations, expectations about future occupations, the occupations of his or her parents, children, spouse, brothers and sisters, friends, neighbours, associates, workmates. Residence and locality would structure some of these class linkages, family would structure others. The growth of female employment, particularly full-time female employment, has significant effects on the occupational links between family and class. The family can no longer be characterised adequately by a single 'head of household occupation' (Andersen 1983).

8.2 *Within-class variations in partisanship*

If the class alignment had been a little less pre-eminent, the natural form of analysis would have been some multivariate prediction scheme in which a number of factors—including class—predisposed respondents to favour one or other of the parties. Yet that was not the way British surveys were analysed. As Birch noted, 'the fact that needs explaining is that 33 per cent of the industrial workers voted Conservative in 1951. Most attempts to explain this phenomenon, be they popular or academic, seem to assume that industrial workers who vote Conservative are people who *have in some way been led astray* from their natural tendency to support Labour' (Birch *et al*. 1959; see also Sartori 1969).

Birch himself stressed the historical dimension and the relatively recent replacement of a religious Liberal v. Conservative system by a class-based Labour v. Conservative system. His ideas were developed later by Butler and Stokes, but other writers put forward theories of embourgeoisement, deference, and public v. private sectoral alignments as alternative explanations of working class conservatism.

8.2.1 *The property owning democracy.* The political impact of the post-war spread of material possessions could take several forms which we might christen (1) the *zero effect thesis*: within classes those blessed or burdened by more possessions might be no more Conservative than those who were more free from the ties of wordly goods; (2) the *property owning democracy thesis*: within both classes those with more possessions might be more Conservative; (3) the *embourgeoisement thesis*: the acquisition of material possessions might make elements of the working class behave like the middle class, but have no effect on middle class people.

In addition, we can distinguish two variants of the second and third theses according to whether the role of property is *causative* or *discriminatory*. Causative versions of these theses imply that the acquisition of material goods would affect electors' political behaviour, probably but not necessarily by acting on their sense of class consciousness. Thus they imply political time trends in response to trends in property acquisition. Discriminatory versions are totally different. They imply that the politically right-wing would be more likely to acquire material possessions, probably but not necessarily because both their right-wing votes and their respect for material goods flowed from the same underlying right-wing philosophy. Thus as some new consumer durable came into mass production we should expect it to be acquired first by the right-wing elements in society, then later by the whole of society. But this tidal wave of possessions would sweep through society without changing political behaviour.

We can further subdivide the causal version into reactive and non-reactive versions. Under the non-reactive versions, material possessions incline some electors towards the Conservatives, but have no political effect on those without them. By contrast, the reactive versions imply a growing polarisation between the 'haves' and 'have nots', the one group tending towards the Conservatives the other towards Labour. Thus the net effect of prosperity on the party balance would be large and pro-Conservative under the non-reactive version, but small and in either political direction under the reactive version. Altogether that gives seven models (see Figure 1), but they by no means exhaust the possibilities for models of the political consequences of prosperity. For example, the seven do not include the 'good times' model which simply postulates a general trend towards the government of the day in times of prosperity and away from it in times of economic adversity.

In the Nuffield study of the 1959 election, Butler and Rose (1960) referred to the 'blurring of some class differences and the spread of middle class standards' eroding support for the Labour party; but they did not make clear whether they proposed an 'embourgeoisement' model or a 'good times' model. Rose worked with Abrams and Hinden (Abrams, Rose, and Hinden 1960) on a special survey for *Socialist Commentary* which Abrams interpreted quite clearly as supporting a 'good times' model and rejecting the 'embourgeoisement' model (Abrams 1960). None the less, many readers of Butler and Rose interpreted their ambiguous statements as advocating the 'embourgeoisement' model, and Goldthorpe *et al.* set out to disprove it.

Their study is unique amongst British political survey studies in its use of 'critical case' methodology. To test the proposition that manual workers were becoming progressively assimilated into middle class society as they achieved relatively high incomes and living standards, Goldthorpe and his associates chose to interview shop floor workers at three leading firms in the prosperous and expanding town of Luton. Their non-random sample of 229 respondents was in no sense representative of the electorate, but was intended to exemplify something close to an 'ideal-type' affluent worker.

Despite the excellence of their theoretical discussions and the plausibility of their conclusions, the limitations of such a sample must be admitted. First, we may doubt whether critical cases exist in political science. The analogy is with the process of mathematical reasoning known as 'taking to the limit'. But the purity and simplicity of abstract

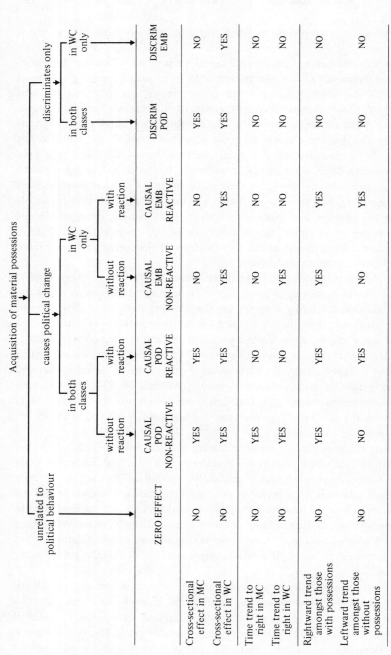

Acquisition of material possessions

	ZERO EFFECT	CAUSAL POD NON-REACTIVE	CAUSAL POD REACTIVE	CAUSAL EMB NON-REACTIVE	CAUSAL EMB REACTIVE	DISCRIM POD	DISCRIM EMB
	(unrelated to political behaviour)	(in both classes, without reaction)	(in both classes, with reaction)	(in WC only, without reaction)	(in WC only, with reaction)	(in both classes)	(in WC only)
Cross-sectional effect in MC	NO	YES	YES	NO	NO	YES	NO
Cross-sectional effect in WC	NO	YES	YES	YES	YES	YES	YES
Time trend to right in MC	NO	YES	NO	NO	NO	NO	NO
Time trend to right in WC	NO	YES	NO	YES	NO	NO	NO
Rightward trend amongst those with possessions	NO	YES	YES	YES	YES	NO	NO
Leftward trend amongst those without possessions	NO	NO	YES	NO	YES	NO	NO

Key: MC = middle class; WC = Working class; POD = Property-owning democracy thesis; EMB = Embourgoisement thesis

Fig. 1 The political effects of affluence

mathematical reasoning is not replicated in the political world, with its multiplicity of social, historical, and local patterns of influence. However well chosen, it is always possible that embourgeoisement might be rampant amongst the British working class yet, by a chance combination of local factors, absent in Luton. If Goldthorpe *et al.* had wanted to prove that some pattern could occur and used Luton as an example, they might have proved their point. But to prove the absence of some pattern by failing to find it in Luton requires more than the belief that the pattern is specially likely to occur in Luton: it requires faith in the certainty that if the pattern occurs on any extended scale, it occurs in Luton. Second, the seven models set out in my diagram imply different voting patterns or different voting trends in the affluent sections of the middle and working classes. Goldthorpe *et al.* could say nothing about trends, because they had no over-time element in their design: it was not a panel survey. They could say nothing about differences between affluent and non-affluent workers, because their sample was restricted to the affluent. They could say nothing about the differential effects of affluence in different classes because their sample was restricted to one class. Third, and it needs to be repeated *ad nauseam*, a sample of 229 does not fit with subtle theoretical distinctions which are to be tested by contrasts between fine subdivisions of the sample.

In their first volume they analysed the *industrial* attitudes of their affluent workers. They found that their sample had predominantly instrumental, rather than affective, orientations to work: respondents were interested in both firm and union, largely for the personal benefits they could get out of them, to be invested in the affective sphere of the family. A second and slighter volume discussed political attitudes. In this they developed the theme outlined in their larger book on industrial attitudes. They expected that their affluent workers would vote Labour, but give instrumental rather than affective reasons for so doing. And much of the text reflects this expectation. However, their data showed quite the opposite.

The overwhelming majority of their affluent workers (80 per cent) did vote Labour, but very few gave instrumental reasons for doing so: 45 per cent quoted general working class identification with Labour; 9 per cent family tradition; 15 per cent preferred Labour policies on economic planning and nationalisation or on the social services; and a mere 8 per cent said they voted Labour because they would be better off economically under Labour rather than the Conservatives.

Goldthorpe also drew attention to a study by Cannon (1967) of one hundred London printing compositors. Despite enjoying a standard of affluence beyond the dreams of even middle class avarice, high levels of house ownership, car ownership, telephone rental, and middle class identification, they still voted Labour by a margin of 5 to 1. Only their objective occupational class grade and the persistence of political traditions could explain their vote.

Butler and Stokes dismissed the theory of working class embourgeoisement: 'The collapse of Conservative strength in the 1960s dealt a rude blow to the embourgeoisement hypothesis . . . the reversal of party fortunes suggested that economic expansion had benefited the Conservatives more as a governing party during a prosperous period than as the party of an expanding middle class.'

However, they did investigate the impact of change in housing tenure and the associated change in neighbourhood class milieu. Council tenants who stayed in council housing throughout the seven years 1963–70 were 62 per cent Labour at the start and 56 per cent Labour at the end. Those other council tenants who were to switch to owner-occupied housing by 1970 were 56 per cent Labour at the start but only 33 per cent Labour at the end. Conservatism did seem to influence tenure change, but tenure change also appeared to have a large impact on partisanship, though whether the effective cause was tenure change *per se* or a change of class milieu, they could not say. Even if tenure change itself was the critical influence, tenure was much more than a question of possession, it also involved questions of sector (public or private) and ideologically motivated party appeals.

Butler and Stokes's basic analyses of the effect of affluence were based upon a 'good times' model, but this appeared in two versions. In their first edition they proposed a simple model under which the party in office was instantaneously rewarded for good times and punished for bad. Goodhart and Bhansali (1970) also used this model in their time series analysis of monthly economic statistics and monthly Gallup-poll ratings of government popularity. Their conclusions suggested extreme sensitivity to unemployment and inflation rates. W. L. Miller and Mackie (1973) pointed to the need to consider expectations and perceptions, and also suggested that the meaning of Gallup-poll ratings changed during the electoral cycle from an essentially non-comparative protest in the mid-term to a more balanced comparison between alternative parties as the date of the general election approached. The coincidence of peaks of unemployment and troughs of government popularity in the mid-terms of parliaments up to 1968 had biased Goodhart and Bhansali's findings. (Since 1968 unemployment has not always peaked in the mid-term.)

In their second edition, based on their full 1963–70 panel, Butler and

Stokes found clear evidence that perceptions were important and that the simple deterministic 'good times' model was inadequate. In 1970 more respondents blamed the 1959–64 Conservative government than the more recent 1966–70 Labour government for current economic troubles: 'what the economy means as a national issue depends on the economic debate between the parties and is capable of changing over time'.

Alt, who worked on the 1974 national election survey, documented the slippage between raw economic statistics, economic perceptions, economic blame, and their varying effects upon party support (Alt 1979). Moseley (1982) has shown that newspaper commentaries about economic affairs have more influence than official economic statistics on political response. The debate matters more than the uninterpreted reality.

The old embourgeoisement thesis was transformed into a new, more plausible, more ideological form by Dunleavy (1979, 1980a, b) with his theory of public and private sectors. He postulated that those who worked in the public sector or who consumed public-sector goods would be more likely to vote for Labour as the party of big-government. He looked at three sectoral cleavages: public versus private industry jobs: cars versus public transport; owner occupation versus council housing. Unfortunately, his empirical analyses uncovered nothing new. He was content to demonstrate once again the partisan differences between those in different tenure situations, for example, but his Gallup-poll data allowed no investigation of the reasons and motivations that lay behind such differences. He seemed unaware of the large number of alternative models that could be advanced to explain them and unaware also of the kinds of survey data that would allow a real test of his hypotheses. Harrop (1980b) used a Building Industry survey for a devastating critique. But the sectoral model is plausible and merits a better investigation. It works well in some continental countries, such as Denmark (Andersen 1983).

8.2.2 *Deference.* Another broad explanation of class deviance advanced during the fifties was the theory of deference. Some, at least, of the working class Tories might be deferent voters willing to accept the rule of their acknowledged superiors. Conversely, middle class elements who supported left-wing parties or pressure groups might be anti-deferents, or radicals, motivated in part by a desire to overturn established authority.

In *The Civic Culture*, Almond and Verba (1963) drew attention to 'Mr H: a good illustration of the deferential British participant. This is reflected in his support for the Conservative party despite his working-class position, and in his attitudes towards government and politics.' Yet there was an important ambiguity in their treatment of deference. The question is 'deferent to what?' There is a world of difference between being deferent to the authority of duly selected leaders in government, party, or trade union, and merely being deferent to the Conservative Party—a difference obscured perhaps by the existence of a Conservative government when the interviews were held in 1959. Mr H. was an authoritarian who was willing to defer to management at work, but expected his family to abide by his decisions at home; an Anglican, a home-owner, a patriot who enjoyed singing the national anthem and wanted a more aggressive foreign policy, a monarchist; and he was closely related to a local Conservative notable. It is difficult to see quite how he could 'defer' to the Conservative Party when it was such a natural choice for him anyway.

Nordlinger (1967) was interested in deference itself, rather than its effects on political partisanship. Deferentials were defined as 'those Conservative voters who manifest a strong preference for men of high status as their governmental leaders'—specifically a respondent had to prefer both a peer's son to a clerk's son, and an old Etonian over a grammar school man, as a Prime Minister. Only 28 per cent of working class Tories could be classified as deferent, despite the use of such party-associated symbols for the deference test (26 per cent of working class Labour voters also preferred the Eton man, but they were not classified as deferential). However, few though they might be, the deferential working class Tories displayed a coherent set of deviant attitudes on other political questions, being notably willing (or so they said, for it was not a panel survey) to change their own views if their party changed its policy and to accept independent unpopular action taken by their own party when in government. But their deference did not extend to Labour governments. These deferent Conservatives were the least deferent group of all when considering the authority of a Labour government.

McKenzie and Silver (1968) criticised early British survey work for being too much bound by its American predecessors: early surveys were 'unhistorical', their enquiries and analysis torn from the context of history. They were too much concerned with the brief election campaign and wrongly sought 'general' findings which could apply to any democratic election anywhere, anytime. This was the criticism of Columbia that produced the Michigan tradition in America. Deference was Mackenzie and Silver's British equivalent of Michigan's party identification—not in a substantive sense, but in a functional sense: it was to be a concept with equivalent significance in a different national and historical context. But by McKenzie and Silver's criteria, only 26 per cent of working class Conservatives were deferential. Like Nordlinger, they found that deferential Conservatives were a small minority of a minority: by itself, the concept could not go far towards explaining working class Conservatism.

Parkin (1968) responded to these studies of deferential working class deviants with an almost perfect inverse: a study of those radical middle class deviants who supported the Campaign for Nuclear Disarmament. Using the CND organisation itself, he obtained lists of active members and sent them a short postal questionnaire. He got 358 responses from this source. He also collected names and addresses of young people (under twenty-five) during the three-day Easter march of 1965 and mailed questionnaires to them afterwards. He got 445 replies.

The premise of his study was the same as that of the working class Tory studies: it was pure natural self-interest that explained working class Labour votes and middle class Conservative votes. Thus right-wing political behaviour by the working class or left-wing political behaviour by the middle class was deviant. And his explanation of deviance was the same as for deferential working class Conservatives. While the deferential working class was attracted to the Conservative party by its veneration for the symbols of monarchy, empire, nation, and House of Lords, Parkin's middle class radicals were distinguished by their antagonism to these same symbols —a sort of inverted deference. He found that his middle class radicals were not alienated from the society around them in the sense of lacking contact with society or of feeling powerless to influence politics, but they were alienated from what Parkin called these 'dominant values' in society.

They were also a specific type of middle class—professional rather than business, irreligious or non-conformist rather than Anglican—and every previous study had shown these groups to be less Conservative than the Anglican, business, and managerial sections of the middle class. They crop up later as the most post-materialist of Inglehart's (1977) social strata, and much earlier as reformist Liberals prior to 1914.

In one sense they were anything but radical, however. Almost two-thirds of the youth sample felt one of their parents approved of the CND. At this very personal level they were acting *in accordance with the dominant values* in their immediate society. Despite this finding, Parking determinedly compared CND activity 'with more common forms of deviance amongst the young—most obviously the increasing tendency towards juvenile delinquency'. He hypothesised that much of the CND's youth support was based on some sort of anti-adult protest; but there was no evidence in his survey for this plausible view.

Butler and Stokes took an even harsher view of the deference thesis than of the embourgeoisement thesis: 'the whole deference argument has proved to be something of a cul-de-sac in British electoral analysis'.

Certainly working class Tories were patriotic and attracted to 'national' institutions like the monarchy; but so, to an even greater degree, were middle class Tories. 'If the Conservatives' appeal as a national party aligned with national institutions is to be styled in terms of deference, it is at least clear that this is not a deference that is peculiarly likely to be evoked among people within the lower social strata by reason of their humble station.' This well-aimed attack by Butler and Stokes points to the dangers in basing conclusions on over-focused samples of subsets of the electorate. Yet while Butler and Stokes were right to reject the deference thesis as an explanation of working class Conservatism, the concept of deference is more valuable than the badly designed studies in which it was used during the late fifties and early sixties. Once deference to leadership and to established authority is distinguished from deference to Conservative party symbols it can play a significant role in studies of direct action and rebellion within states, within parties, and even within trade unions. One may defer to leadership of the left as well as leadership of the right.

For their own analysis of working class Conservatism, Butler and Stokes took up the views expressed by Birch in his analysis of the 1951 election in Glossop: Labour was still a relatively new party and the class alignment had only recently replaced the sectarian alignment as the basis of British politics.

Interpreting their respondents' age-groups as historical cohorts, Butler and Stokes pointed to the 'decline of working class Conservatism' from the earlier cohorts to the later; and the simultaneous decline in sectarian polarisation across the cohorts. To extend their analysis backwards, they added two pseudo-cohorts consisting of their two oldest cohorts' memories of their fathers' partisanship, sect, and class.

Intergenerational social mobility was also important. Offspring carried with them a remarkably persistent party identification across class boundaries: so the very processes that helped to maintain the class alignment also helped to sustain within-class deviance.

Although they relied over-much on respondents' memories, this was a most impressive integration of past and present, portraying the patterns in the current electorate as the product of a century of past history. But we must be clear about the limitations of cohort analysis. It is logically wrong to use cohort analysis as evidence of both history itself and of the imprint of history on the current electorate. It should properly be used only for the latter. Sectarian polarisations evident in Butler and Stokes's oldest cohort referred to 1963 questions about 1963 partisanship, even though the cohort consisted of all respondents who had come of age prior to 1918. Providing we accept independent evidence that sectarian divisions were significant at the turn of the century, these patterns in 1963 partisanship reveal the persistence of historical patterns. Conversely, if we assume persistence, they reveal the nature of early twentieth century partisan divisions; though the evidence on persistence of partisanship is not so strong as to allow precise backwards historical projections. Thus elderly respondents' 1963 partisanship cannot be identified with their pre-1918 voting patterns. Indeed, most of them would not have been permitted to vote prior to the extension of the franchise in 1918.

Butler and Stokes provided no single explanation of working class Conservatism, and strongly rejected the notion that it was 'deviant'. Far from being deviant, cross-class partisanship was apparently growing between 1963 and 1970. It was particularly strong in the most recent cohorts and was associated with a declining belief in politics as a conflict of class interests.

8.3 *The workings of democracy*

Apart from the investigation of social alignments, early British surveys also adopted Columbia themes related to the proper functioning of the democratic system. To this end they looked at popular participation and the influence of the media; they charted the development of opinion during the election campaign, gauged the rationality of voters' choices and changes, and measured the extent of agreement between party voters on the one hand and party leaders or official policies on the other. Historically, several of these themes can be traced back to the Columbia Office of Radio Research's original interest in the power of radio to influence consumer choice.

Behind all these studies was a naive model of democracy which could be summarised as follows. In an ideal democratic election there would be a high level of interest, knowledge, and participation shown by the electorate. Some electors would find one or other party the perfect expression of their policy attitudes, and they would actively support that party by attempting to persuade their fellows to vote for it. But the most important electors would be those who constituted the floating vote: those who were not bound to any party, who would stand above the party battle, and who would carefully assess the rival policy packages on offer before casting their vote and thereby deciding the outcome. No one postulated the existence of such a model. Its status was that of a straw man to be knocked down or, more usefully, a reference point for comparison with reality.

Benney's 1950 Greenwich survey paid close attention to the media. A hundred students reported on speeches and audience reactions at election meetings, on the number of houses displaying window cards, on loud-speaker tours, and the distribution of party literature. During the campaign itself, there were special quota-sample surveys on a daily basis to measure reactions to the previous evening's radio broadcasts. The number of respondents who read election addresses, read other pamphlets, went to meetings, knew the candidates' names, read different daily newspapers, and listened to each particular radio election broadcast were noted. Benney *et al.* found that radio broadcasting reached far more electors than any other form of election communication, that it reached the apolitical, and that unlike audiences for all other types of campaign propaganda, radio listeners were not drawn primarily to the spokesmen of their own party. On average only a minority of listeners to an election broadcast sympathised with the speaker. It was a media-election: only one respondent in twenty actually attended a political campaign meeting of any kind—far fewer than the numbers who attended campaign meetings during the by-elections of 1982, for example (see Chapter 12).

A campaign panel format made it possible to characterise the electors on the first round of interviews as Conservative, Labour, Liberal, or un-decided. Then by comparing voting preferences at the start of the campaign with actual vote choices recorded just after election day, electors could be divided up into (1) constants (2) crystallisers (3) converts (4) disintegrators and (5) indifferents—a set of terms derived from the 1948 Elmira questionnaire.

Typically, British campaign studies found that the bulk of the electorate already had a party preference at the start of the campaign and held on to it through to polling day. Too much stress was probably put on the stability of voting preferences, perhaps because more change had been anticipated and also because much of the change cancelled out at both the individual and aggregate level—some people wavered between a couple of voting options and ended up where they started, while parties traded vote preferences in both directions simultaneously. Yet only two-thirds of Greenwich electors actually held to the same preference over three panel interviews between December 1949 and February 1950—incidentally showing more gross volatility than a campaign panel in 1979.

Change between elections was grossly underestimated, because none of the early studies was an interelection panel. They all relied on memories of vote at the last election, for their analysis of interelection change. Unfortunately, such memories have since been proved to be grossly biased towards present political choices.

More important than the quantity of change was its quality. What sorts of people were these floating voters? They fell into no single well-defined social or attitudinal group. Rather they were best identified as individuals whose initial voting preference was at odds with their social background, political opinions, previous voting choices, or family and social environment: in short, those who were under some form of cross-pressure. It was not so much a matter of being located at the centre of some spectrum as having a multiplicity of links to different points on the spectrum.

Those who did change their minds, and especially those who made up their minds late on in the campaign, or who wavered between voting and abstaining were characterised not by a high degree of political interest, involvement, and knowledge, but by indifference, ignorance, and rejection of the unwelcome choice they were being encouraged to make. Even at the level of following the campaign in the media, floaters were significantly less involved than those who held constant to their original party preference.

Few voters showed great interest in, or knowledge of, the details of party policy. Manifestos were not read with great attention to the fine print. For example, the 1955 Labour manifesto contained a crisply worded paragraph pledging the party to abolish the '11-plus' examination and introduce comprehensive secondary schools. Yet the 1955 Bristol survey found that fewer than a third of all respondents could attribute this policy correctly to the Labour party.

Milne and Mackenzie (1958) stressed the importance of images rather than issues. By *image* they meant some generalised policy orientation or some symbol associated with a party. They attempted to identify party images by asking their respondents what they thought each of the three parties stood for. Labour's image had two elements in the eyes of its own voters—'for the working class' (68 per cent) and 'for the welfare state' (18 per cent). The Conservative party was simply 'for the rich and big business, and against the workers', according to 85 per cent of Labour voters; but Conservatives saw their party as 'for all classes, the whole country' (30 per cent), 'for free enterprise' (26 per cent), and 'for individual freedom' (14 per cent). The Liberal party was seen as a 'centre' party, or a 'compromise' party. Those who voted against it saw it, in addition, as a 'political has-been'. Respondents who changed their voting preference attributed their own change of preference to the pull of party leadership or to these very general images but seldom to specific, detailed issues. Labour voters, especially, emphasised images rather than issues.

Milne and Mackenzie explicitly adopted the Columbia group's notion (and their terminology) of issues coming to a gateway—a time slice in which they were decided. Images were issues which were in or just through the time gateway and which had been 'plugged' (their word) so much by one or other political party that the party had 'annexed' (their word) the issue; so that 'after a time the issue is identified with the party' and becomes a 'symbol'. This symbolic identification persisted and remained electorally significant even when the issue as a real policy choice had faded. They quoted Democrat/Republican images on the Civil War as an example.

Voters' rationality could not be challenged on the grounds that they voted on images rather than issues, provided that images were merely wide and general in scope. But if images retained their electoral potency when they had declined into pure symbol, divorced from or even at variance with real current policy choices, then the voters could indeed be accused of irrationality.

The same question of image and issue voting could be considered from a more systemic viewpoint. If voters voted for the party whose policies they supported, then, admitting some mechanical imperfections, the electoral system could be described as a means of converting policy attitudes into a parliament and government. Conversely, parliament and government could be said to represent the policy view of the electorate.

Various sorts of agreement were measured. Voters had social characteristics and policy attitudes; parties had official policies, and various levels of élite personnel—leaders, MPs, local officials, activists, and finally inactive supporters—all of whom had social characteristics and policy attitudes. The Labour party was founded to put 'working men' into parliament, not socialist or even class policies: its pre-1918 constitution explicitly defined its representational objective in social rather than policy terms—an appropriate ambition in a state which is governed by men, not laws.

Benney et al. in the Greenwich study arbitrarily defined what they took to be ten official Labour and Conservative party propositions or themes (five each) and then compared support for these amongst party voters. A great deal of cross-support existed in Greenwich. However, Labour voters generally approved Conservative themes more than vice-versa—on average 41 per cent against 31 per cent; and Labour voters agreed with their own party less than Conservatives—on average only 61 per cent compared to 75 per cent. Using four pre-specified issues, all with an ideological flavour about them—controls, free enterprise, comprehensive schools, and nationalisation—Milne and Mackenzie showed that only 34 per cent of British Labour voters in 1955 averaged a pro-Labour position, while 82 per cent of Conservatives averaged a pro-Conservative position. Taking each voter's rating of the parties on the issue that he or she rated most important, only 71 per cent of Labour voters, but 84 per cent of Conservatives thought their own party was best. Birch, in his 1951 Glossop study, went further and found that on fourteen pre-specified issues (ten of them involving the nationalisation of some industry, however) only 44 per cent of Labour party *members* compared with 73 per cent of Conservative members, were in agreement with the party line.

Birch also considered the social representativeness of the parties. Dividing his Glossop respondents up into leaders, members, and voters, he catalogued the socially unrepresentative nature of party members and still more, party leaders as compared with their voters. In all parties the higher echelons were drawn disproportionately from middle class groups—the Conservatives from business proprietors, the Labour élite from professional and white-collar groups, and the Liberal élite from both. None the less, only Labour had more than a handful of working class leaders. The pattern was reminiscent of the nineteenth and early twentieth century Liberal party, which was non-conformist only in the sense that its leaders included a large proportion but still a minority (about a third) who were non-conformists (Blewett 1972).

Just as the last chapter of Columbia's *Voting* was titled 'Democratic practice and democratic theory', so Milne and Mackenzie's last chapter was headed 'The implications for representative government'. The theme was the same: were the British (or American) electors good enough for the democratic system? It seems to put the question the wrong way round, but it was the question that great nineteenth century British political theorists had asked as they were confronted with successive extensions of the franchise. In contrast to the situation that faced those who framed the American constitution, Britain started with the system and added the people to it, which made their qualifications for entry all the more relevant. Mackinnon had written that 'public opinion' was the 'sentiment on any given subject which is entertained by the best informed, most intelligent and most moral persons in the community'. Mill, Bryce, and Bagehot guessed there were few such people around in nineteenth century England. Milne and Mackenzie now had evidence that the twentieth century electorate was prejudiced, ignorant, and uninterested. They pointed to the high participation rates in the 1950/51 elections with some dismay. Apathy was the one remaining defence the system had against electoral choices made by the ignorant and uninterested. Worst of all, the system was steered and guided by the changing electoral behaviour of floating voters, who turned out to be the most ignorant and uninterested of the lot, their vacillation and indecision arising from rootlessness or conflicting pressures, rather than deep reflection, rational judgment, or moderation.

However, Milne and Mackenzie also suggested that their own characterisation of floating voters might depend too much on a small sample which made it difficult to distinguish between 'illiterate' and 'intellectual' floaters. What was evident, even in their small sample, was that those who had switched to a Liberal vote during the 1955 election campaign scored well on political knowledge and activity. More generally they suggested that even ignorant and apathetic floaters might behave in accordance with more widespread changes of opinion. Certainly one pervasive finding of all the early studies was the social nature of voting. Individual electors did not in fact make their own independent voting choices: influence and pressure was everywhere. So that collective rationality might be greater than the rationality of the poor instruments that registered the collective mood.

Columbia's original interest in the power of the media was maintained in two studies by the Granada Foundation Television Research Unit at Leeds University. Throughout the fifties, roughly 69 per cent of electors listened to at least one party political broadcast during each election campaign. But whereas in 1950 and 1951 this exposure was entirely to radio broadcasts, in 1955 it split equally between radio and TV, and in 1959 it divided almost 4 to 1 in favour of TV. And while radio had never been able to challenge the press as the main source of political information, TV proved able to do so. Trenaman and McQuail (1961) took up Milne and Mackenzie's discussion of political images, but they now used the term quite explicitly in the adman's sense as something that could be manipulated by media advertising.

However, the findings of their 1959 Leeds election study in many ways replicated the 1940 Columbia findings. Despite the advent of a new and apparently more powerful mass communications media, 'the electorate was not influenced directly in its voting or political attitudes, either by the amount of the political campaign to which it was exposed, or by the presence or absence of any part or of virtually all the campaign'. Several years later their study of the 1970 election reached a similar conclusion: 'nowhere was there a sign that any object of partisan evaluation—a party or a leader—had profited from the opportunity to direct persuasive messages to the electorate (young or old) through the mass media . . . the most powerful single communication variable in the analysis was a measure of interpersonal contact—family based political discussion' (Blumler, McQuail, and Nossiter 1975, p. VIII. 15).

But in their 1964 study they found 'public attitudes towards the Liberal party and its leader became more favourable during the campaign and in the greater part of the sample this movement of opinion was associated progressively with exposure to election television', and 'the most important single influence on the development of pro-Liberal views was exposure to television news (Blumler and McQuail 1968). Reanalysis of the previous British campaign panels showed the Liberals gaining 1.5 per cent during the 1950 campaign, 3 per cent in 1951, 4 per cent in 1955, 5 per cent in 1959, and 5 per cent again in 1964. Clearly this could not all be attributed to television, which reached few households in the early fifties, but it could have been the result of a heightened level and more equal balance of media exposure during election campaigns. The Granada team went on to confirm this tendency in studies of later elections (Blumler, McQuail, and Nossiter 1976).

Blumler and McQuail disputed the by now received wisdom that floating voters in Britain 'resemble abstainers more than they resemble the image of the perfect voter'. The electors gained by the Liberals in 1964 were high on motivation for following an election campaign: 'well above average in knowledgeability when the campaign opened; they nevertheless acquired more political information as a result of the campaign than did any other voting group in the sample, and they watched a remarkably large number of political broadcasts . . . In fact the new Liberal in 1964 seemed to embody some of the classic virtues of the rational democratic voter'. The Leeds authors noted that Milne and Mackenzie in 1955 had also found that protest Liberals were 'far superior to (other floaters) in political knowledge and activity . . . they compared favourably with other Liberals who had voted Liberal previously; their exposure to propaganda was actually slightly higher and their attribution of propositions more acute'.

Butler and Stokes had relatively little to say about participation and media exposure. Echoing Blumler and McQuail's lament that there were few research-supported generalisations about the political impact of the media, they noted 'our own findings in this field are for the most part surprisingly negative'. They drew attention to the strongly partisan structure of newspaper readership, but were faced with the difficult question of whether choice of party influenced choice of paper or vice versa. By chance, the 1974–79 panel survey of the Scottish electorate conducted by W. L. Miller *et al.* spanned the period in which the best-selling Scots paper, the Conservative-oriented *Scottish Daily Express*, switched its printing to England and lost over half of its Scots readership. In 1974 those *Express* readers who were later to stop reading the paper were already 20 per cent less Conservative than those who would stay loyal to the paper. But in 1979, after they had stopped reading the *Express*, they were still only 20 per cent less Conservative than those who continued to read it. Partisanship in 1974 predicted later defections from the *Express*, but switching papers had no subsequent effect upon partisanship (Miller *et al.* 1982).

Following Converse (1964), Butler and Stokes set out to show that in the British mass electorate issue attitudes did not conform to generally accepted ideological patterns: issue constraint was low. First, issue attitudes were not tightly determined by party identification. Electors had fairly stable attachments to parties, and fairly stable perceptions of party policy, but not so stable attitudes on policy issues.

A second way of looking at ideology was to look at attitude correlations irrespective of party policy. Did electors tend to accept or reject whole packages of policies even if those packages did not correspond to the packages offered by the parties? Looking at nationalisation, nuclear arms, EEC entry, immigration, hanging, the Queen, TUC power and big business power, Butler and Stokes found that the only two which were usually either jointly approved or jointly disapproved were TUC power and nationalisation.

Butler and Stokes then turned to images as described by Milne and Mackenzie or Trenaman and McQuail. 'In the 1960s, as for a century past, the behaviour of the electorate was shaped by generalised attitudes and beliefs about the parties far more than by any specific policy issues. People respond to the parties to a large extent in terms of the images they form of them from the characteristics and style of party leaders and from the party's association, intended or not, with the things governments may achieve.' 'Some of the most general and salient beliefs about the parties are very slow to change . . . other elements of the parties' images, however, are much more plastic.' Accordingly they followed the Leeds studies in looking at images that included a class image, but also 'ability to govern', 'modernity', 'youth', 'excitement', and other malleable images. Using open-ended questions on likes and dislikes about the parties, they found during the sixties a sharp decline in Labour's image as a class party and increasing attention given to its ability (or not) to govern. Conversely, for the Conservative party, there was a sharp rise in references to its class image. Over the sequence of interviews between 1963 and 1970, Labour's image of competence, strength, modernity, youth, and excitement rose from 1963 to 1966, dropped back sharply in 1969, then recovered in 1970.

But the theme of images was disappointly under-developed, as indicated by the weak conclusion that 'in all likelihood such (image) changes are an important feature of the popular attitudes on which the alternation of governments rests'. Such transient, cyclical, correlated image movements tell us little more than the fluctuations in monthly opinion poll ratings, and Butler and Stokes never used images as an independent predictor variable. Thus their analytical status remained as a dependent variable, yet another symptom of general political trends.

As possible influences on political change, they examined in more detail images of party leaders, images of the parties' association with 'good times', and the issues of social service expenditure and immigration. Breaking down voting choice by attitudes to parties and attitudes to leaders showed that in 1964 and 1966 party rating was a far greater influence on voting, but in 1970 a favourable attitude to Wilson counter-balanced negative attitudes to party much more effectively than in the past.

There were three elements to Butler and Stokes's analysis of the impact of issues: the electorate had to perceive party policies as being different, they had to rate the issue as important, and they had themselves to take up positions more on one side than the other. This last condition reflected Butler and Stokes's view of issues as causing electors to deviate from their basic alignments sufficiently to alter the balance of party support and perhaps swing an election one way or the other. It also reflected the classic Michigan concern with elections as political systems with political consequences, rather than merely as convenient scientific tools for looking at patterns and relationships amongst individuals. Hence, Butler and Stokes were not much interested in issues that caused some electors to deviate to the Labour party but others against it, with little net effect on Labour's overall strength.

Butler and Stokes concluded that 'in the mid-1960s the social services provided the one issue that fully satisfied the three conditions (salient, party differences perceived, skewed opinions)' and 'this issue worked strongly to Labour's advantage'. However, 'in the period when we collected our evidence, social services and, to a much smaller extent, strikes, may have ceased to fully satisfy our three conditions for impact'. While their conclusions may or may not be correct, their evidence was extremely weak. They noted that in 1964 there was a 4 to 1 majority in favour of spending more on social services, but they relegated to the appendix the information that when offered the choice in 1963 of more social service spending or tax cuts, a majority chose tax cuts.

During the sixties they noted the rising potential of immigration as an issue. There was always a 7 or 8 to 1 majority (roughly 84 per cent v. 12 per cent) thinking too many immigrants had been let in to Britain. Opinion was always skewed. It was also salient. That only left the question of which party was more likely to keep the immigrants out. In 1964 there was very little difference in public perceptions of party policy except in areas with a high local concentration of immigrants, where the Conservative party was seen as more likely to keep them out. However, after Powell's 1968 speeches—not in response to any great changes in official party policies—the view formerly confined to areas of high local concentration became quite general, and extremely intense. The Conservative party was overwhelmingly seen as more likely to keep immigrants out. Using their

1966–70 panel, Butler and Stokes showed that Labour defections to the Conservatives were twice as heavy amongst those who perceived (in 1970) the Conservative party as the more likely to keep immigrants out.

Generally their treatment of issues, images, and ideology was a lot less satisfactory than their treatment of social alignments. The analysis was frankly patchy, inconsistent, and at times superficial. Not nearly enough use was made of their panel as panel wherein a cross-lagged panel methodology might have exposed the interplay of partisanship and issue attitudes. Perhaps they felt the panel intervals were so long that cause and effect would necessarily appear simultaneous. Certainly their standard use of the panel was to show volatility, variable by separate variable. Even when, as with immigration, they used the panel to relate party swings to attitudes, it was to attitudes at the later wave, not the earlier, which brings in all the ambiguities of causal direction. (See Schuur 1983, for a masterly review of the problems in issue voting analysis.)

8.4 *Party identification*

Most British surveys followed Columbia in giving scant attention to party identification. Yet the need for an imaginative use of this concept was apparent all the way through their accounts of British politics. Benney's description of the background to his Greenwich survey gave numerous examples of partisanship affecting the attitudes and behaviour of party members and workers—like the Conservative councillor who declared that 'the rising suicide-rate amongst old age pensioners is only one example of what happens under a socialist government', or Benney's general observation that the lower the status of a party speaker within the party and the less formal the occasion, the less regard was given to accuracy. Now, apart from their charm as anecdotes, these stories imply a certain causal direction, namely that the attitudes expressed were the *result*, rather than the *cause* of party preference, at least for these party workers. But partisanship extended far beyond the ranks of party workers: Benney *et al.* noted that 'almost three-quarters of those who, in general, disagreed with their party on the statements summarised in the political issues index, nevertheless voted for it. *Loyalty to a party appears to be compatible with almost any degree of disagreement with its formal electoral policies*'.

In Bristol, Milne and Mackenzie found that 43 per cent of voters could give no reason for their vote, and a further 6 per cent named family tradition. At various points in their analysis they referred to evidence that 'some electors were pulled in different directions by (party) loyalty and self-interest'; that 'voting the same way as family and friends bore no relation to agreement with propositions: this suggests that the similarity of voting behaviour in small groups did not arise to any great extent from similarity of views on issues'; 'apparently the removal of the party label from issues made quite a big difference to the voters' opinions'. They also found evidence that electors manipulated their perceptions of party policy to resolve conflicts between their policy attitudes and party preference. A long list of indications, therefore, that partisanship was an independent causal force, rather than a mere dependent result of policy or image considerations.

Even the classic Michigan terms 'identification' and 'partisanship' were used in a speculative paragraph: 'First the mere fact of an elector having committed himself to, and *identified* himself with, a party by voting for it would tend to produce an increase in *partisanship*. Second if there were any general movement of opinion from one party to another . . . this might well be accompanied by increased partisanship in the party gaining support and diminished partisanship in the party losing it. Finally once the election has been won, there is probably an increase in confidence in the superiority of the winning party, just because it has won; this would tend to *increase partisanship* among its supporters and *decrease partisanship* among its opponents' (Milne and Mackenzie 1958). This was a very perceptive paragraph, but the concept of partisanship was not carefully thought through and appeared in tables represented by the percentage of respondents naming their party as the best party on what they took to be the most important issues—a figure which is the joint product of partisanship and policy evaluation mixed together in unknown proportions. Milne and Mackenzie themselves had given clear evidence that party loyalty could survive policy disagreements very well: so it was absurd to measure partisanship by policy agreement.

Goldthorpe *et al.* defined 'party attachment' in terms of stated voting history, combined with voting intentions. While these are undoubtedly related to current sense of attachment to party, they are equally certainly not the same as it.

Trenaman and McQuail, and Blumler and McQuail used the term 'partisanship' to apply to their measure of relative party images—the respondent's image index of the Conservative party minus his or her image index for Labour. But like previous issue-based measures of partisanship, that also confounded cause and effect, and failed to isolate the specifically emotional attachment to party which was implicit in Trenaman and McQuail's own finding that there was some 'definite and consistent barrier between sources of communication and movements of attitude'.

The whole analysis of British political attitudes and voting would have been greatly improved by an explicit articulation of the party identification concept along Michigan lines, coupled with direct survey measures of the concept so defined. Whether Michigan's measure would have been adequate is another matter.

Party identification, in the Michigan sense, meant an affective emotional link to a party, a conscious feeling by the respondent that he or she was a 'Labour person' or the Labour party was *his* or *her* 'party'. Such an identification has to be distinguished from previous voting (which is an influence upon it) and current voting (which is partly a product of it). Party identification has to be distinguished from policy agreement and from approval of the party or its leaders. We also need to know the strength of identification, as well as the name of the party with which the respondent identifies.

If such a concept can be measured adequately by survey questions, the analytical gains are enormous. It becomes possible to speak of the natural governing party, and the normal level of party support, distinguished from the accidents of transient circumstance. It becomes possible to speak of 'Labour' electors abstaining, of 'Liberal' electors voting Conservative or Labour to avoid a wasted vote, of parties gaining the votes of the uncommitted, of the strain and tension associated with a poor party leader, a scandal in high places, an unpopular policy or whatever. The vote itself is the product of many factors. Party identification plays the role of one of those factors. Its dominance or weakness as a cause of voting reveals the strength of other factors. However, it is essential to have as direct a measure of party identification as possible; so that we do not confound it with one of its partial causes or one of its only partially determined consequences. The practical difficulties in formulating and applying such a measure should not be under-estimated. None the less, it was a major failing of the early British surveys that they did not try.

Butler and Stokes described what Michigan meant by party identification and applied the standard Michigan question to measure it, but they noted that 'in transferring their votes from one party to another British electors are less likely than Americans to retain a conscious identification with a party other than the one they currently support' and they treated party identification as a dependent variable, rather than a causative variable. Much of their book in both editions presented the patterns underlying 1963 party identification, but very little indeed would have required any revision if they had chosen to use 1964 voting choice instead of 1963 party identification as their basis for analysis.

Paradoxically, therefore, it was the survey analysts in the Conservative Research Department who first used the concept to good effect in Britain.

They found in their private surveys between 1967 and 1969 that although Labour ran far behind the Conservatives in current voting intentions, Labour always enjoyed a lead in terms of party identification. This finding tempered Conservative party expectations during the late sixties and influenced party strategy. It also prompted Butler and Stokes to undertake a similar analysis of their own surveys for their second edition. (See Butler and Pinto-Dushinsky 1971: 346; but compare similar conclusions based on Gallup questions which distinguished 'by-election' and 'general election' voting intentions.)

They then found Labour votes or preferences running ahead of identifications, particularly in 1964 and 1966, but lagging behind identifications, especially in 1969, though they did not find the extreme divergence that had occurred in the Conservative party surveys. Thus in their second edition they remarked that 'an increasing proportion of the British electorate seemed capable of retaining partisan self-images (identifications) to which their electoral choices returned after a period of disenchantment'. But they still noted that 'this pattern was much less marked in Britain than in America. We suspect that the distinctiveness of the American pattern is derived from the distinctiveness of the American electoral system', and they still did not stress party identification as a causative variable in their analysis.

When they wished to illustrate the impact of images and issues on party voting, the party control they used (if any) was the traditional Columbia control—vote preference in the preceding wave of the panel. They seldom analysed the simultaneous pull of issue and party attachment. Where they did so, as in their chapter on the 'Pull of the leaders', they measured party attachment not by the supposedly deep-seated party-identification, but by a transient measure of party ratings based on the number of spontaneous favourable and unfavourable references to party given in answer to the open-ended questions on likes and dislikes about parties and leaders, a measure which was closely analogous to Trenaman and McQuail's measure of partisanship and conceptually very different from party identification as understood by Michigan.

Crewe (1972, 1976) launched a weighty criticism of *Political Change in Britain*. He accepted it (wrongly) as a good account of political change in the twenties and thirties. Actually it assumed such changes and then explained patterns in the 1963 electorate in terms of the imprint of this assumed history. More significantly, Crewe argued that Butler and Stokes concentrated on the Labour/Conservative divide which had shown little net change in recent years, but they had neglected the topic of participation where changes had been greater. They had also neglected the secular trend away from the two-party system as a whole.

But the core of Crewe's criticism was that what he called the 'Michigan model' implied increasing support for the two-party system at a time when it had, in fact, fallen. Crewe called for a return from the Michigan model to the more sociological model of the Columbia tradition. Crewe's 'Michigan model' was as follows: (1) electors inherit a sense of party attachment from their parents, which is only gradually changed by their other social and political experiences, with parental partisanship remaining the dominant influence; (2) the direction of this party identification is the main determinant of voting choice; (3) the strength of this party identification is the main determinant of turnout to vote; (4) transient issues deflect electors temporarily from the vote implied by their party identification, especially if it is a weak identification, but only cataclysmic events shake party identification itself. A party's electoral success therefore rests on a majority of loyal partisans, plus a minority composed of temporary defectors from other parties, plus a few non-identifiers; and in addition it will fluctuate as a result of new partisans entering the electorate or old partisans leaving it.

Now Crewe argued that this was a model of ever-increasing stability, not of change, despite Butler and Stokes's title *Political Change in Britain*. As the two-party system became established in Britain after the war, increasing numbers of respondents should have had parents who identified with one or other major party. This itself should have increased the level and strength of party identification among the electorate as a whole, leading to ever higher turnout rates and ever more support for the two-party system amongst those who did turn out to vote. But turnout had dropped and support for third parties increased. Why, he asked, had a growing allegiance to the two main parties, in terms of party identification, been accompanied by their growing rejection at recent elections?

Advocating 'a return to the sociological themes of the Columbia voting studies', Crewe claimed that partisanship was best understood as something rooted and nurtured in social milieux, rather than as a psychological learning process. Volatility could then be the result of more voters entering primary social groups that were more heterogeneous. Geographic mobility in search of work, the car, the phone, the new privatised style of working class life, the decline of socially isolated communities, the blurring of social differences and freer choice of life-styles suggested a decline in the types of milieux likely to sustain and reinforce strong partisanship.

Critical though Crewe was, his critique was more in the Michigan tradition than was Butler and Stokes's book. Butler and Stokes had done no more than pay polite lip-service to the Michigan concept of party identification, had never used it in the analytic role assigned to it by Michigan, and had contrasted the social base of British voting with the psychological base of American voting. Crewe was puzzled, disappointed, and worried, because he tried to apply the Michigan concept in the Michigan role. Butler and Stokes were already in the Columbia tradition and there was no need to 'return' to it. What was also true, however, was that Butler and Stokes's book is better described by its secondary title *The Evolution of Electoral Choice* rather than its primary title of *Political Change in Britain*. It was indeed about how British political patterns had come to be what they were, rather than about what they were turning into.

According to Crewe's critique of Butler and Stokes, the critical variable requiring explanation was turnout, not party choice, and a Michigan-style model based upon party identification could not do this. However, when he undertook his own analysis of turnout patterns after the 1974 elections, his fascination with party identification remained, though his evidence now seemed to show that it was precisely the Michigan model—which in my view, Butler and Stokes did not use—that *did* explain declining British turnout rates. Crewe and his associates used their own and the Butler/ Stokes surveys to analyse turnout trends between 1964 and October 1974, concluding thus: 'we have discovered two particularly sturdy sources of *irregular* voting: relative youth and a weak or absent party identification . . . both age and strength of identification are independently related to turn-out levels . . . (and) on the basis of this comparison strength of partisanship appears to have a greater bearing than age on turnout regularity' (Crewe, Fox, and Alt 1977).

And the same explanation applied to changes in turnout: 'a persistent and substantial drop in turnout is a phenomenon unique to Britain since the war. Part of the explanation may lie in the parallel erosion of partisan commitment in the British electorate over the last decade . . . Although an overwhelming majority of respondents continued to volunteer a party identification, the proportion declaring themselves *very strong* identifiers steadily fell from 41 per cent in 1964 and 1966 to 29 per cent in February 1974 and then down again to 23 per cent by October of the same year.' It fell a bit more in 1979 (Crewe, Särlvik, and Alt 1977; Crewe 1981b).

Party identification, measured by the standard Michigan question, has proved a useful over-time predictor of individual political behaviour. Panels have shown that those who switch votes without switching party identification are more likely to switch back than other defectors. The strength of party identification does predict an individual's turnout and volatility. In 1982, British media polls used measures of partisan strength to reveal the weakness and contingency of attachments to the Liberal party and the new Social Democratic party.

But while Michigan's measures of the strength and direction of party identification have worked well at the level of individuals, they have not performed well in the aggregate, either in Britain or America. So far, the Conservative party's pollsters in 1968/69 have been the only ones to score a predictive success with aggregate partisanship. The Butler/Stokes survey series clearly shows their measure of the *strength* of party identification follows an electoral cycle: strong Labour and Conservative identifiers comprised only 29 per cent of the electorate in 1963 and 25 per cent in 1969, but roughly 40 per cent in the election years of 1964 and 1970. Just as the pervasiveness and strength of party identification in 1970 failed to predict voting trends in 1974, so the low level of strong party identification in 1963 and 1969 did not predict voting behaviour in 1966 and 1970 well. And the sharp reduction in levels of strong party identification between 1970 and 1979 hardly explains a significantly higher turnout level in 1979. LeDuc's (1983) analysis of dealignment in Britain, Canada, and the USA suggests that its effects may be limited.

As an aggregate level, the Michigan measure of the *strength* of party identification has not served as some prior warning signal. It is no more than another indicator, an alternative to voting itself, which tells us what is happening as and when it happens. A partisan identification which changes massively in response to a general election campaign is little defence against flash parties, and a poor guide to the future. Michigan's favoured measure of party identification does not correspond to the Michigan concept of something so deeply held that it is part of the individual's means of self-identity, a means by which he knows who he is. I fear we have not yet solved the problem of measuring Michigan's concept in Britain, but the value of the concept is indisputable.

8.5 *The denationalisation of British politics*

British politics in the fifties was characterised not only by high turnout and a two-party system, but also by the appearance of cultural and political homogeneity. Early British surveys therefore used cheap local samples to investigate general laws of political behaviour or to replicate and confirm findings from other local surveys. But like their Columbia predecessors, British analysts were ambivalent about locality and took advantage of the local survey format to study and describe the locality in great detail.

Yet they lacked a good rationale for devoting so much attention to Greenwich or Glossop or Bristol or Newcastle or Clapham or Glasgow. I am reminded of a famous incident when Harold Wilson was addressing a rally in the naval dockyard town of Chatham. 'Why do I emphasise the importance of the Royal Navy?' he asked rhetorically. 'Because you're in Chatham!' came a loud reply from the audience. Many localities were surveyed in the fifties simply because they were conveniently close to the survey director's university.

By the late sixties, however, Britain's lack of political homogeneity could no longer be ignored, and local or other regional surveys were needed to investigate that heterogeneity, not to save money. Indeed they required national surveys to provide a benchmark for comparison. Thus they were an extra expense, not a cheap alternative.

Race relations stimulated numerous surveys of public attitudes both among the general population and the ethnic minorities themselves. Abram's (1969) chapter in Rose's *Colour and Citizenship*, based on a national sample of 2,250, supplemented by five samples of 500 respondents taken in immigrant areas, is one example of the first type. National samples such as Butler and Stokes's were obviously inappropriate for studying ethnic minorities themselves and Anwar (1975, 1980) used a variety of alternative techniques for his *Participation of Ethnic Minorities in the General Election of October 1974*, and *Votes and Policies: Ethnic Minorities and the General Election of 1979*. In 1979 he sampled in twenty-four constituencies with a high concentration of immigrants or an ethnic minority candidate, comparing attitudes towards racial matters and perceptions of party policies held by whites, Afro-Caribbeans, and Asians. Anwar also measured trends in ethnic registration and turnout rates.

Rose planned *Governing without Consensus: An Irish Perspective* (1971) as a study of legitimacy in Northern Ireland, focused on the related but independent concepts of support and compliance. He made no attempt to survey the totality of Irish politics, but concentrated on a single theme whose significance tragically increased during the fieldwork in 1968. His standard form of analysis compared Catholics and Protestants, rather than social classes or party identifiers. The existence of a sharp religious divide could be taken for granted, but he used the survey to study the nature and consequences of that division. How did attitudes towards the churches, towards doctrine, towards religious tolerance differ between Catholics and Protestants? How did the local balance of the sects influence attitudes? On this, for example, Rose found Ulster shatteringly different from Elmira or England: the religious balance in primary groups, or in the locality, or in the school had very little influence on attitudes. On many matters Catholics and Protestants held similar views, but on those constitutional and political questions on which they were divided, contact did not breed consensus in Northern Ireland as it did between the classes in England or classes and sects in Elmira.

Generalised attitudes towards authority did not have the expected link with political compliance. Catholic attitudes towards authority were unrelated to political compliance and among Protestants, those who *generally* favoured obeying authority were the *most*, not the least willing to break the law for political ends. Only a quarter of the Northern Irish— under a third of Protestants and under a fifth of Catholics—were fully allegiant, in the sense of supporting the regime and rejecting illegal action.

Since 1968 there have been many survey studies of Northern Ireland, particularly focusing on proposed solutions to the area's endemic crisis. Ten years later, Moxon–Browne (1979) replicated Rose's Loyalty Survey and almost unbelievably, found an intensification of sectarian political divisions beyond the levels discovered by Rose.

Madgwick's survey for *The Politics of Rural Wales* (1973) was located entirely within the constituency of Cardigan, not so much because Cardigan was typical of Wales but because it was a caricature of Welshness: Celtic, non-conformist, rural, and agrarian. Three quarters of the population spoke Welsh, half were non-conformists, the largest social-class grade consisted of farmers and their families, and the constituency had elected a Liberal for eighty years until Labour won it in 1966, only to relinquish it back to the Liberals in 1974. And, in addition, Cardigan enjoyed that most Welsh of characteristics: a large number of English immigrants.

In a wide-ranging analysis, Madgwick looked at the influence of religious non-conformity on Welsh sympathies and voting. Some impression of the richness of his survey questionnaire may be conveyed by his analysis of the dimensions of specifically Welsh culture. He factor analysed some thirty or so different Welsh-attitude variables to produce five dimensions to Welsh political culture—Welsh cultural identity, consciousness of English differences, protestant socialism, separatism, and anti-authoritarianism. 'Radicals' and 'radicalism' were terms often associated with Welsh politics. Madgwick measured radicalism by means of sixteen variables covering seven aspects of radicalism: individualism, socialism, non-conformist conscience, nationalist sentiment, anti-authority attitudes, acceptance of change, and protest potential.

The peculiarities of rural Welsh conditions also shone through Madgwick's analysis of social class. Every other British political survey found it possible to put respondents into two or more social classes, ranging from employers and managers through professionals, white collar workers, and skilled manuals down to unskilled manual workers. Even Rose, in *Government without Consensus*, found that 'the decline of agriculture's significance in Northern Ireland makes it practicable to analyse class differences by placing farmers and those in industry in common occupational categories'.

Not so Madgwick in Cardiganshire. He put 20 per cent into a farming class and divided the rest into seven fairly conventional occupational strata. Despite the significance of class in British voting, Butler and Stokes had only found half their sample spontaneously willing to reply 'yes' to the question, 'Do you ever think of yourself as belonging to a particular social class?' However, in Cardigan the figure dropped from a half to a fifth, though nearly all Cardigan people, like other Britons, would choose a social class label if pressed. The farmers had a distinctive voting pattern. They were the least Labour and most Conservative of any strata, but they gave more votes to the Liberals than to either of the governing parties. Indeed, they contributed over a third of the Liberal total. Though the farming class contained both rich and poor, it was the most homogeneous, occupationally, of all the social grades; it was the most highly organised; and the most politically distinctive.

Madgwick's survey was rich in specifically Welsh social and political variables, well suited to an analysis of a distinctive but multi-faceted culture. In complete contrast, the Scottish survey which W. L. Miller (1981a) used in *The End of British Politics? Scots and English Political Behaviour in the Seventies* was, in essence, merely a regionally boosted sample of 1,200 respondents forming part of the October 1974 British Election Study survey. Very few of the variables other than attitudes to Scottish devolution were specifically Scottish, and the format of Miller's analysis reflected its title by stressing the British context of Scottish political attitudes and behaviour. What this survey lost in specifically Scottish information, however, it gained in comparability with England.

Scots and English social characteristics and political attitudes were compared across the full range of variables in the 1974 election study. In addition, English respondents were divided into four broad regions— London, the North, the Midlands, and the South excluding London; and Scottish conditions and attitudes were compared with those in the regions of England to see whether Scots differences were truly national or whether Scotland merely represented the end of some centre-periphery spectrum centred on the cultural heart (i.e. the South) or the administrative centre (i.e. London) of England.

Support for the SNP was linked to two broad types of variable: first, all those measures which indicated a balanced connection to both or neither of the two governing parties; second, variables which indicated a special interest in Scottish issues like oil and devolution, or a particularly pro-Scots position on these issues. The first category of variable indicated, and often explained, weak attachment to the two-party system facilitating desertion to *any* new party; the second category indicated a positive attraction to the aims and objectives of the SNP. Facilitating variables which opened up the possibility of an SNP vote in Scotland generally had a similar effect on tendencies to vote Liberal in England.

SNP votes were particularly high among the young and irreligious; among those who had not voted in the 1970 election, or who had voted Liberal in the past; among those who denied the importance of issues like prices, strikes, public expenditure, or redistributing wealth; among those who saw little difference between the parties, rated Heath and Wilson equally—even if moderately highly; or among those who trusted both governing parties equally—again, even if they trusted them equally well; among those whose social class was contradicted by their attitude to public expenditure, by their parents' class, or by their parents' partisanship.

However, even with a very strict control for balanced attitudes towards the two governing parties, there was a strong correlation between attitudes to devolution and SNP voting. Devolution also seemed a more powerful influence on voting than attitudes on North Sea Oil, or the EEC, on which the SNP also had distinctive policies. With the data available in this single-wave cross-sectional survey there was no way of statistically determining whether attitudes on devolution were caused by SNP voting or, conversely, influenced voting choice. However, the meteoric rise in SNP voting between 1970 and 1974 was accompanied by a small drop in support for devolution. This suggested that SNP voting did not increase pro-devolution attitudes, nor was it the product of an increase in devolution sentiment; instead it appeared that when British conditions were ripe for a switch to third-party voting, the SNP was able to appeal specially strongly to those who approved of devolution but was unable to attract the votes of those who did not. While this might seem obvious after analysis, almost all British surveys had noted that very large numbers of Labour voters disagreed with that party's most fundamental policies; and it was not obvious that anti-devolutionists might refuse to vote SNP, when anti-nationalisers voted Labour in huge numbers.

Miller broke down his Scottish sample geographically by area, class, rurality, peripherality, and partisanship. Individuals had a higher tendency to vote SNP when their own social class contradicted the class environment in which they lived. More surprisingly these geographic breakdowns showed that attitudes towards oil revenues, EEC membership, and devolution scarcely differed between SNP seats and those won by Labour or the Conservatives. The SNP won certain seats not because devolution sentiment was higher there, nor by gaining the votes of anti-devolutionists, but by winning roughly 60 per cent instead of 30 per cent of the pro-devolution vote. Miller confirmed this finding by reanalysing three other Scottish surveys which Opinion Research Centre had carried out for the *Scotsman*.

In 1974 both Labour and Conservative parties proposed to set up a devolved Scottish Assembly to handle internal Scottish affairs. The SNP proposed outright independence. At that election attitudes to Scottish self-government correlated strongly with SNP voting, but not with the choice between Labour and Conservative. By the time of the 1979 election however, self-government attitudes did correlate with the choice between Labour and Conservative. In the interval the Conservative party had reneged on its commitment to devolution. But it would be quite wrong to attribute the increasing correlation purely or even mainly to a Conservative loss of support amongst pro-devolutionists. Miller's analysis (1983) of the 1974–79 Scottish election panel survey shows that in resolving the tension between party choice and issue attitudes, issue attitudes had more influence on SNP voting than vice versa; but Conservative and Labour voters mainly adjusted their issue attitudes to fit their parties' changing policies. (Compare Verba and Nie 1972: 106–9 on the power of issues to influence *third party* voting.) All parties had tried quite explicitly to influence their supporters' issue attitudes at the devolution referendum only two months prior to the 1979 general election. It seems reasonable to suppose that issues would matter more than partisanship for SNP supporters, most of whom had voted SNP for the first time in 1974; but Labour and Conservative supporters had a much longer-standing partisanship and so were more influenced by party appeals to change their issue attitudes. They may also have been influenced by the widespread but not fully justified presumption that a devolved Scotland would be governed by Labour.

This interpretation is supported by evidence from numerous media-commissioned polls in the weeks and months before the 1979 referendum on devolution, though none of them was a panel survey, and they did not provide conclusive evidence by themselves. When a referendum was first proposed in 1976, Conservative and Labour parties were both still officially in favour of devolution, and their partisans were indistinguishable in their referendum voting intentions. However, as soon as Thatcher issued a three-line whip in parliament urging her MPs to vote against Labour's devolution proposals, Conservative supporters in Scottish opinion polls became significantly less inclined to vote for devolution in a referendum. And in the final weeks of the referendum campaign, in January and February 1979, weekly opinion polls showed a progressive change by

Conservatives towards a negative referendum vote. (W. L. Miller 1981a: 250–2; for comparison, see the party politicisation of the abortion issue in the Netherlands—Eijk and Outshoorn 1980 or Eijk and Niemoller 1983: 208.)

Earlier, a sequence of polls in 1975 showed that Wilson constructed the pro-EEC majority in the EEC referendum by persuading Labour supporters to switch from a negative to a positive vote intention in that referendum (Butler and Kitzinger 1976).

Both these British referendum experiences in the seventies are hauntingly similar to that American experience with attitudes to foreign policy in the late forties which originally prompted Belknap and Campbell (1951) to stress the significance of party identification as a concept. If the seventies provided evidence that party identification measured by the Michigan question had become extremely weak, the decade also furnished new dynamic evidence of the electorate's continuing responsiveness to party-based appeals. A balanced analysis must take note of the power of partisanship to influence referendum votes, as well as the power of issue attitudes to influence electoral choice.

9 The multi-nationals: cross-national surveys of political participation

The fundamental motivation for multi-national or cross-national survey research was an interest in systems—social systems, institutional systems, cultural systems, or political systems, but systems rather than individuals. Among the early criticisms of survey research was the claim that, by interviewing individuals, surveys could only describe and analyse the individual components of political life; that surveys were irrelevant to the study of cultures and institutions; and that surveys even gave a misleadingly restricted view of individuals, because individuals were embedded in a cultural and institutional setting which lay outside the scope of the surveys.

Multi-national survey designs were intended essentially as multi-system, multi-cultural, or multi-setting surveys. Analysis required variation within the data set. Thus surveys could be used to study cultural variation, but only if the sample was spread sufficiently widely to draw respondents from a number of different cultural settings. Cross-national surveys were only one way of doing that. Within a single nation or a single state, there might be significant variations in cultural and institutional settings. British election studies made very good use of this fact by contrasting political behaviour in working class and middle class environments, or in Scots, Welsh, Irish, and English environments. Similarly, students of American voting behaviour often found it difficult to regard the USA as a cultural and institutional unity. At the very least, the South appeared radically different from the rest of the USA, both culturally and institutionally.

From another perspective, however, cross-national survey designs might sometimes seem too narrow rather than unnecessarily wide. On some cultural dimensions Britain and America, or even Europe and America were too similar to provide the degree of cultural variation necessary for analysis.

In short, the basic requirement was that the object of study must vary across the elements of the data set. Multi-national designs necessarily incorporated more variation than single nation designs, but whether they incorporated enough or more than enough would depend upon the precise details of the subject being studied. Multi-national designs were an attempt to realise multi-cultural or multi-institutional designs. They were only incidentally multi-national.

Broadly speaking, there are three reasons for using a multi-national design, and I shall discuss one outstanding example of each kind of multi-national survey study. First, we might wish to show the influence of individual attitudes and behaviour upon political institutions. That was the motivation for Almond and Verba's *Civic Culture* study, which sought to explain why some democracies were stable and others not. Second, we might wish to show the influence of the cultural and institutional setting upon the attitudes and behaviour of individuals. That was the motivation for Verba, Nie, and Kim's study of *Participation and Political Equality*, which sought to show why class influenced participation rates more in some countries than in others. Third, we might wish to establish the generality of a finding by showing how little it was affected by the social and political setting. That was the motivation for Barnes and Kaase's study of *Political Action*, which sought to reveal the psychological motivations for political protest and show that these were the same in many settings.

But as well as illustrating the different uses of cross-national survey designs, these three studies also illustrate the development of our understanding of political participation. Almond and Verba's original classic dealt with conventional participatory attitudes. Verba, Nie, and Kim's follow-up study stressed participatory behaviour instead of attitude, and distinguished between four 'modes' of participation—all of them peaceable, conventional, and élite-controlled, however. Barnes and Kaase's study widened its scope to include élite-challenging protest behaviour and support for police and military repression.

9.1 *Substance and method: cross-national analysis, political participation, and multi-national surveys*

It would be unrealistic to suggest that political scientists have problems and devise methods to solve them. Sometimes like a plumber or a carpenter they acquire some tools and seek an outlet for their skills. A revealing comment in *The Civic Culture* noted that 'in order to compare political behaviour cross-nationally, one must be able to specify dimensions of political behaviour that apply to all the systems studied'. So cross-national analysis and political participation were linked in two ways: political participation was so closely bound up with culture and institutions, both as cause and effect, that cross-national analysis was a good way of studying participation; but equally important, participation was so comparable from one nation to another, that participation was a particularly good subject for cross-national survey analysis. There is no way of doing a cross-national analysis of Democratic versus Republican voting choice, since these parties are unique to the United States. Even a cross-national analysis of left-wing versus right-wing voting choice raises all manner of difficult problems about cross-national comparability. There are certainly problems with comparing participation in different nations, but they are less severe than the problems associated with comparing party choice cross-nationally. Verba, Nie, and Kim even extended their analysis of participation to countries where the choice between political parties did not exist at all.

The topic therefore provided a means of access for the method. A focus on participation let the Survey Method contribute to comparative politics. It is no accident that the most outstanding surveys of voting choice have been national, and the most outstanding surveys of participation have been multi-national.

However, although multi-national surveys and comparative politics are closely related, they are not the same. Barnes and Kaase explicitly admitted that their five-nation study of political protest was 'not a comparative study', although they misguidedly claimed that it was none the less 'a study in comparative politics'. In fact there was nothing comparative about it. Their object was to use a variety of national settings to establish general principles and relationships that would apply everywhere (or at least throughout their five nations). Structurally and methodologically their study was much less interesting than the work of Almond, Verba, and Nie. Barnes and Kaase's main contribution was to extend the topic to include forms of political participation not considered by the other studies.

If a multi-national survey need not imply comparative analysis, the converse is also true: comparative analysis can be done without multi-national surveys. Lipset's *Political Man* (1960) was a good example of comparative analysis based upon collecting and synthesising results from a variety of non-comparative single-national surveys. More systematic was Rose's *Electoral Behaviour* (1974b, 1974c) in which a dozen authors each contributed a survey-based analysis of a single country, but all authors worked (partly) to a common format. Alford's *Party and Society* (1963) was based on his reanalysis of Gallup surveys from Canada, Australia, America, and Britain, while Budge and Farlie (1976, 1977) raided the British SSRC's Survey Archive for surveys from ten countries to reanalyse for their comparative work on *Voting and Party Competition*.

Synthesis and reanalysis have their virtues. They are certainly cheap. But they have important defects, which I discuss in Chapter 10. And reanalysis of sets of surveys, particularly multi-national collections of surveys, suffers from all the problems that afflict reanalysis of a single survey, multiplied and magnified by the need to maintain comparability.

We can only base a cross-national analysis on ten national surveys if each of them asked the same (or equivalent) questions. Put another way, we can only analyse what they have in common. That tends to mean restricting the analysis to social and electoral variables—neglecting psychological and attitudinal variables. It often means restricting political choice and participation variables to turnout and voting choice. Even with these restrictions, cross-national reanalysis tends to require a lax approach to problems of comparability and equivalence.

Unfortunately for cross-national analyses of participation which are not based on multi-national surveys, there is a big difference between voting turnout and democratic participation in the wider sense; and this difference varies from nation to nation. Consequently the United States comes almost at the bottom of Powell's list of turnout rates in thirty democracies (Powell 1980), yet other studies show that America is the most participatory of democracies, when other forms of democratic participation are taken into account. At the very least that means turnout rates cannot be used by themselves as a sufficient index of cross-national variations in participation.

A multi-national survey, planned as a unified enterprise, makes it possible to ensure that all the required questions are asked in each of the nations. And it forces explicit consideration of question equivalence at a point in the research process where action can be taken to maximise that comparability.

In principle the problems of question equivalence are the same in a multi-national survey as in a national survey, but they are worse in quantity and degree. The Kilbrandon Commission survey on attitudes to devolution in various parts of the UK asked the people of East Anglia 'should East Anglia completely run its own affairs?' In Scotland it asked 'should Scotland completely run its own affairs?' Though the words were the same the meanings were entirely different. Scots naturally thought they were being asked a familiar question about national independence, East Anglians thought they were being asked an obscure question about local government. In a multi-national and multi-cultural survey such problems of equivalence are only made more difficult by the need to translate words into different languages and find cross-cultural equivalents for concepts like wealth (cash in one culture, cattle in another?) or campaign activities (displaying posters in one culture, bumper stickers in another?).

9.2 The Civic Culture *and democratic stability*

Early voting studies in Britain and America tried to link survey research to political theory by comparing survey information on the electorate with classic philosophical statements of the qualifications necessary for being an elector in a democracy. The ideal democratic citizen was expected to be 'active in politics and to be involved . . . to be rational in his approach to politics, guided by reason, not by emotion . . . well informed and to make decisions on the basis of careful calculation as to the interests and the principles he would like to see furthered.' By that standard, British and American electorates did not show up very well in the surveys of the 1940s and 1950s.

But Almond and Verba noted that 'British and American democracy had somehow weathered the crisis of the 1920s and 1930s: Germany and Italy had not.' So instead of judging the British and American electorates against some theoretical, abstract standard for democratic participation, they set out to see why British and American democracy had been success-ful while German and Italian had not. Implicitly they took British and American reality as their standard. By definition, the actual characteristics of the British and American electorates and not some textbook norms were to be the 'political culture of democracy': *The Civic Culture* (Almond and Verba 1963). By empirical analysis they would uncover a definition of what the democratic citizen was like *in reality* to replace speculative notions of what he *ought* to be.

But Almond and Verba were not only motivated by a concern to study the stability of democracy. 'The development of survey research method-ology was the immediate and more powerful stimulus. It had now become possible to establish whether there were indeed distinctive national charac-teristics' (Almond 1980). Cross-national surveys could 'do much to bring more closely together the analysis of individual political behaviour with that of political systems'. Cross-national designs allowed surveys to contribute to a form of 'micro–macro' analysis. Too often in the past, comparative political analysis had suffered from 'an unfortunate circu-larity. In the absence of direct data on political attitudes one often infers political attitudes from political structures. The stability of the British political system, for example might be explained in terms of a basic consensus among the British people. But what is the evidence for the consensus? If one looks carefully it is often the existence of a stable party system.'

The Civic Culture was based upon roughly a thousand interviews in each of Britain, America, Mexico, Germany, and Italy. All the surveys were done in 1959 or 1960 and a limited number of respondents were selected for follow-up, in-depth interviews about their 'political life-histories.'

If methodological developments prompted the study, methodological under-development also restricted the analysis. '*The Civic Culture* was perhaps the last major social investigation to be analysed by a statistical card-sorter' instead of an electronic computer. Consequently most of the analysis consisted of cross-national comparisons of marginal frequencies, or at best a comparative breakdown of attitudes by class within each nation. These were supplemented by very extensive quotations taken from the depth interviews.

Almond and Verba's central question was this: 'Is there a democratic political culture—a pattern of political attitudes that fosters democratic stability, that in some way fits the democratic political system?' By way of an answer, they simply contrasted attitudes in Britain and America, 'the two relatively stable and successful democracies' with attitudes in Germany, Italy, and Mexico.

They defined three political 'orientations': 'parochial', 'subject', and 'participant' orientations. Unlike rational choice theorists, they stressed the need for a *mix* of orientations, even for an inconsistent and contradictory mix. 'The civic culture is a mixed political culture. In it many individuals are active in politics, but there are also many who take the more passive role of subject. More important, even among those performing the active role of the citizen, the roles of subject and parochial have not been displaced.'

While the *participant* orientation focused on the inputs to democratic government, on politics and on law making, the *subject* orientation focused on coping with the outputs of government—on administration, on 'deference to the independent authority of government', on fair and sympathetic treatment by the bureaucracy, rather than access to policy making. The *parochial* orientation focused on largely non-political concerns about the locality, and family or social contacts.

British and American respondents expressed very much more confidence than Italians, Germans, or Mexicans in their own ability to do something about an unjust law. By contrast, the British and Germans (not the Americans) had the most confidence in fair treatment by their bureaucracies. So British and Americans were 'competent participants', while British and Germans were 'competent subjects'.

The British and Americans also scored particularly high on 'open partisanship'—defined as a combination of emotional involvement in political campaigns coupled with an indifference towards cross-party marriage: that is a lively yet not too personally antagonistic attitude towards party divisions.

Thirdly, the British and Americans scored particularly high on feelings that they could 'trust most people'. By contrast Italians, Germans, and

Mexicans not only displayed 'levels of interpersonal trust that were relatively low, but what interpersonal trust there was, was not related to the willingness or ability to cooperate with one's fellow citizens'.

Lastly, only the British and Americans showed high levels of activism within organisations. Mexicans and Italians tended not to belong to voluntary organisations. Germans were often members of voluntary organisations but seldom active within them, just as they had high rates of voter turnout but seldom discussed politics or formed political groups. German participation was formal and passive.

Almond and Verba characterised Italy as an *alienated political culture* afflicted by 'unrelieved political alienation; social isolation and distrust' with a low level of national pride and only a moderate amount of open partisanship. Germany combined *political detachment and subject competence*. It was the only nation in which the sense of subject competence occurred more frequently than a sense of participant competence. Hostility among party supporters was high and not tempered by any general social trust. Germans were 'satisfied with the performance of their government but lacked a more general attachment to the system' on a symbolic or emotional level.

Both British and American cultures approximated to the civic culture. Participant and subject orientations were widespread; the political cultures were 'permeated by more general attitudes of social trust and confidence'; 'open patterns of partisanship predominated'. Yet there was a difference between British and American cultures: in America 'there was some imbalance in the direction of the participant role', while the 'British political culture represented a more effective combination of the subject and participant roles . . . Despite the spread of political competence and participant orientations, the British had maintained a strong deference to the independent authority of government'.

Almond and Verba's survey provided evidence that experiences with non-political authorities in the family, school, or especially workplace affected perceptions of political competence. High levels of education also increased respondents' sense of political competence. Similarly, but without any direct survey evidence, they attributed the difference in overall national political cultures to overall national experiences, that is to history.

These were grand themes. No one could accuse Almond and Verba of confining their attention to 'miniscular problems of uncertain relevance to the sweeping institutional complexes of politics' (Leiserson 1958: 371). Perhaps they were overambitious. Verba (1980) later described *The Civic Culture* as a 'bold and incautious book', even 'foolhardy'. The connection between a micro-analysis of individual attitudes and a macro-analysis of political systems was not fully realised. There was a 'large inferential leap from that on which they had data to that about which they wanted to generalise'. 'The dependent variable of system stability . . . was not precisely measured and not directly linked to the survey data.' Moreover, 'there was no clear understanding of the process by which basic political values affected the operation of a political system'. Yet *The Civic Culture* was a most impressive attempt at connecting survey research with broad questions about theory and institutions. If the connection was not perfect, it was not a total failure either. Later studies did connect data to conclusions more closely, but at the cost of restraining their ambitions and tackling much more limited questions.

In contrast to the classic voting studies which I discussed in earlier chapters, *The Civic Culture* made little impact in Britain, Germany, or Italy (see Kavanagh 1980, Conradt 1980, Sani 1980). Political scientists in each nation felt they knew its findings already. Germans and Italians found them unpalatable, especially in the context of an American book. The British found them altogether too comforting to evoke much reaction. European readers tended to see it as a book about five nations, rather than about the conditions for democracy, and the layout of the book reinforced this non-comparative, gazetteer image. It was a mistake to characterise national cultures with pithy phrases when the book was about the relationship between culture and system, and nations were mere units of analysis.

The Civic Culture illustrates well some of the special difficulties with multi-national surveys. Despite all the efforts to achieve cross-national comparability, some problems remained unresolved and others were exposed as inherently insoluble. There were simple errors of translation. There was the logical impossibility of conducting the surveys at the same point in historical time and also at the same point in each country's electoral cycle—simply because different countries had elections at different times. The samples were *not* national samples: 63 per cent of Mexicans were excluded by limiting the sample to urban areas, and selection was biased within urban areas (Craig and Cornelius 1980). The British sample was variously described as 'English', 'British', or 'UK'. In fact it was a sample of the British mainland—neither a state nor a nation. Completion rates were specially low (only 60 per cent) in Britain and Mexico compared to America (83 per cent)—which was specially unfortunate in a survey about participation, since those who do not participate in surveys may well be the ones who do not participate in other ways. The Italian sample was afflicted by 'reticence' (Sani 1980): only half the sample would say which party they voted for. So while the Italian Communist Party won 23 per cent of the vote in the 1958 election, only a mere four per cent of Almond and Verba's sample admitted doing so. There were also very high levels of 'don't knows' or refusals on attitude questions in the Italian sample. Consequently cross-national comparisons of marginal percentages depended very much on whether they were made with or without the exclusion of missing data codes.

More generally, the basic analytic technique used by Almond and Verba —comparing total national percentages giving particular replies—was highly sensitive to question wording, linguistic conventions, and even the sequencing of questions within the interview. It was especially inappropriate to cross-national analysis.

We can usefully compare the relative strengths and weaknesses of the survey methods used for *The Civic Culture* with those of the Columbia and Michigan election surveys. The chief virtue of the *Civic Culture* study was that its sample was spread over a wider variety of cultural and institutional settings; so that culture and institutions could then be studied by precise survey methods. But in several other respects the *Civic Culture* survey was markedly inferior to the election surveys, notably because it did not employ a panel or even time series design; because it failed to over-sample interesting subcultures; and because its variables were not so well defined, not so closely related to the concepts under investigation. These three defects are worth some attention.

First, the multi-national structure of the *Civic Culture* survey made it so expensive, and so difficult to organise, that it consisted of a single wave of interviews (supplemented admittedly by a few in-depth follow-ups). That meant the study had no time dimension. In turn, the lack of a time dimension made it impossible to determine directions of causal influence, and it subtly implied that the differences between nations at one point in time reflected enduring differences between cultures.

Almond and Verba were trying to explain the German and Italian failure to sustain democracy in the 1920s and 1930s by investigating their political culture in 1959. Unless culture is almost totally invariant over time, the mere fact of time sequence suggests that their study may well have revealed the effect of defeat and occupation on German and Italian culture, rather than the effect of culture on democratic institutions. Indeed, they themselves speculated that culture derived from long-term history. It may well have been strongly influenced by short-term history. Nothing in their single wave study allowed them to determine causal direction. In Germany especially, the occupying powers made an extensive and sustained attempt to alter German political culture, monitoring their success by conducting several hundred surveys that employed questions remarkably similar to those used by Almond and Verba (see Merritt and

Merritt 1970). It was not at all obvious that culture was the cause, rather than the effect, in its relationship to institutions (see Barry 1970; Pateman 1970, 1980).

Not surprisingly, some Marxist critics took the view that all significant mass attitudes were structurally determined, and political culture was thus so very dependent upon objective structural realities that it hardly merited serious research (see Craig and Cornelius 1980). Much more surprisingly, other Marxists took the opposite view and suggested that Communist governments might use political culture surveys to monitor progress towards the creation of a 'new socialist man' (Wiatr 1980; Brown and Gray 1977).

Criticisms of Almond and Verba for assuming that culture influenced institutions rather than vice versa are simply wrong: they did not. They suggested that culture and institutions influenced each other, that they might sometimes be 'congruent' or in harmony, but at other times they might contradict each other and the tension would spark off changes in culture, institutions, or both. Congruence would imply stability, contradiction would imply instability. Moreover, the function of political culture might be like that of a starter battery in a car engine: at any one time the culture might be derivative from past history, but once established it could exert an independent influence over behaviour at least for a short time— a democratic culture would be a resource, built up by history, that could support democratic institutions through a short-term crisis. The proper criticism of the *Civic Culture* survey is not that its authors failed to imagine a two-way process of influence, but that a single-wave survey did not permit dynamic analysis and could not discriminate empirically between causes and effects, or between influence in one direction and influence in the opposite direction.

Ideally, these important questions of causation required panel surveys applied to communities with incongruent cultures and institutions, though Barry's suggestion of a panel survey spanning a period in which a democratic regime is replaced by an authoritarian regime conjures up some practical difficulties.

A much more modest ambition would be a time series of regular surveys repeating some of the same questions (instead of a panel), and spanning a period in which an authoritarian regime is replaced by a democratic one (instead of vice versa). Germany provides just such a case.

Sequences of surveys in Britain (Kavanagh 1980) and America (Abramowitz 1980) but especially in Germany show how much Almond and Verba underestimated the flexibility, indeed malleability, of political culture. Since the *Civic Culture* survey, crime in the streets, black militancy, student protest, Vietnam and Watergate have influenced American culture, economic decline has influenced the British. Resilient though they are, both cultures have lost some of their confidence; trust and pride have declined.

In Germany persistent efforts to manipulate political culture, coupled with sustained economic success, have produced decisive changes (Conradt 1980). Germans had shown some pride in their economic performance in 1959, but over the next two decades they also recovered their lost pride in governmental institutions and in their social welfare system. Their sense of participant competence rose to British levels, and their trust in government surpassed British levels. By the seventies even those Germans who thought the performance of their parliamentary system was unsatisfactory still thought its existence was necessary. Their attitudes were no longer purely instrumental. Their involvement in politics was no longer purely formal: interest in politics was high and they proclaimed (at least) a determination actively to oppose any new Nazi party. They no longer looked back to pre-Weimar days as the best period in German history. They had lost interest in German unification and gained an interest in European unification. By the seventies, a concern for the security and stability of German democracy had been replaced by a concern for the quality and extent of German democracy. Criticism now came from the left rather than from the right.

Almond and Verba never assumed that culture remained unchanged as time passed, but their lack of a time series format tended to imply—more to readers perhaps, than to the authors—that political culture could change only slowly unless there were traumatic upheavals to accelerate the process. Kavanagh (1980) underlines the faults of the readers as well as the authors, however: 'if students of British politics have fed off Almond and Verba's descriptive data for too long, this is largely because later writings have been based on so little empirical research.'

The second major defect of the *Civic Culture* survey, which made it inferior in design to the election surveys, was its lack of attention to subcultures. In one sense the book did admit the significance of subcultural variation, but analysed it only in terms of education, and not in terms of race or region. Rokkan (1964) was especially critical of the *Civic Culture's* 'strong nation-orientation' and its tendency to present 'straight comparisons between national cross-sections'. Burnham (1974) quotes a reworking of the *Civic Culture* data by Jacob and Vines which showed that the 'attitudes towards political life among inhabitants of the Southern region of the US were much more similar to those encountered in Italy or Mexico than those encountered in the rest of the US or the UK'. *The Civic Culture* gave a clue to this cultural similarity between Mexico and the American South when it reported that some interviewers had been arrested and jailed in Mexico and in Louisiana—but the jailing of interviewers was not used as a formal measure of political culture!

Almond (1980) later admitted the fault, but claimed there was no way of analysing subcultures when costs restricted each national sample to about a thousand respondents. There were only about a hundred blacks in the American sample and a hundred Scots in the British. However, small numbers did not prevent Almond and Verba splitting each sample by education into low, intermediate, and university educated groups. And in each of Britain, Germany, and Mexico the university-educated group comprised a mere twenty-five individuals.

Even within a limited total number of interviews it is possible to analyse subcultures by using a 'modified quota' or 'scope' sample rather than a 'representative' sample. Election studies in America over-sampled sparsely populated but theoretically interesting regions; election studies in Britain over-sampled in Scotland and Wales; election studies in Wales over-sampled in the sparsely populated Welsh-speaking parts of the principality. There was no reason why *Civic Culture* samples could not have been designed as multi-cultural rather than merely multi-national. That would have meant more interviews in Scotland, Wales, and the American South, balanced by rather fewer interviews in England and New England; more interviews with American blacks and rather fewer with whites; some interviews (instead of none) with rural Mexicans and fewer with urban Mexicans. Especially when the analytic target is theory rather than mere historical description, purely unmodified representative national samples are inefficient and inappropriate.

Similarly, it could be argued that some people's participation and some people's democratic culture was more important than others (Stouffer 1955). If cultural values were to be used to explain the stability of the democratic system, then perhaps some of the *Civic Culture* interviews should have been directed at élites rather than masses—though Almond and Verba took previous work on élite/mass differences into account when planning and analysing *The Civic Culture*.

The third respect in which *The Civic Culture* was inferior to the election studies was in its conceptualisation and measurement of critical variables, though that inferiority was largely the result of focusing attention on concepts and variables which were inherently more difficult to measure. The dependent variable in *The Civic Culture* was *democratic stability* and the number of *cases* available for analysis was *five*. Barry (1970) and Pateman (1980) attacked *The Civic Culture* for failing to 'address the question of *how democratic* these five countries were'. Even if Almond and Verba had produced some numeric measures of democratic stability in each of their five countries, a statistical analysis of only five cases would necessarily prove insignificant. The problem is a real one, but easier to recognise than solve. Quantitative measures of democratic stability, instead of a dichotomy between stable and unstable would have helped. So would more cases—though that would have required surveying more nations or more times.

The civic culture was a *mixed* culture, according to Almond and Verba. But they used the idea of a *mix* in several different ways: confident élites mixed with passive citizens; participant norms mixed with passive behaviour; a mixture of activists and apathetics in the general public; and finally a mixture of participant and subject orientations within the same individual. Yet their analyses tended to quantify the levels of both participation and deference, rather than the mixture or co-occurence of the two. We know how many people had 'subject competence' and how many had 'participant competence', but not how many had both. We do not know whether subjects and participants were the same people or different.

Deference itself was ill-defined. They occasionally used the term in the text (though it does not appear in the index) as an approximate synonym for 'subject orientation'. It was particularly unfortunate that they should characterise Britain as '*a deferential civic culture*' and refer to the British having a 'strong deference to the independent authority of government', yet without specifically defining deference and without devising a specific measure of deference. The concept provoked considerable interest in Britain though, as I suggested in Chapter 8, its potential was never fully realised because successive researchers followed Almond and Verba in confusing deference to the 'independent authority of government' with deference to the Conservative party. Paradoxically we know that it is the Labour party that needs to rely on deference to the 'independent authority of government' much more than the Conservative party, because it is the Labour party that persistently gets elected to power despite popular disagreement with its basic policies. In private conversation at party headquarters, it has been Labour, not Conservative, officials who have expressed the need to understand deference, and the limits of deference. Conservatives may find social deference useful in getting elected, but Labour needs political deference to survive in government and implement its policies.

Class was also badly conceptualised in *The Civic Culture*. Quite shockingly to European readers, Almond and Verba divided their samples by level of education and then described the result as a 'class' analysis.

Education reflects educational institutions. Outside America very few respondents fell into the 'university-educated' category. Worse, the two other education categories—'primary' and 'secondary'—took no account of changing institutional arrangements. Close to half the occupationally defined middle class in Britain fell into Almond and Verba's minimum education category and hence were treated as lower class. There is a lot to be said in favour of analysing participation in terms of education, but nothing to be said for calling education 'class'.

Lastly, the notion of *participation* was conceptualised far too narrowly. From a Marxist standpoint, Wiatr (1980) criticised Almond and Verba for defining 'citizen participation as participation within the established system alone and according to the norms of that system'. But one does not need to be a Marxist to appreciate that political activity may consist of more than participating in the electoral process or going to petition bureaucrats with private grievances. Craig and Cornelius point out that Mexican peasants who may not be consulted in the formulation of policy, and may be unsuccessful in getting preferential application of specific policies, none the less possess a formidable 'capacity to resist policy initiatives emanating from Mexico City'. And in the other four countries there is also ample evidence of protest and disruption as forms of political activity. Indeed, *The Civic Culture* surveys were conducted just after the foundation of the British Campaign for Nuclear Disarmament, at a time when Bertrand Russell was advocating a campaign of civil disobedience, and when Gaitskell was proclaiming the need to 'fight, and fight and fight again' to save the Labour party from being taken over by extreme leftists and nuclear disarmers. It was written up in a year when one and a half times as many British citizens were involved in strikes as in the General Strike year of 1926.

But having listed all these criticisms, *The Civic Culture* was a pathbreaking study that brought survey methodology to bear on major questions of comparative politics, political institutions, and political theory in a more systematic, more empirical, and more realistic way than before. Some later surveys improved on its treatment of the active side of political participation, but not on the subject/deferential side; and Kavanagh was right to note that too many political scientists in Britain either quoted it or criticised it without advancing its empirical contribution to our knowledge.

9.3 *Democratic participation and political equality*

Fifteen years after *The Civic Culture*, Verba, Nie, and Kim published *Participation and Political Equality: a Seven-Nation Comparison*. Their 'original goal was to replicate the *Civic Culture* study in some other nations', but in the event they developed some of the themes touched upon in the earlier volume, neither replicating *The Civic Culture* nor switching to entirely new themes.

In several respects *Participation and Political Equality* avoided the faults and failings of *The Civic Culture*, while retaining the same objectives. Despite its subsidiary title, the new book avoided those simple cross-national comparisons which had diverted attention from the theoretical objectives of *The Civic Culture*: 'though our data came from seven nations this is not a book about these nations so much as it is a book about some general social processes for which each nation is the setting. This is not to say that we ignore context. As we shall try to demonstrate, certain general social processes lead to different results within different contexts.' 'In most cases our analysis involves relative rather than absolute measures . . . We avoid some of the problems of establishing equivalence by *avoiding direct cross-national comparisons of marginal results* . . . (which) are sensitive to question wording, question order, and the way in which the interview is administered.'

Compared to the *Civic Culture* study, Verba, Nie, and Kim posed a much more modest question, but answered it in a much more methodologically sophisticated way, specifying it with precision and answering it with data that were closely related to the question.

In their introduction to *The Civic Culture*, Almond and Verba had noted: 'the proposition, derived from numerous studies of voting behaviour in the US, that higher status individuals participate most in politics might, for instance, not hold in political systems with other party structures'. Fifteen years later this became the central theme of *Participation and Political Equality*. Why did status or education correlate with participation more highly in one country than another? Why in particular was the correlation especially high in America, India, and Yugoslavia—an unlikely collection of nations in which to find any similarities; but especially low in Austria, Japan, Nigeria, and the Netherlands—another seemingly heterogeneous collection of nations? Rokkan (1970) had pointed out that the correlation between education and political activity was actually negative in Norway, and he had speculated that Norway's highly class-polarised party system explained this reversal of the usual relationship: a strong working class party mobilised the working class and also provided opportunities for those in the working class who wished to participate in politics. So neither Verba, Nie, and Kim's question, nor their answer, was very original. What was new, however, was their powerful and systematic empirical analysis of highly relevant data.

Verba, Nie, and Kim's model 'juxtaposed individual characteristics with institutional constraints'. Unlike *The Civic Culture*, it was more about the influence of the system on the individual than the influence of the individual on the system. It also differed in a number of technical but significant ways: the new book was about participatory *behaviour*, rather than participant *attitudes*; it distinguished four *modes* of participation—voting, campaigning, community activity, and the pursuit of personal favours (see also Verba, Nie, and Kim 1971 on modes of participation); it explained participation in terms of contemporaneous characteristics rather than in terms of history and socialisation; it distinguished (correctly) between class and education, instead of confusing the two; and its samples were better designed. Samples were roughly twice the size of those used for *The Civic Culture*; they included national cross-sections plus boosted samples in a subset of communities and élite samples drawn from local notables in those same communities. Most of the analysis, however, was based on the cross-section samples. (See Verba and Nie 1972 for more emphasis on the élite and community samples.) Fieldwork was spread over a five-year period, 1966–1971.

But despite its improved methodology, the new survey stuck to the fundamentals of *The Civic Culture* study. It was still about conventional participation: 'those legal acts by private citizens that are more or less directly aimed at influencing the selection of governmental personnel and/or the actions they take'. It did not deal with protest, violence, or rebellion. It distinguished between 'group-based' and 'individual based' motivations for participation, but not between 'élite directed' and 'élite challenging' modes of participation.

Secondly it was still about participatory systems, rather than participating individuals. At one level it did describe the way individual characteristics and institutional constraints or opportunities combined to make individuals participate. Yet Verba, Nie, and Kim stated unequivocally: 'we are *not* interested in explaining the decision on the part of the individual whether or not to take part in politics . . . Our ultimate dependent variable is the *shape of the participant population*.' They argued that whatever the reasons for it, social bias in participation rates lowered the *quality* of democracy even if it restricted the participating population to those with more democratic ideals. Political inequality was an important characteristic of a system, as well as a guide to the behaviour of particular individuals within it.

The seven nations involved in the study were a deliberately heterogeneous collection. It followed what Przeworski and Teune (1970) called a 'maximum difference research design'. Any uniformities found in such a varied collection of nations could well be described as generally applicable findings. The nations were Austria, India, Japan, the Netherlands, Nigeria, the United States, and Yugoslavia.

Although many questions about specific acts of participation were asked in each country (fifteen questions in the US, for example), Verba, Nie, and Kim were always able to group these by factor analysis into four modes of participation: voting, campaigning, community political activity, and personal petitioning. They noted that other studies in Norway, Costa Rica, Peru, the US, and Japan had also been able to group specific acts of participation under these same four headings. They paid most attention to the first three modes; that is, voting, campaigning, and community action. But they stressed that multi-dimensionality of political activity, participation in one mode of political action, neither precluded nor implied participation in other modes.

Critical to their analysis was a comparison between patterns of political activity and patterns of political involvement, where 'involvement' was measured by questions about respondents' awareness of politics, interest in politics, level of information, attention to the media, or participation in political discussions.

Activity and involvement were dependent variables. The two independent or predictor variables were SERL and the institutional setting. SERL stood for 'socio-economic resources level'. It was based on the individual's education and his or her family income. The authors made no claim that SERL represented some abstract concept of class or status. Rather, they claimed that education and income were important motivations and resources for those who wished to participate in politics. The second influence on political activity was the nature of the political and party system. SERL was an 'individual-based' motivation for participation; institutional factors were 'group-based' motivations.

In all nations, and in all social segments within them, there was a natural tendency for those higher up the SERL scale to participate more. Indeed, in every nation there was a strong correlation between SERL and political involvement in the psychological sense. But institutions mobilised and/or constrained political action, even if they did not constrain psychological involvement.

The institutional system might be *dominant*, if institutional affiliation was a necessary and sufficient condition for activity; *restrictive*, if it was a necessary condition; *mobilizing*, if it was a sufficient condition; or *additive*, if institutional affiliation helped to increase participation without being either a necessary or sufficient condition for it. And the same political system might be dominant with respect to one mode of participation yet additive or restrictive with respect to other modes.

In all nations except the United States, institutions were dominant with respect to voting: 'If one had strong ties to political institutions, one's voting participation was high no matter what one's level of socioeconomic resources'. In the United States, institutional affiliation operated in a way that was intermediate between the mobilising and the additive: it increased the voting participation of those with low socio-economic resources more than those with high resources, but not sufficiently to make SERL levels unimportant.

But with respect to campaigning, institutions were dominant only in the Netherlands. In India and the United States they were additive, in Austria and Japan they were restrictive.

Different social segments could also be classified into *committed*, *apathetic*, *mobilised*, or *inhibited*, by looking at their combination of activity and involvement. Committed segments would have high levels of both, while apathetic segments would have low levels of both. Mobilised segments would be active but uninvolved, while inhibited segments would be involved but inactive. In the absence of institutional influences, people would be either committed or apathetic, but institutions might mobilise some of the uninterested into activity or lock some of the interested out of the system.

Such institutional effects might or might not affect the correlation between SERL and political activity. As Rokkan had speculated, a class-polarised party system might reduce the SERL/activity correlation by mobilising the working class. But other mobilisations or lock-outs might have no effect on the SERL/activity correlation, or might even increase it. Conversely, mobilisation and lock-out could reduce the SERL/activity correlation, even in institutional systems that were not based upon class-polarised parties: 'Political conflict in a society does not have to be about stratification. It can be about religion or race, or it can be about urban–rural conflict, or a conflict between traditional and modern values. Such conflict can nevertheless have consequences for stratification of political activity, especially when the conflicting groups differ in their position on the socio-economic scale. What counts is that there be some explicit basis for the mobilisation of citizens to conteract the implicit bias built into a participatory system on the individual level.'

Thus the SERL/activity correlation was depressed in Austria by a lock-out of the high-resource irreligious middle class (who had no party to represent them) and the mobilisation of the low-resource religious farmers (by the Catholic People's Party). So *religious* polarisation altered the relationship between SERL and activity in Austria.

In the United States, black consciousness mobilised low-resource blacks, but the consequent reduction in the SERL/activity correlation was out-weighed by other factors which mobilised right-wing groups with high SERL levels.

Verba, Nie, and Kim did a social breakdown of partisanship in each of their nations. Some social groups were closely linked to a political party but others were not—either because they had a combination of social characteristics associated with different parties, or because no party was specially linked to their social characteristics. A close link between party and social group implied mobilisation and a relatively high activity level. No link always implied no mobilisation, and sometimes it implied exclusion or lock-out in addition.

In Austria, Japan, and the Netherlands, significant social segments were mobilised by the party system. In India and the United States the dominance of catch-all parties prevented mobilisation and allowed indivi-dual socio-economic forces relatively full play. Hence the stronger SERL/activity relationship found in those two nations.

Yugoslavia was a special case. Institutions were dominant. Affiliation was both a necessary and sufficient condition for very high levels of political activity. Controlling for institutional affiliation, there was virtually no correla-tion between SERL and political activity, though the usual correlation with psychological involvement remained. But here is a paradox: the raw corre-lation between SERL and political activity was high, not low—as high indeed as for India or the United States. But there was a simple explanation for this paradox: the Yugoslav League of Communists had become a thor-oughly middle class party! Since institutional affiliation was so strongly linked to high SERL levels, the dominance of institutions did not attenuate the class stratification of political activity: it imposed that stratification.

Generally Verba, Nie, and Kim took political equality, that is a low correlation between SERL and participation, as a measure of the demo-cratic quality of a participatory system. Towards the end of their book, however, they modified that position by considering the quality of partici-pation itself. Systems which achieved political equality by mobilising low-resource citizens mobilised them into activity, but not into psychological involvement. So participation was spread more widely, but its quality was reduced. Whether that added up to a better structure of participation was open to debate.

Methodologically, an important feature of the *Political Equality* survey was its use of boosted samples in selected communities, coupled with a parallel survey of élites in those same communities. Verba and Nie made more use of this feature of the survey design in their earlier *Participation in America* (1972) than in their later comparative book.

First they asked whether larger, more urban communities increased participation by increasing interpersonal contacts (the mobilisation model), or reduced it by increasing the individual's sense of alienation from his or her community (the decline of community model). To answer this question they did not divide communities into large and small. Instead they measured the 'boundedness' of different American communities by the density of their external media connections and the proportion of commuters in the local population. Then they corrected or adjusted participation scores to take account of the SERL levels in the community. Finally they compared these adjusted participation scores with the boundedness of the local community.

High commuting rates produced low levels of community political activity. High reliance on external mass media also produced a low level of community activity, but a high level of campaign activity. Verba and Nie concluded that their data supported the 'decline of community' model. A less sophisticated test of these models in the full seven-nation survey also tended to confirm the 'decline of community' model, at least for community-oriented political activity.

Parallel élite surveys were used to test the effect of political activity rates on the concurrence of view between élites, activists, and non-activists. Verba and Nie found a correlation between local activity rates and the concurrence of leaders' and activists' views. However, there was a curvilinear relationship between activity rates and the concurrence of leaders' and non-activists' views: a moderate amount of local activity brought leaders' views into line with the views of the few unrepresentative activists, rather than with the views of the masses; only a large amount of local activity brought leaders' views into agreement with mass views.

Cross-nationally, the study showed that where political activity correlated most highly with SERL 'local leaders came disproportionately from the haves' and there was the greatest gap between the views of leaders and masses.

In short, just because class was so unimportant in American studies of *voting choice*, it was more important in America than almost anywhere else in its influence on political participation and *political choice*. Britain might be a class-ridden party system, but America had a class-ridden political system. The choice was between class polarisation and middle class domination.

Participation and Political Equality was technically much better than *The Civic Culture* and corrected many of the faults in the earlier work, but some technical problems remained and its narrow scope underlined the need for additional studies of other forms of participation.

Samples were still less than national in coverage. Just as the *Civic Culture's* survey of Mexico was limited to urban areas, so *Political Equality's* survey was limited to southern Nigeria, to four of the Yugoslav republics, and to four of the Indian states. Indeed, there was a government ban on interviews in some Indian states. Luckily the methodology of *Political Equality* was not based upon simple cross-national comparisons of aggregate percentages. They would have been thoroughly misleading.

Surveys for *Political Equality* were carried out by collaborating but independent national teams, at various times between 1966 and 1971. Verba, Nie, and Kim wrote scathingly about 'safari research' done internationally by a single research team. But 'comparative survey research is a slow and complex business. Cooperative research designed and conducted by an international group is slower by a factor probably equal to the number of collaborating groups.' For many political science purposes this leisurely time scale is both inappropriate and unnecessary. We might accept the need for collaboration to take priority over speed in a study that spans America, India, and Japan. But many multi-national surveys could be done much more speedily by a single team. A Europe-wide survey should not be that much more cumbersome than a survey covering the fifty states and vast area of the USA. The EEC'S Eurobarometer surveys provide an alternative model. Indeed, for surveys of advanced countries, telephone polling now provides the technology for doing multi-national surveys in as many days as *Political Equality* took years, using a single team of interviewers centralised in one location.

Political Equality's analysis was fully computerised and consequently much more sophisticated than *The Civic Culture's*, but it was still not fully multi-variate (Rusk 1976). It was essentially hierarchical, dominated by the SERL variable, like early British election survey work. The book never specified the relative explanatory weights of all the influences in a directly comparable form. Regression analysis was noticeably absent. In addition, social class could have been more carefully operationalised. In contrast to *The Civic Culture*, the main improvement was to re-label education as 'socio-economic resource level' instead of labelling it as 'class'. The text often substituted the word 'stratification' for SERL and read as if the authors still viewed education as class.

But the main shortcoming in this seven-nation study was its limited scope. In one sense it is very unfair to criticise Verba, Nie, and Kim for limiting themselves to a discussion of their four modes or dimensions of participation. What they did, they did very well. Yet the limitations of their study are very important for a proper understanding of the full range of political activity.

First of all, the whole idea of participation was only one half of the subject raised in *The Civic Culture*. The other half was deference, governability, acquiescence, coping with the outputs of government rather than trying to influence the inputs. This whole side of *The Civic Culture*'s topic was lost in the follow up study.

Second, and this drew much more widespread criticism, there was at least a missing fifth dimension to mass political participation: namely, protest behaviour of one kind and another. Verba, Nie, and Kim did well to discount cumulative ideas of participation, and to stress its multidimensionality. But there was nothing fixed and absolute about *four* dimensions. The reason that numerous factor analyses in different countries turned up the same four modes of participation was quite simply that the specific activities input to the factor analyses were limited to activities within these four modes. Verba, Nie, and Kim themselves quoted Welch's (1975) factor analysis of Canadian data which produced a clearly differentiated 'protest factor' when protest activity questions were included in the survey. Moreover, the reason they could not extend their survey to northern Nigeria was just because there was so much political activity there, of a kind which did not fit into any of their four modes.

Rusk (1976) suggested that many of the central findings about the relationship between stratification and participation, or between community size and participation, might be reversed for protest participation. Demonstrators were often young and left-wing, in contrast to the old and right-wing who participated so much in Verba, Nie, and Kim's version of political 'campaigning'. Verba, Nie, and Kim measured 'campaigning' by 'working for a party', 'attending rallies', 'contributing money to a candidate', and 'being a member of a political club or organisation', but not by anything less electorally oriented.

9.4 *Democratic or violent protest?*

Starting in 1952, Michigan's presidential election surveys regularly asked respondents whether they agreed with the proposition that 'voting is not the only way to influence government'. In 1952 only 17 per cent agreed. At each of the next three presidential elections and as late as the 1966 Congressional election, roughly 26 per cent agreed. But there was a sharp discontinuity in 1968 (see Inglehart 1977). In 1968 fully 42 per cent agreed, and the figures dropped only slightly thereafter. Converse (1972) has argued that until the mid-sixties answers to such questions were 'education driven', reflecting a growing personal sense of efficacy; there-after they were 'system driven', reflecting a declining respect for conventional political channels and authorities. Inglehart wrote of a 'growing readiness to use unconventional techniques of political participation' and claimed that 'mass politics were increasingly apt to be élite-challenging rather than élite-directed'. He attributed this change to a shift in the balance of political skills between élites and masses, brought about by a vast increase in education, by the spread of television as a means of up-to-date information, and by the decline in the numbers living in rural isolation. The course of political events—notably the spread of nuclear weapons and US involvement in Vietnam—may also have had a catalytic effect.

Certainly by the time Verba, Nie, and Kim's fieldwork was being done —between 1966 and 1971—'protest' or 'unconventional' participation was widespread and widely publicised. The nature and extent, if not the novelty, of support for protest participation was studied in *Political Action*, based on a multi-nation survey of the Netherlands, Britain, the United States, Germany, and Austria in 1974, with subsequent surveys in Finland, Switzerland, and Italy a year later (Barnes and Kaase 1979).

For this Marsh (1974, 1977) developed a series of questions designed to measure respondents' approval of, and willingness to participate in, various protest activities (see also Marsh and Kaase 1979). Earlier he had worked with Madgwick on a survey of Cardiganshire in the cultural heartland of Wales (Madgwick 1973).

Wales had seen an unusually large amount of direct action, linked to the activities of the Welsh Language Society. Madgwick asked whether various forms of direct action were 'ever justified'. Only 4 per cent justified blowing up the pipelines which took Welsh water to English cities, but 13 per cent justified homicide, 16 per cent pulling down sign-posts, 17 per cent disrupting sports, 32 per cent blocking traffic, 33 per cent keeping children off school, 50 per cent refusing taxes, 63 per cent demonstration marches, and 66 per cent strikes. The fluent Welsh-speaking Welsh were the least willing to justify strikes and marches, but were the most willing to justify attacks on (English language) road signs and water pipelines— two standard routines from the Welsh language protester's repertoire. This last finding was significant because it indicated that protest action was not a single mode of participation, a fifth dimension, but rather another *set* of modes of participation.

Madgwick himself made little use of this protest index beyond incorporating it as one of seven facets of Welsh radicalism—and radicalism rather than protest was his theme. Marsh, however, was primarily interested in protest itself, and he developed the battery of protest questions and eliminated that distinctively Welsh flavour. He showed that his revised protest scale was a undimensional scale of political aggression, whose various components differed essentially in degree rather than kind (Marsh 1974).

Most Britons were willing to accept or reject various degrees of direct action without qualifying their answers by spontaneous reference to some specific political scenario. Marsh suggested that the 'potential for protest' was a characteristic of the individual, a level of political aggressiveness independent of the situation in which that aggressiveness might be expressed in action. Young people were the most willing to accept direct action, though the middle class, the highly educated, trade unionists, and men were also relatively favourable towards protest action (Marsh 1977).

Marsh's *protest potential* scale was based on attitudes towards petitions, lawful demonstrations, boycotts, tax strikes, 'sit-ins', blocking traffic, and wildcat strikes. These items formed a 'cumulative scale' in the sense that respondents who approved one of the later items on this list (almost) automatically approved all the earlier, less violent, items. So a respondent's protest potential could be measured simply by how far down the list of items he or she was prepared to go or, equivalently, by noting the most aggressive action he or she was willing to approve. In that sense, protest was unidimensional.

In a similar way, Marsh and Kaase constructed a 'cumulative scale' of *conventional participation* from: reading about politics, discussing politics with friends, working with others in the community, working for a party, convincing friends to vote one way or another, attending a rally, or contacting officials. And they defined a third scale of *repression potential* from support for four items: severe treatment of demonstrators by courts, use of force by police against demonstrators, use of troops to break strikes, and laws to ban all demonstrations.

With all three scales, the precise ordering of items varied a little from country to country and the authors of *Political Action* used country-specific variants of each scale.

Kaase and Marsh (1979) argued that 'the emergence of direct action techniques did not in itself signal the end of stable liberal democracy'. In all countries they found a moderately strong *positive* correlation between protest potential and conventional participation; a strong negative correlation between protest and repression potential; and very little correlation at all between conventional participation and repression potential. So to a significant extent the protestors overlapped with people who participated in conventional election-oriented political activities. The overlap was very far from perfect, but direct action and conventional participation were clearly not polar opposites, not in any way exclusive alternatives.

Farah, Barnes, and Heunks (1979) used multiple regression analysis to determine the relative weights of various social and psychological influences on protest potential and conventional participation. A comparison of their two regressions revealed the similarities and differences in motivations towards the two kinds of action. Youth was a powerful influence towards protest, but a moderate influence against conventional participation. But other influences tended to operate in the same direction on both protest potential and conventional participation: the highly educated, the ideologically sophisticated, the 'post-materialists' who gave priority to liberty and participation rather than material or physical security, those who expressed dissatisfaction with policy outputs, and those who had a high sense of personal efficacy were all of them likely to show above-average levels of both protest potential and conventional participation.

Age effects might either be life-cycle or generation effects. However, Inglehart (1977, 1979) argued on the basis of Eurobarometer surveys that post-materialism was growing, partly in response to a spread of higher education. Since post-materialist values had a relatively large influence on protest potential compared to its influence on conventional participation, he concluded that social change was producing value change which in turn would increase the propensity to participate in more élite-challenging modes of political activity.

Direct action was an original topic for survey research, but the methodology of *Political Action* was unexciting. The basic form of analysis was purely replicative——the same analyses were performed in each nation and the results listed in a five-nation table. Table entries were often correlation and regression coefficients rather than marginal percentages, but the method remained closer to that used in *The Civic Culture* than that used in *Political Equality*. When table entries were different for different countries, the explanation of the differences had to be purely speculative. However, the authors of *Political Action* stressed cross-national similarities rather than cross-national differences; so cross-national comparisons carried much less of the analytic load than in *The Civic Culture*.

Much of the text was about trend and change, about new ways of political participation. Yet the data were drawn from a single wave of surveys that allowed no analysis of either aggregate or individual change.

Like the *Political Equality* survey, each national component of the *Political Action* survey was funded and directed by an independent national team. The book had chapters by various teams but on topics, not on countries—each chapter reported findings about all five countries. Thus all the teams preserved their academic equality without writing a political gazetteer. But the multiplicity of authors produced inconsistencies in the analysis and made the result a collection of essays which lacked the strong analytic backbone of *The Civic Culture* or *Democratic Participation and Political Equality*.

Various chapters in *Political Action* discussed the measurement of protest potential and its relation to a variety of social and psychological factors. But in measuring participation, the authors were overcommitted to achieving unidimensional scalability and over-satisfied by their distinction between conventional and protest modes of participation. They failed to appreciate the multi-modal nature of both. That failure was relatively unimportant for convention participation because Verba, Nie, and Kim had already analysed its modalities so well; but it did cause Barnes and Kaase to exclude the act of voting from their scale of conventional participation—defined as acts 'directly or indirectly related to the electoral process'—because voting would not fit into a unidimensional scale of conventional electorally-oriented activity!

More important was their stress on the unidimensionality of protest potential. In a study of the 1979 Scots and Welsh Election Surveys, W. L. Miller and Madgwick (1982) found that protest items did scale as Marsh and Kaase claimed, yet there was none the less a very important distinction to be drawn between what they called *democratic protest* and *violent protest*. Miller and Madgwick used five protest items: petitions, demonstrations, sit-ins, hurting people, and damaging property. These certainly formed a unidimensional scale in the sense that almost all respondents who approved of violence approved of petitions, demonstrations, and sit-ins; almost all who approved of sit-ins approved of demonstrations and petitions; and almost all who approved of demonstrations approved of petitions. They did indeed form a scale which measured 'how far respondents were willing to go'. Yet paradoxically that kind of unidimensionality was not inconsistent with multi-modality or multi-dimensionality in another important sense.

Multi-modality was revealed by a consideration of the causes and consequences of protest, not by an examination of the scale itself. Different causal factors influenced respondents towards different points on the scale; and action at different points on the scale, different forms of protest, could have consequences that differed in kind rather than degree.

Thus Miller and Madgwick, like Barnes and Kaase, found that the middle class and trade unionists gave above-average support to protest action—but only to the milder forms of protest action. The middle class and trade unionists coupled above-average support for demonstrations with below-average support for political violence. Other groups coupled below-average support for demonstrations with above-average support for political violence. Miller and Madgwick argued that this was not, in fact, surprising, because there was a theoretical difference in principle between protests which contributed to the democratic process and more violent protests which disrupted it: a good democrat in late twentieth century Britain should in theory support demonstrations but oppose violence.

Almond and Verba had claimed 'the role of social trust and coopera-tiveness as a component of the civic culture cannot be over emphasized. It is, in a sense, a generalised resource that keeps a democratic polity oper-ating.' And the *Civic Culture* survey showed that Britain and America were distinguished by high levels of social trust as measured by a question on whether 'most people can be trusted'. When Scots were asked in 1979 whether they could 'usually trust ordinary people' those who said 'yes' were notable for their especially high level of support for demonstrations but their especially low level of support for political violence. Conversely those with 'no interest' in politics were the people least likely to support demonstrations, but most likely to support violence. Social and political alienation decreased support for moderate methods of élite-challenging action, but increased support for outright violence. So the limits of demo-cratic participation should be drawn, on empirical as well as theoretical grounds, so as to include demonstrations and sit-ins but exclude violence.

Miller and Madgwick also reintroduced the notion of scenarios for protest and found that even hypothetical issues and circumstances had a major effect on support for political protests. Protest potential was not a purely psychological characteristic buried in the individual. On a collection of ten realistic scenarios, Miller and Madgwick found large numbers of respondents who were willing to support protest action related to specific issues, despite having rejected protest action in principle. They were nearly always greatly outnumbered by those who supported protest action in principle but not in practice. Two patterns emerged. First, the introduc-tion of hypothetical scenarios usually reduced (on balance) support for protest action. Second, support for protest under a specific scenario often correlated with issue positions on issues relevant to that scenario. So, for example, support for protests against nuclear power was coherently related to attitudes about energy policy, as well as to the individual's psychological aggressiveness. Political protest could not be dismissed as mindless disrup-tion or generalised dissatisfaction.

Approval, of course, is not the same as active participation. Marsh and Kaase's measure of direct action potential was a composite based upon approval and stated willingness to act. Miller and Madgwick's analysis focused exclusively on approval. However, Muller (1979), in a most impressive survey study of actual participation in direct action in various parts of Germany, showed that approval influenced action in three ways: first, those who felt that protest was justified were more likely to protest; second, a general climate of approval encouraged particular individuals towards active protest; third, a general climate of approval had a particularly strong influence towards action on those who themselves felt there was cause for protest. We might add that a general climate of approval makes detection and repression more difficult, both technically and politically. In short, although approval is certainly not the same as active participation in protest, it is an important condition and facility for it.

We have now seen how the theme of participation in combination with the method of multi-national surveys developed from its early use in *The Civic Culture*. In some respects later surveys could claim a wider coverage of the topic, a closer connection between data and theory, and more sophisticated multi-variate approaches to analysis. In other respects the development was marked by cumulation instead of improvement: there were some things that *The Civic Culture* did better than its successors. Overall, the most encouraging feature of this collection of studies was the extent to which each connected with the others, extending the topic, or improving the method, yet remaining sufficiently connected to its predecessors to qualify and deepen our understanding of the earlier findings.

A few criticisms might reasonably be directed at these surveys as a whole. They were too expensive and too cumbersome to be timely: speedier ways of doing multi-national surveys and cheaper ways of doing series of multi-national surveys are needed. Some further modes of political participation require investigation—participation in pressure groups, in trade union activity, and in quangos like Health Boards, for example. We need to give more attention to the effects of participation, both on élites and on those who take part in the campaign, protest, or whatever. Does participation influence policy? Is it educative? How far does it cause a sense of efficacy as well as derive from such a feeling? Do different modes of participation (lobbying versus demonstrating, for example) have different effects on élites and on participants? Lastly, we need more integrated studies of combinations of various kinds of political activity. Ideally it should not be quite so easy to divide studies into those which focus on party choice and those which focus on participation: is the class alignment in America between parties, between participation and non-participation, or in some other less simplistic political orientation? (For a discussion of the political *direction* of alignments, see W. L. Miller 1981b.)

PART IV

TOMORROW'S WORLD—NEW OPPORTUNITIES FOR THE SURVEY METHOD

It should now be evident that political surveys have been neither completely trivial and irrelevant to theory nor incapable of improvement. They have addressed important questions concerning the nature and health of our political system, the basis and stability of our party system, and the political imagination of our fellow citizens. They have been used to develop complex theories whose postulated mechanisms were not mere verbal analogies. They have gone beyond and sometimes against the obvious. And while some findings have been overturned by later research, there have been important lines of cumulation, such as the treatment of social and environmental influences which developed from the Columbia studies through Butler and Stokes and beyond, or the growing conceptual and methodological sophistication in analyses of political participation. Surveys covered the electorate as a whole and important subgroups within it. They traced the evolution of political patterns over several decades with a wealth of subtle indicators. Though samples were often too small, important findings remained quantitative through to the conclusions—quantifying, for example, the numbers of ideologues and strong party identifiers, or the individual and environmental components of class polarisation. Panels provided the opportunity for some causal analysis: though the causal and predictive element was small, it was far from non-existent.

In many studies, though not all, there was a close connection between the data and the conclusions. Samples were increasingly well matched to the populations under analysis. However, analysts were frequently driven by a lack of data to expedients they would have preferred to avoid. Thus they based conclusions on excessively small numbers of respondents, they imposed too few analytic controls, and they treated memories and perceptions as factual reports—all because samples were too small or survey series did not stretch back far enough in time or cross-section samples had to do duty for panels. Theory, speculation, and analysis were forever pushing data to their limits and often beyond them. On the credit side: academic studies measured perceptions, identifications, psychological intervening variables, and indicators of milieu in an effort to reduce the role of speculation and close the gap between theory and data.

No developing discipline can ever reach the stage where previous work appears entirely satisfactory, and the failures of imagination and analysis that have afflicted political science afflict the hardest of hard sciences as well. The record of surveys in adding to our understanding of politics is a good one, however incomplete that understanding remains. The question for the future is whether we can improve on the past by finding better or cheaper ways to increase our knowledge.

Part IV looks to the future. However much we can justify or excuse the cost of surveys, they remain expensive. So the quantity and nature of the surveys that get done is determined by people with access to large funds. If the survey is part of a large-scale money-making or money-spending enterprise—marketing or government, for example—survey funds will be plentiful. Many academic studies, however, are not directly related to making or spending huge sums of money. Grants for survey research are difficult to obtain and usually inadequate. Lack of sufficient funds distorts and corrupts survey designs as much as any other factor. Chapter 10 looks at cheap alternatives to doing surveys—analysing aggregate statistics such as census returns, re-analysing the existing files of survey data which are steadily accumulating in data banks round the world, or relying upon government, party, pressure groups, and the media to sponsor surveys that ask the right questions in the right way at the right time. Academics already rely heavily on these external resources, but it would be dangerous to rely on them exclusively and perhaps we already depend too much on analysing questions framed by others.

Chapter 11 ignores cost and asks what kind of surveys we need in order to answer important questions about politics and society. Ideally we need a lot more interviews, with a lot more people, a lot more frequently. And we need more expensive survey designs. By ignoring costs for a while, we expose the restrictions, the distortions, the damage done to Survey Methods by inadequate funds.

There are only two ways to get more surveys and more expensive survey designs—either a vast increase in survey funds or a new, more efficient survey technology. Chapter 12 describes the new technology. It begins with a review of cheap methods for doing surveys. Only one is both cheaper and potentially better than conventional methods. Mechanically, it is based on Computer Assisted Telephone Interviewing (CATI for short), but the essence of the method is neither computers nor telephones. The critical features of the new technology are centralisation, control, flexibility, and speed. Computers and telephones are but means to these ends.

Telephone interviewing is not new. It was already in use when Gallup established the conventional survey norm in the early thirties. For half a century survey textbooks have mentioned the method in footnotes and dismissed it as useless except for very special applications. Two things have changed since most of these books were conceived. First, over 90 per cent of Americans can now be reached by phone, and other countries are also coming close to saturation telephone coverage. Moreover, electronic facilities like phone calls are rapidly getting cheaper relative to interviewers' travel costs or even relative to postal charges. Secondly, we have made significant conceptual advances in the design and control of surveys which can now be implemented by centralising the interviewing and using computers to control the interviewers. Only telephones allow that centralisation and control. A combination of factors, none of them very dramatic in itself, adds up to a revolutionary change in survey technology. Even the concept of an interview as a unit has to be abandoned and replaced by the idea of a quantum of interviewing time. Similarly the concept of a survey as a unit must also be abandoned and replaced by the idea of a quantum of survey activity. In Chapter 12 I describe the new technology and highlight its revolutionary features. I show how it solves many of the problems of conventional surveys, meet the requirements specified in Chapter 11, and opens up radically new opportunities for new types of survey design. I also indicate the new problems which it poses, and some of the basic research needed to provide infrastructural support.

10   Cheap alternatives to doing more surveys

There are at least two relatively cheap ways of attempting to answer some of the same questions that surveys answer: we can either analyse aggregate data of the sort available in official statistics, or we can obtain someone else's survey data for re-analysis.

10.1 *Aggregate data*

Aggregate data—census statistics, voting returns, election expenses, local government taxes and the like—are readily available in official publications and can be put into machine-readable form at a very modest cost. By 'aggregate' I mean data about groups of individuals which are not available on an individual basis. Aggregation overcomes problems of confidentiality and reduces the quantity of data to be processed. We can easily obtain, and cheaply process, data on parliamentary constituencies. The parliamentary volume of the census publishes the percentages of each constituency's workforce who are in each socio-economic and sectoral group. By comparing this census information with published election results, we can determine the extent to which relatively middle class constituencies vote Conservative, or relatively agricultural constituencies vote Liberal. What we cannot determine from these data is what kind of individuals *within* constituencies are the ones who vote Liberal. Agricultural areas may tend towards the Liberals because professional people have bought out-of-town houses and vote Liberal, for example. Some Welsh areas with relatively large numbers of English immigrants in them give relatively high votes to the Welsh nationalist party, but certainly *not* because the English incomers vote Welsh nationalist.

Official statistics at least appear to be direct, objective data, often taken from a full population instead of a sample, which eliminates the massive uncertainties introduced by sampling. But in practice that is not so. Official data include a surprising amount of uncertainty and error, even in highly developed societies. I still recall attempting to correlate Balance of Payments statistics with monthly Gallup poll figures on government popularity and being shocked at the way successive editions of government publications altered the original figures given for the Balance of Payments. Checks on the census have shown that surprising large numbers of people misreport even such 'objective' data as the number of rooms in their dwelling.

There are other problems, besides sheer error and uncertainty. There is usually a long delay between taking a census and publishing the relevant tabulations. There is a large difference between population, which is the subject of the census, and electorate, which is the more usual object of political enquiry. Still more significant is the chaotic state of electoral and administrative boundaries in Britain: they cross-cut at any one time, and they change frequently and totally without co-ordination, so as to hinder even the simplest over-time analyses. By the time census data are available by parliamentary constituencies, the constituencies may be changed or abolished and there is a further delay before census statistics are recalculated according to the new boundaries. This happened with the 1971 census.

A special impediment to British political research is the fact that election results are only counted and published by the areas corresponding to the representatives elected—Euroconstituencies, parliamentary constituencies, regional electoral divisions, or district wards as appropriate to the particular election. (Or whole counties and regions in the EEC and devolution referendums.) These boundaries cross-cut each other and generally enclose far too large an area to be designated a local social or political environment. British political science suffers from the lack of precinct-level vote counts.

Then there is the problem of content. Aggregate data are mainly socio-economic. This ties the analysis to one aspect of politics and worse, it may tie the imagination also: so that we begin to believe the available data are the desirable data. Even such a simple statistic as religious affiliation is not available in the British census (Northern Ireland has its own census which does include religious questions) and there is nothing at all on feelings, perceptions, motivations, attitudes, opinions, or personality factors. Again, much of the variation that exists at the individual level is washed out by the aggregation. Even quite large sex differences in voting behaviour are unlikely to appear very significant in an aggregate data analysis because the proportions of males and females vary so little from area to area. Aggregate data provide no information on cancelling cross-currents of change; so that absolutely stable statistics of party support in a constituency, as in the nation as a whole, may cloak extreme volatility at the level of individuals. Indeed, it is now thirty years since Robinson published his famous paper on the 'ecological fallacy' which showed that it is statistically impossible to infer individual level patterns of political behaviour from aggregate level patterns (Robinson 1950). The converse, of course, also applies: individual level patterns discovered in sample surveys cannot be used to infer aggregate level patterns unless the survey has been designed to measure the influence of environment as well as the influence of one individual-level characteristic upon another.

All of this does not mean that aggregate data are useless for analytic purposes. Sometimes we are primarily interested in the behaviour of aggregates, and appendices to successive Nuffield studies, Miller's *Electoral Dynamics*, or Key's study of partisan persistence illustrate what can be done at a purely aggregate level (Steed 1966, 1971, 1974, 1975; Curtice and Steed 1980, 1982; Dogan and Rokkan 1969; W. L. Miller 1977a; Key and Munger 1959). Occasionally official data may provide us with essentially individual-level information like the cross-tabulations of voting by age, sex, occupation, and marital status which Tingsten (1937) found for various scattered parts of pre-war Europe, and which is now regularly available throughout Germany.

But aggregate data can be most useful when combined with survey data. They can be used to place individuals and their personal characteristics in a spatial context to facilitate an analysis of milieu; or in a temporal context, as in the many studies which relate survey-based figures on monthly government popularity to aggregate economic statistics. An early and very simple example of this combined survey/aggregate approach was Cleary and Pollins's study of where the ex-Liberal vote went in 1951. The Gallup poll said it divided 60 : 40 in favour of the Conservatives. Cleary and Pollins (1953) worked out the implications of this division in different constituencies and compared the poll-based prediction with the actual result. The discrepancies indicated that Labour had probably picked up a higher proportion of the ex-Liberal vote in rural areas than in urban.

10.2 *Data banks*

The second cheap alternative is to use someone else's survey data, always provided that we can get them at little cost and without offering data of our own in return. Sometimes it has been suggested that political science could do with a moratorium on collecting new survey data and should devote itself to more intensive reanalysis of the vast amount of data it has already accumulated in its data banks. During a period of general financial constraint this argument is unusually seductive. The Chairman of the British Social Science Research Council recently introduced a book on secondary analysis with a very explicit statement of this theme:

> At times when the funding climate for research veers towards the wintry
> —as, unhappily, is the case just at present—we look to the squirrels of
> social science to turn to such carefully accumulated stores with a more

than ordinary relish. For it is at these periods that secondary analysis, so *refreshingly inexpensive* compared with almost all other forms of research, can be expected to come into its own [Posner 1982, my italics].

There is no shortage of material for re-analysis. The *Index to International Public Opinion* (Survey Research Consultants International, 1981) lists twenty political data archives offering access to survey data from over forty countries. And re-analysis is a worthy task. But if the only motivation for re-analysis is cheapness, then re-analysis is a bad bargain. Hyman (1972) lists some of the benefits of re-analysis: it is undeniably cheap; it may be a useful preliminary stage in designing a new survey—a means of stimulating the imagination and suggesting new hypotheses to be tested; it opens research possibilities to young, unestablished researchers who may not be able to obtain large funds; it permits historical analysis—'unconsidered aspects of the past become interesting in the light of the changing present' (Lazarsfeld 1957: 249); it forms the basis for analyses of changes and trends; it lets us view our own primary research findings in a comparative perspective; it can overcome some of the problems of sample size by replication. Re-analysis has many virtues of its own. Undoubtedly some very good work has been based purely on re-analysing the contents of the data bank: I have already described *The Changing American Voter* by Nie *et al.* and Pomper's *Voters' Choice* which follow that rationale.

But what re-analysis cannot do is provide an adequate substitute for new survey research. The early hope of establishing scientific laws of political behaviour has not been realised in any precise sense. The laws of electoral behaviour are not immutable; the historical dimension is important. We need to capture information when it is fresh, if only as a resource for future historians and future re-analysers of data bank material. Pre-war history is based on private memoires, press-cuttings, and aggregate data analyses. The views expressed in letters, leading articles, and élite speeches are not necessary widely held. Aggregate level socio-political relationships cannot be assumed to apply at the individual level and aggregate data provide no information on attitudes and opinions at any level. Hence numerous speculative and inconclusive attempts are still being made to discover, for example, the social and attitudinal bases of Nazi votes in Weimar Germany when survey data, if they had existed, would supply a definitive answer.

Nor can we rely on picking up data about the present at some time in the future when we wish to analyse it. Panel studies have shown quite conclusively that future surveys could not be used to reconstruct current patterns of attitudes, since memories are wildly inaccurate and wildly biased. Already by 1979 our 1974–79 panel showed that almost half the Scottish National Party voters of 1974 had forgotten they had ever voted SNP. Recall-data are a very poor and unreliable substitute for contemporary surveys. There would be no possibility of analysing the surge and decline of the Social Democratic Party in 1981–82 by asking questions in surveys conducted in 1983 or 1984.

Moreover, there is a scientific value as well as an historical value in maintaining survey series: they provide evidence of trend and change. Trends in levels of trust, alienation, identification, issue salience, and issue polarisation have more important implications for theory and prediction than do levels in these variables at any one time: in a sense, it is trends that calibrate the data and identify certain levels as high or low.

Simply because political patterns can and do change, there is a value in monitoring even previous null findings. For example, the notion that very little change occurred during the election campaign became established in British political science just as it was falsified by events. So as soon as Butler and Stokes established their new norm of inter-election panels rather than campaign panels, it became apparent that campaign trends determined the outcome—in 1970, February 1974, and probably 1979 also.

Finally, old survey data like existing census data restrict the range of analyses that are possible and may restrict the imagination also. We can too easily assume that existing surveys ask the right questions, in the right way, about the right topics.

10.3 *Government, party, or pressure group surveys*

It would, however, be possible to rely on other people's surveys without necessarily restricting attention to the past. We could, as political scientists, rely on others with an interest in politics to fund surveys which might cover the topics we want to analyse.

Hakim (1982a, b) argues strongly for more use of government survey material since 'the scale of social research in government is such that there is almost no practical possibility of such research being carried out by independent researchers in universities and research institutes', and 'surveys carried out by professional social scientists in government are of better quality . . . than surveys carried out by academic social scientists'. Indeed, she advocated a division of labour between data-collectors and data-analysers: 'a data-producers' responsibility for the quality of the statistics should not be blurred by other work; they should be allowed to specialize in data-collection methodology'.

While we cannot be certain about the future, we can make informed guesses about the likely range of future information by considering the surveys that have been funded in the past by government, parties, pressure groups, and the media. Many of these were later made available to academics for re-analysis at little or no cost.

Notable examples of recent *ad hoc* government-sponsored polls of interest to political scientists include various surveys on race by the Community Relations Commission; the survey for the Houghton Committee on *Financial Aid to Political Parties*, which investigated party membership as well as finance; the Building Economic Development Committee's *Housing Consumer Survey*, which Harrop used in a critique of Dunleavy's consumption sector theory; the Fulton Committee's *Social Survey of the Civil Service*, which Halsey and Crewe analysed for a book-length report; the *Community Attitudes Survey* for the Wheatley and Maud Commissions on Local Government in Scotland and in England; and especially the Kilbrandon Commission's survey on *Devolution and Other Aspects of Government*.

But Hakim is more concerned to advocate use of continuing, regular government surveys like the *Census* itself, the *General Household Survey*, the *Family Expenditure Survey*, the *Labour Force Survey*, the *National Food Survey*, and the *Workplace Industrial Relations Survey*, or at the international level Rabier's *Eurobarometer* surveys. Another example is the government-commissioned *National Child Development Study* by the National Children's Bureau, which is following a cohort born in 1958 through their adult lives by re-interviewing them at intervals.

Even the notoriously secretive British government is gradually relaxing its restrictions on access to government-produced surveys. Many have been deposited in the SSRC's Survey Archive at Essex University. Up till now the British government has refused to follow the American example and release a Public Use Sample of the census—only aggregate census results for areas have been released; but attitudes are changing, and public use samples are likely to be available before the end of the eighties.

Government data can be very useful for policy-related analyses—that is, after all, the purpose for which they are collected. But they are not much use for analysing other aspects of government and politics. Despite the claims of Hakim, government sponsored surveys are *not* well designed for theoretical studies. They place too much emphasis on the technicalities of data collection and fail to grapple with the real problems of understanding. They stress accurate measurement of objective characteristics. From a theoretical standpoint, they waste resources on over-accurate measurement of irrelevant variables. They focus on supposedly objective behaviour and neglect the measurement of attitudes, values, beliefs, and perceptions. Very often they omit the most politically central variables. While polls conducted by the Community Relations Commission, National Children's Bureau, and EEC do ask questions about political partisanship, most government surveys do not—not even those for the Commission on the Constitution. Far too often their focus is so narrow that while government surveys cover many relevant topics in different surveys, important inter-related variables cannot be analysed together. Finally, government usually appears to be as slow-moving as politics is fast-moving. Many political variables need timely investigation or continuous monitoring. To take one example, the Kilbrandon Commission was appointed in 1969 as a response to events in 1967. It surveyed attitudes towards devolution once only, in 1970. By contrast the *Scotsman* newspaper, reacting to changing circumstances, repeated the Kilbrandon investigation twice in 1974, twice in 1975, once in 1976 and 1977, and three times in 1979. (See the *Scotsman*, 28th September 1979 for the full series.)

In short, government pollsters devote enormous funds and enormous expertise to measuring what are often the wrong variables at the wrong time. They serve government, and while the interests and concerns of government overlap with those of the academic community, the degree of overlap should not be exaggerated.

Party and pressure-group polls suffer less from these defects, though some have deliberately excluded vote-intention questions so as not to distract or depress their sponsors. The direct incentive to find out more about the battle which determines their own future often encourages parties and pressure groups to speedy, timely action, backed by lavish funding. The standard of expertise used in designing their surveys is high and when they are made available to academics, access is usually at negligible cost.

However, while the polling may be timely, open access is not. Favoured academics are soon permitted a peep at some of the findings, but it can be a long time before free, open, academic-style access is granted, and then it may be to only a subset of the data. It has to be stressed that political actors do not sponsor polls with the object of improving our general understanding of politics: they do so as an aid to planning their political campaigns and sometimes as a means of generating suitable ammunition for the political struggle. I have described some of the consequences of this in Part I. Pressure-groups, especially, generate biased or repetitiously favourable polling percentages to quote back at the public. Similarly party leaders sometimes commission polls to quote at their followers. The major parties tie their polls to questions of influencing public opinion, and the polls are linked tightly to advertising and television broadcasts. The more efficient they become at spending party funds, the less they will invest in replicating the more general information gathered by media polls.

10.4 Media-sponsored surveys

Media polls, those commissioned by the press or television for open publication, come closest to academic requirements. They have been very widely used for re-analysis and open publication in academic books and journals. The combination of commissioning journalists and commissioned commercial polling agencies like Gallup, NOP, or MORI brings together a formidable array of experience and expertise which is likely to exceed that involved in many academic enquiries; and the huge quantity of media poll interviews makes them extremely valuable for detailed analysis.

Given this combination of quantity and expertise, we could rely on media polls to ask most of the obvious questions on party preference, issue salience, issue position, and social background; to ask them frequently, and to make the data available for re-analysis. Thus they constitute a cheap source of basic political survey information and will probably continue to do so. Rose's chapter on Britain in *Electoral Behaviour*, his *Class Does Not Equal Party*, Lipset's *Social Bases of Politics*, and Alford's *Party and Society* are good examples of academic work based on this cheap resource.

But media polls also have a number of more specialised virtues. I will list seven that come readily to mind. Most of them derive from the sheer quantity of media polling (see Gallup Poll 1972). First, media polls are especially good for measuring trends on voting preference, salience of issues, attitudes on issues, or approval of the government and the party leaders, because they ask these questions as frequently as once a month, or even once a week. Gallup can provide thirty-year time-series on several questions and ten-year series are not at all uncommon. Such series have been used especially for time series analyses of politico-economic models (Moseley 1982) but also, for example, to chart sharp changes in public opinion on the EEC or on devolution and relate them to changes in official party policy. (See W. L. Miller 1981a on devolution; Butler and Kitzinger 1976 on the EEC.)

Second, media polls can be cumulated to produce very large numbers of respondents and then broken down into regional, area, or even constituency subsamples. Butler and Stokes used this method to quantify the influence of the class milieu. Third, these large media poll cumulations can be broken down so as to analyse small but politically interesting groups like

National Front voters (Harrop *et al*. 1980) or ethnic minorities (Anwar 1980). Fourth, large cumulated samples permit relatively complex analytic procedures. This may mean no more than, for example, Bonham's very finely cut middle class strata, i.e. analysis by a single variable with many categories; or it may involve a multi-variate analysis with a moderate to large number of variables and interactive relationships between them—for example, Rose's AID tree analysis in *Electoral Behaviour* or Dunleavy's application of Goodman's highly interactive log-linear modelling. Fifth, large media poll cumulations can be used as a means of identifying subsets of respondents for further, more intensive interviewing, as in Nordlinger's analysis of working class Tories.

Sixth, the sheer quantity of media polls has helped to close gaps in survey coverage. Thus the *Scotsman*'s excellent series of ORC polls on devolution permits analysis in some depth and with some frequency, over the years 1974–79. Similarly, the London *Times* expressed its special interests by commissioning a 1974 campaign panel survey of school and university teachers. Granada TV's 1972 *State of the Nation* poll is another good example of a special topic surveyed in considerable depth by a media poll. Methodologically as well as substantively media polls have filled gaps. When academic polling methodology shifted from campaign panels to inter-election panels, the media filled the gap by sponsoring campaign panels. Butler and Stokes quote the NOP campaign panel findings for 1964 and 1966. In 1979 Granada TV sponsored a campaign panel in Bolton, and the *Sunday Times* sponsored a national four-wave campaign panel of a thousand respondents, despite the fact that a strike prevented publication of the *Sunday Times* itself. Very generously the *Sunday Times* allowed publication elsewhere.

Lastly, the dictates of their sponsors ensure that the main findings are published very quickly indeed, often with sufficient standard cross-tabulations to form the basis for academic commentary. Thus Butler's Nuffield Election Studies have included a great deal of survey-based information, but exclusively gathered from party and especially media polls, even when he was directing academic election surveys. Similarly Crewe's chapter in Penniman's AEI study of the 1979 election uses media polls, including a last-minute eve-of-election and election-day poll which Crewe directed on behalf of the BBC, but no data from Crewe's own academically funded election survey.

In short, media polls not only serve their sponsors, they provide an invaluable resource for academic analysis. But having said that and admitting their special virtues, one must emphasise that they provide no real substitute for academic political surveys. With media polls, the medium literally determines the message. Teer and Spence, who spoke from personal experience as media pollsters, were a little harsh, but no more, when they wrote that 'unlike academic enquirers whose objectives will be to reach a basic understanding of the mainsprings of opinion, the (media) pollster's function is simply to report that opinion as succinctly as possible. He is seldom concerned with its depth, intensity or origin.' 'The requirements of the sponsor must impose severe limitations on the scope of the enquiry . . . survey research organisations undoubtedly all have the capability to carry their enquiries to the root of opinion formation and to reach a closer understanding of the motives for political behaviour . . . that they do not do so is because of the nature of the task rather than a lack of capacity or interest. A poll is an item of transient news. Its sponsors are not concerned with reaching an understanding of electoral behaviour or opinions. They are concerned solely with that behaviour and these opinions for their own sake or, in so far as the latter coincide with their own policy stances, as a weapon in their political campaigning . . . Because of the nature of the medium and its audience, the newspaper is concerned with the sweeping statement, the firm conclusion and the clear-cut perspective rather than the nuances and shading which are the almost inevitable consequence of deeper enquiry' (Teer and Spence 1973: 21–2).

Since Teer and Spence wrote that harsh judgment on media polling, increasing familiarity with poll findings—on the part of both journalists and their readers—has led to some improvement. But it remains true that the media still regard polls primarily as an expensive way to get an exclusive headline and attract an audience. The twin constraints of cost and inability to print very much material largely determine the nature of media polls, though media organisations can use unpublishable detail and subtlety to give their editors, correspondents, and commentators a more thorough background briefing.

Their focus is on predicting and interpreting election results and, at non-election times, gauging reactions to topical events or publicising issues of concern to the editors. Polls have to be very cheap—usually under £3,000, with perhaps a maximum of £10,000, exceeded only very rarely. They have to be fast and newsworthy. The maximum depth of analysis usually consists of all questions in the survey cross-tabulated against party preference, social-background variables, and perhaps also against some topical variable. For example, polls during 1981 in some inner-city areas added participation in riots to the set of standard background variables used for analysis.

Media polls give great attention to issue attitudes *per se*, despite all the academic evidence that issue opinions are often lightly held, volatile, or determined by partisanship. Many surveys are repetitive, their news content being the fact of a new poll, rather than the detection of a new finding. In keeping with the media's concern for news there is an absence of theoretical concern, deliberate avoidance of materials that require complex analysis, and a focus on the concrete and the immediate. Questions must have at least the appearance of self-evident meaning and implication, since the mass audience still has only a marginal interest and little skill in interpreting survey findings.

The range of series questions is limited and wordings vary between polling organisations, and even within the same organisation. While they may cover a vast range of topics in aggregate, each poll tends to ask relatively few questions. Thus it is easy to quote levels for variables, and to analyse relationships between any one of the vast number of political variables and standard background variables; but it is frequently impossible to relate one political variable to another, because the relevant questions were put to different samples of respondents.

Media polls have also been criticised for being extremely atomistic in design, giving social characteristics but not social structure, social context, or social meaning. Despite the paradox that Butler and Stokes's use of cumulated NOP polls greatly advanced our knowledge of social structure and social context, the criticism remains valid for media polls themselves, for they do tend to treat each man as an island. They were virtually useless for testing Dunleavy's theory of consumption sectors, because tenure could not be distinguished from milieu. The fact that Dunleavy himself failed to grasp the inadequacy of his data is no defence. Cumulated Gallup polls gave him a large enough sample for sophisticated analysis, but not the necessary variables.

The marginal distributions and elementary cross-tabulations which comprise the usual analytic output from media polls represent only a first step towards a proper analysis. (See Webb and Wybrow 1981 for a typical pollsters' report.) Yet because it is so easy to reproduce these elementary findings and so troublesome to secure the original data files for re-analysis, the media's own analyses are often incorporated in academic work without academics playing any real part in the analysis. Now it can be thoroughly misleading to accept these media analyses at face value. First, the desire for news and topicality means that media polls are frequently mounted at the most atypical times, when their findings depend quite excessively on heated but transient reactions to topical events. Media polls about the major parties have been keyed to party conferences, media polls about the minor parties have been keyed to by-election successes, media polls on immigration have been keyed to dramatic public speeches by Powell or Thatcher.

Secondly the desire to predict political responses, especially voting, means that media polls are more often centred on voting preference or voting intention than on voting itself. This is not always true: in 1979 for example, the *Sunday Times* panel's last wave of interviews took place after the election, and the Conservative party commissioned a post-election poll, which shows a remarkable ability to act professionally during a period of post-election euphoria. But none the less, the weight of media polling done in connection with a general election is spread over the month or so before the vote and very little is done after election day. Thus the cumulated Gallup election surveys which Dunleavy and Rose, among others, have used to allow detailed analysis of large samples unfortunately give a very large number of voting intentions but no votes. In the days when it appeared that the campaign produced little or no systematic change, that discrepancy might have been overlooked, but in the last four elections at least, aggregate voting intentions early in the campaign differed so much from later voting that the campaign determined the outcome. And attitudes changed during the campaign even more than voting intentions. Moreover, the full quantity of change during the campaign exceeds the net aggregate change: the 1979 *Sunday Times* panel found that over a quarter of its respondents changed their voting intention in the month before the election. Thus there is no guarantee that very fine analyses of huge cumulated data sets spread over the month before the election can really explain the result itself with any precision.

A third problem with media polls is the difference between published figures and actual, unpublished survey results. Let me give two examples. Butler and Stokes presented a number of indicators to show increasing political volatility from the late sixties onwards. One indicator of volatility was the variation in Gallup poll figures during the year. But they did not mention the trend to smaller sample size, nor the fact that Gallup at one time averaged out the findings of one poll with those of others before publication. Recent Gallup monthly poll figures have been derived from single samples of around a thousand respondents, except during election campaigns.

My second example concerns weighting. Weighting can be a perfectly legitimate procedure. Suppose that we double the rate of sampling in Wales so as to allow enough respondents for a special study of Wales. Then when we are analysing the full British data set we should weight all respondents outside Wales twice as heavily as those within Wales in order to achieve a properly balanced sample. No one would quarrel with that procedure. The problem arises when we analyse a data set which was not deliberately and intentionally biased at the sampling stage. Then we may feel that we have discovered an unintentional under-sampling. Perhaps there are fewer women in the sample than census data would suggest. So we weight women in the sample more heavily than men to correct the bias. Any such after-the-analysis weighting procedure amounts to manipulating data that we do not like. It is inevitably more or less subjective—perhaps even the sex ratios in the census are wrong, for example. That does not mean the procedure cannot be justified. It means, on the contrary, that the procedure has to be justified in some way before weighting is applied.

During the 1979 election campaign, Gallup, NOP, Marplan, and RSL all used weighting. This reduced the forecast Conservative lead by 4 per cent for Marplan and 3 per cent for NOP, though it had less effect on Gallup and RSL figures. None of the newspaper reports nor the 1979 Nuffield Election Study, which quoted the adjusted figures, mentioned the fact that they had been adjusted, still less how. Marplan weighted their sample to conform to an interlocking quota of sex, region, and class; then 'the data was re-examined and there was found to be more people in the sample who claimed to vote Conservative in the last election than who claimed to vote Labour. In order to enable comparison with the earlier polls the data were then weighted to the profile of the claimed past voting behaviour reported in our first two surveys.' NOP found 'the proportion working full time and the percentage of trade unionists were both about 3 per cent short of expected figures. The differences between voting intention of unionists and non-unionists observed in the previous poll were used to calculate weights which were applied to the survey. This resulted in a reduction of the Conservative lead by about 3 per cent'. RSL worked on 'the assumption that the Liberal and other voters at the 1974 election would have been drawn in the ratio of 3.3 : 1 from people now claiming to have voted Conservative and Labour. Consequently to restore our results to this assumed distribution, we weighted claimed Conservative voters in 1974 by 0.952 and claimed Labour voters by 1.054. The 3.3 : 1 ratio was based on the finding that Liberal and other claimed voters in 1974 divided in these proportions in their 1979 voting intention.' However, RSL only applied this weighting procedure to the first of their four campaign surveys. Gallup weighted only by region and constituency marginality. MORI did not weight any of its election forecasting polls but had weighted similar surveys in the past and been heavily criticised for it. (Quotations are from letters by Clements of Marplan, Barter of NOP, and Cornish of RSL to Worcester of MORI and appear in Worcester 1980: 39–49).

All these weighting procedures had some kind of logic—of a rather Heath-Robinson kind—to them; but weighting procedures which would not automatically command universal approval were applied without public comment and substantially altered some of the findings. The media format does not permit lengthy description of boring but important details of data adjustments, and media figures then get transferred over to academic studies.

Often media pollsters give access to fuller findings than appear in the media—basically their own working tables which they use for writing the media articles. And they will also supply the original data, though that takes longer and is more troublesome. But the commercial nature of media polling agencies, the degree of public exposure accorded to their findings, their own encouragement of the notion that they purvey concrete facts, and their often tenuous links to their media sponsors, all combine to make the polling agencies nervous of criticism. Academics who have been given speedy access to pollsters' data can then be under explicit or implicit restrictions on the range of findings they are allowed to report, especially if they hope to receive more data from the same source.

If there is any case for academics continuing to comment on political surveys or analyse them in any depth, there is a strong case for their generating at least a major part of the survey data they analyse. If they rely totally, or even excessively, on government, party, or media-sponsored data, then they accept the right of government, parties, and media to set the agenda for political science investigations.

In the first place that means restricting analysis to the topics or facets of topics pre-specified by the survey sponsors. Second, it implies a time-delay before the start of academic analysis; and when academic analysis begins, it begins in an intellectual climate governed by the survey sponsors' initial analyses. All too often the easy option is simply to incorporate media findings into academic commentary. Third, skills which are not exercised tend to atrophy: so that dependence upon second-hand data becomes addictive. Fourth, it is entirely natural that when we receive expensively collected data for free, we tend to gloss over the deficiencies in the data, partly to enhance the significance of our own work, partly in gratitude for access to a free resource, and partly to keep the future supply of free data available. No doubt academics also gloss over the deficiencies in their own surveys, but at least they can take care to do better next time, whereas they are in no position to force improvements on external bene-factors.

Certainly free resources, or cheap resources should be used. And some of the problems with academic use of non-academic surveys can be solved by better liaison. But it remains true that divorcing data collection from data analysis is profoundly anti-theoretical and must tend to corrupt the imagination. Perhaps there is a case, as Hakim claims, for a division of labour between data-collectors and data-analysts, but the essential questions are about means and ends, not division of labour. Are we to collect data to answer research questions, or are we to analyse data merely 'because they are there'? Who is to determine the focus of the research and the explanatory models which may be applied? Effective freedom of ideas requires effective freedom to collect data, not merely free access to predetermined data.

11 Surveys for the future

I have argued that there is no adequate substitute for survey data; and no adequate substitute for new, custom-built surveys—second-hand survey data are valuable but insufficient. But if we do accept that new surveys must be designed and controlled by future researchers for their own research purposes, is there anything that can be said about the kind of surveys they should attempt? Are existing survey designs sufficiently good that the main requirement is just enough stamina to keep at it? Or is the future so unknowable that we cannot specify now what surveys will be required in the future? Or are there some obvious but curable faults in existing survey work which suggest at least some broad lines of advance in the near future?

Academic political surveys in Britain have gone through two phases. The dominant model has always been some kind of election survey, though there have also been special surveys on general attitudes towards government, on affluent workers, working class Conservatives, CND activists, relative deprivation, National Front supporters, racial tensions, sectarian Irishmen, cultured Welshmen, and separatist Scots. However, the typical election survey during the fifties followed the Columbia model by concentrating on the attitudes and behaviour of about a thousand electors in a single locality during the short election campaign and on election day itself. Since the early sixties the typical election survey has followed the Michigan model, introduced to Britain by Butler and Stokes in 1963–64: a nationwide sample of two thousand respondents interviewed shortly after a general election. Butler and Stokes originally carried out run-up panels in 1963–4 and in 1969–70, as well as inter-election panels, but since then the emphasis has shifted to cross-sectional election samples, without campaign panels, or run-up panels and with less emphasis on inter-election panels also. Even if we accept the need for further academic political surveys, we may or may not accept the need for more surveys in the Michigan mould. Whether or not there are specially commissioned academic surveys at election time we can guarantee there will be no shortage of other political surveys around that time which will certainly include many relevant questions on party preference, issues, and demographic background. Should scarce academic resources therefore be aimed at other objectives? And if so, at what other objectives?

11.1 *Topics*

Ultimately the case for investigating new topics must rest with specific research proposals. Politics is distinguished from the natural sciences and even to a degree from other social sciences by the speed with which its subject matter changes. So it is not possible or even desirable to be too specific about future research topics.

However, a corollary of this variability in subject matter is that truths are not true for all time, levels and relationships change, null findings resolve into patterns and vice versa. So the truth must be constantly reassessed, not only because the original investigations may have been deficient—as is the case in the natural sciences—but also because the truth may have changed. Hence there is a general need to monitor the strengths of established patterns and to recheck null findings. We need regular benchmark surveys and trend-monitoring surveys. At a minimum such bench/monitor surveys in Britain should be keyed to parliamentary elections, Euro-elections, referendums, and mid-term times. Michigan has regularly surveyed American opinion at presidential and Congressional election times, that is at two year intervals.

For monitoring purposes (as distinct from benchmark purposes) there is also a need for some high-frequency surveys on a monthly or quarterly basis like the media polls. There is now no possibility of using academic surveys to study the 1981–82 launching, surge, and decline of the Social Democratic Party, or public reactions to the 1978 Winter of Discontent or the 1982 Falklands Affair, because academic research reaction times are so much slower than political reaction times. Unless regular high-frequency surveys are already operating, it is exceedingly difficult to study fast-moving events, however significant they may be. In Britain, unlike America, even general elections occur unexpectedly, and the start-up time for conventional academic polls can be far too long. Obviously it would be prohibitively expensive to mount something similar to a Butler/Stokes survey at monthly intervals, but I will come back to that point in the next chapter.

We also need to know something about the impact of the campaign. The old view that change during the short campaign itself was small is no longer tenable. Recent elections have been decided during the campaign. It would be wrong to assume that nothing prior to the campaign itself is important, but it has become very clear that short-term as well as long-term change is important. Earlier I distinguished three critical time spans associated with different sorts of political change: the long period of a full parliament; the swing-back period of six to twelve months prior to an election when politics is transformed from a mid-term to an election foot-ing, usually to the benefit of the governing party; and the short three weeks of the campaign itself, when opinion may move in any direction but usually against the leading party, whichever that may be. Ideally we should continue to monitor change over all three time-spans, using panel surveys. All three have been studied at one time or another in the past, but never all three at once.

A fourth interesting time span is the run-down period after an election when the elected party more or less rapidly—and in 1979 very rapidly—loses support, so that we are normally governed by the party which lies second in the opinion polls, and sometimes third. This period has received little attention. (But see Blumler *et al.* 1975.) Yet the response of the elec-torate to the election result is extremely important in terms of political theory. I do not think that classic advocates of democracy envisaged a system whereby the people so persistently and speedily repudiated their own electoral choice. In a similar way, EEC and Devolution referendum votes were at variance with opinion, both before and after the referendums. Should there be another referendum, a run-down survey of post-voting opinion change would be useful after the referendum also.

Because surveys are bad at reconstructing the past, it is important to catch important political responses as and when they happen. Naturally, importance is easier to assess in the long run, well after the event. So at the time we may well fail to spot important topics, or concentrate attention on topics whose importance we later come to doubt. None the less, viewed from the standpoint of the eighties, several topics on parties, the electoral system, and policy issues seem worthy of survey investigation.

First the very idea of party has been called into question by the vola-tility of recent years, splits and divisions in the major parties, flashes of support for minor or new parties, the collapse of party membership, and the growth of television, opinion polls, and referendums as channels of élite/mass communication. American states have increasingly adopted populist devices, such as the mandatory primary election to inflict a candidate on a party. Britain hardly conforms to a perfect populist model, but recent changes are sufficient to justify attention being paid to the notion of party as a means of structuring British politics. We need surveys of the mass elec-torate to study their attitudes towards party and party government. To find out what they mean by party, for example. Do they agree with Wallas that 'party is primarily a name'? What is the essence of a party to the elector?—its historic continuity, its organisation, its top leadership, the lower ranks of its élites, its policies, its recognition by non-party organisa-tions like the unions, or what?—especially when these various elements are in mutual conflict. What is the Labour party?—the thing led by Michael Foot or the breakaway rival led by David Owen, the thing backed by the TUC, or some distillation of Labour voters? We need to study the electors' feelings of relationship towards party. The Michigan concept of party identification is important here, but the Michigan measure has not quite performed the analytic role assigned to the concept. Other techniques need to be considered.

A second party theme would be a spatial study of the penetration of the party idea. In particular we could do with comparative studies of politics in the party and the non-party areas of the country. What is politics like, what are political attitudes and feelings like, in those areas where party politics exist only at the parliamentary level, or not even at that level. I am thinking of areas like the rural parts of Scotland or alternatively the pocket-borough territory of the English metropolitan north and suburban south. In the past, rural areas have been neglected, partly because they had small electorates and partly because no technology existed for surveys at reasonable cost. Yet, as the SNP breakthrough showed in 1974, they can be both interesting, different, and politically significant for the wider polity: the soft underbelly of the two-party system. So often radical change occurs in supposedly 'safe' constituencies, not the marginals, because party has decayed in the absence of regular competition.

A third party theme concerns the internal affairs of the parties. Now that the Labour party has given more direct and immediate powers over leaders and policy to its conference, there is an increased value in studying lower level activists, minor officials, and conference delegates. Too often such studies have tended to be small scale, statistically unsound, and crudely conceptualised. Work like Searing's (1978) on MPs, Bochel and Denver's (1983) on candidate selection, or more especially that by Whiteley (1981) on Labour Party Conference delegates represents a major advance on previous studies, but more work needs to be done, including work on change and trends. As Whiteley noted, his was the first national sample study of Labour party activists. Simple comparisons of élite versus mass attitudes are not enough. The survey needs to be national in coverage, capable of being broken down into regional subsamples, and relational at a very low level of aggregation, if we are to understand how the party lives and functions. How are the conference delegates connected to the activists, the activists to the membership, and the formal membership to the party identifiers, who may well feel the party is theirs without ever paying membership dues? I stress the word 'connection' rather than 'contrast'. Are left-wingers within the party perceived to be left-wingers? Are they evaluated in ideological terms, even if they are perceived in ideological terms? Do they achieve status and influence within the party despite their ideology, or because of it? How does the structure of relationships survive shocks like a disastrous electoral performance? (For an earlier generation of party studies that used too few interviews, in too unsystematic a way see, for example, Hindess 1974 or Minkin 1978.)

Another collection of themes relates to the electoral system. Past survey research has taken a rather cavalier stance towards the electoral system, producing representative samples of the national electorate—an entity with no constitutional significance on either side of the Atlantic; or samples of the adult population which has even less status in the electoral process.

First, we could do with a thorough investigation of the accuracy and biases in the electoral register. The Scotland Act referendum of 1979, with its notorious 40 per cent rule, prompted a lot of hasty research into the state of the register and uncovered much evidence about inaccuracies: dogs and cats were registered, people were registered at their front door address and again at their back door address. But a fully systematic study has yet to be made. The problem is that at present we do not know whether turn-out levels are low or high, because the register is known to be defective but we do not know how defective; nor do we know how its defects vary from area to area. Crewe has stressed declining turnout as one of the key variables in need of explanation, yet the turnout rates usually quoted are the joint product of individuals' motivation to vote and the quality of the register. Both need investigation. Registration in Britain is not nearly so defective as in America, but that contrast has blinded us to its imperfections. The British register is sensitive to geographic mobility and its inaccuracy may well be increasing. A 1982 survey by OPCS for the Home Office found that 7 per cent of eligible voters in England had been omitted from the register—twice as many as in 1966. Nearly a third of coloured immigrants, and a quarter of young electors were omitted in error. Only half the young unemployed in London were properly registered (Todd and Butcher 1982). While some of those omitted from the local register may have been registered elsewhere, postal voting facilities impose more partisan bias than they eliminate and more politically sensitive surveys than those done by OPCS are needed.

Secondly, we need studies which take account of Britain's spatially structured electoral system. That implies regional and national (Scots, Welsh, Irish) analyses; studies of differences between politics in politically marginal and non-marginal areas; studies perhaps on why certain constituencies deviate from general patterns—why the Liberals retain some by-election gains but not others, for example. Some of these studies might adopt the Conservative party pollsters' approach of multi-subgroup samples which attempt to survey several relatively homogeneous groups of constituencies, making sure there are enough respondents drawn from each type of area. Let me illustrate the difference between a survey which takes account of the electoral system and one which does not by quoting a statement made by one of the Labour party's senior researchers: he felt that Mrs Thatcher's promise of cheap mortgages in 1974 had damaged the Conservative party's credibility and perhaps on balance lost the party some votes, but at the same time he thought it had appealed especially to the voters in marginal seats and so perhaps helped the Conservative party in terms of seats while hurting it in terms of votes. This is not the place to discuss whether he was right or wrong. The point is that his argument raises the very plausible notion that political reactions may vary between one area and another; and that under a spatially structured electoral system, reactions in different areas have different consequences in terms of parliamentary representation. Most past surveys have aimed at explaining the popular vote rather than the composition of parliament and although these two aims are closely related, they are not the same. There is something rather absurd in using a representative sample of the electorate in February 1974 (when the Conservatives beat Labour in terms of popular votes) to explain the election of a Labour government.

A third collection of possible themes is loosely related to problems of public policy. We need political science oriented surveys on the issues involved in political debate—matters like education, race relations, health systems, unemployment, crime, or inflation. These matters, like war, are too close to the centre of politics to be left entirely to subject specialists in the policy area themselves. Among currently important issues we need surveys on the political impact of unemployment as the world faces qualitatively new levels and patterns of unemployment; surveys on the political impact of housing milieu, housing type, and housing tenure as large numbers of council tenants are persuaded to change their tenure without changing their spatial location; surveys of attitudes to local government at a time when it is coming under increasingly open central control; surveys of attitudes towards direct action as political violence increases; surveys on the role of trades unions which have played such a large part in the downfall of recent governments of both parties.

Finally, there are other topics of general interest, not specially relevant to present conditions and problems. Despite all that has been written about class definitions and class alignments, there is still scope for an improved and extended treatment of class politics, partly because the nature of class politics is visibly changing (see Andersen 1983). And the same could be said about issue and ideological analysis. We need to relate issue attitudes more closely to media output; to research emotional involvement with issues; to improve our measures of issue salience—an area where previous work is outstandingly weak; to discover those issues on which voters are willing to defer to politicians, and those on which they demand representation; to deal with the question of intense minorities; to find out more about the effects of different issue presentations, and simulated debates; to look for potential new issues, not already incorporated in the party battle; and to carry through a much more thorough investigation on the two-way flow of influence between issue attitudes and partisanship.

11.2 Surveys for benchmark purposes

The existing series of election surveys directed by Butler and Stokes or Crewe and Särlvik provide one model for regular, authoritative benchmark surveys, but they were not designed primarily as benchmark surveys. Although a benchmark survey needs to cover a fairly wide range of topics, the emphasis has to be on continuity, not originality; on breadth, not depth. A shorter questionnaire than that used by Butler and Stokes would be tolerable, especially if it could be traded for a larger sample of respondents. With existing technology no such trade-off is possible: using personal interviews with a random sample, it is so expensive to make contact with respondents that the length of the questionnaire is not a critical element in the cost. With the new technology discussed in the next chapter, a trade-off between sample-size and questionnaire-length is possible, however.

One clear advantage of the Butler/Stokes series over most media polls is that it questioned respondents *after* the election, and so recorded vote rather than vote intention. I have shown that the distinction between the two is important, because recent elections have been won or lost in the campaign and issue salience has also fluctuated enormously during the campaign. However, if time is important before elections, it is also important after them. There is no way to justify using party identification, as expressed a month or two after the vote, as a means of explaining the vote. Furthermore it is beyond doubt that issue salience, attitudes, feelings, and perceptions must be changing almost as quickly after the vote as before it. Some work on survey reporting indicates that even reports of recent past behaviour, including voting and party choice, may become inaccurate after only a week or two. The forecasting pollsters have been driven to mount their final prediction surveys on the day before the vote itself. There is a strong argument for changing benchmark election survey methodology so as to complete the interviewing very much more quickly than in the past. Again, this may be incompatible with personal interviewing of a random sample.

11.3 *Surveys for heterogeneous polities*

It is obvious in the eighties, if it was not before, that the UK is not a single uniformly homogeneous polity and, further, that the sources of heterogeneity are multiple. In that respect Britain has become more like America. Moreover, the electoral system makes heterogeneity critically important for the election of MPs and the alternation of governments. Whereas a Britain-wide proportional representational system, with a modest 5 per cent threshold, would automatically exclude all Irish, Welsh, and Scottish nationalist parties from representation at Westminster, Britain's territorially based system gave them twenty-six MPs in 1974, and under the new arrangements for Irish constituencies a similar voting pattern in future elections would give them thirty-one MPs. Similarly, internal migration has no effect on a proportionately elected parliament, but can have a major effect on parliamentary representation under the British system. Again, deviant electoral behaviour in marginal and non-marginal constituencies may cancel out in the electorate but not in parliament. This list of the political consequences of heterogeneity under a territorial election system could easily be extended.

The significant implication for survey design is this: we need to have large enough samples at the critical point of analysis, not at the point of data collection. Academics soon find that the complexity of their theories and investigations leads them to analyses of relatively small subsamples of the population. Given the heterogeneity of current British political behaviour, they require even finer breakdowns than in the past. And given the territorial nature of the British electoral system, British political analysis requires specially fine breakdowns. There are only two ways of ensuring enough respondents at the point of analysis: either the sample size in national samples has to be large and the sample unclustered; or we need specially targeted surveys aimed at well-defined sub-populations.

Sample sizes in most British academic political surveys—under a thousand in most, rising to two thousand in Butler and Stokes's Cross-sectional surveys (but not in their panels)—are just too small. They may be good enough for the purpose for which they were originally devised—forecasting party shares of the national vote; but they are not good enough for the more advanced analyses that most academic investigation requires. Moreover, national samples, particularly in the national electoral surveys since Butler and Stokes, have been far too clustered, with every constituency in the sample represented by a single polling district. That design is efficient in cost/effectiveness terms, providing we wish to estimate national percentages of the vote, or of attitudes or whatever. But it is not a good design if we wish to subdivide the sample along spatial or geographic lines. Polling districts are far too homogeneous internally and unrepresentative of the wider constituency in which they are situated.

Hence academics frequently have to face the choice between using academic election study surveys, with their wealth of variables, or opinion poll surveys with their wealth of respondents. Bonham, Rose, and Dunleavy all used cumulated Gallup polls with approximately 10,000 respondents in order to apply only moderately complex analytical breakdowns; Harrop, Husbands, and England used NOP cumulated surveys of over 43,000 respondents to look at National Front voting; Butler and Stokes used NOP cumulated surveys of over 120,000 respondents to look at the effect of the local milieu. It really is enormously wasteful for a great deal of academic time to be spent thinking through theoretical questions and devising appropriate measuring instruments and analytical techniques, only to find that the size of the sample is too small to sustain the depth of analysis required.

Until now, the technology of academic survey research has dictated few respondents and heavy clustering, because samples have been random and interviews have been by face-to-face contact. Whatever the statistical text-book advantages of these techniques, they have to be weighed against the fact that these designs made contact with respondents, possibly after several call-backs, very expensive and so dictated a format of long inter-views with few respondents heavily clustered together.

The only conventional alternative to large unclustered samples is to make more use of custom-built specially-targeted sampling. Election surveys have tended not to focus too sharply on particular topics, sub-groups, or theoretical questions, because they had a benchmark function to perform. They had to contribute to the historical record of elections. The motivation was: 'If it's part of the election we must have a question on it'. Indeed, this motivation is reinforced as the years go by, and the survey directors are bombarded with numerous questions from the parties, the media, and their fellow academics, all requesting information about highly disparate aspects of political attitudes and behaviour. This is a very important function of authoritative benchmark surveys, but we deceive ourselves if we imagine that the best format for benchmark surveys is also the best format for theoretical investigations; or if we contend that one or other is sufficient to maintain and advance our knowledge of political behaviour.

There is a very considerable difference between a benchmark election survey and a survey planned as a carefully designed test of some aspect of political theory. Reading through Butler and Stokes's report on their election surveys, we must be struck by how often their data are sufficient to stimulate speculation without being sufficient in either quality or quantity to help very far towards definitive answers—for example, I have described in some detail the way their impressive theoretical discussion of the influence of housing tenure outran the potentialities of their data purely because of sample size.

Since Butler and Stokes, there have been several examples of relatively large-sample targeted surveys. The study by Goldthorpe *et al.* of the affluent worker was targeted but very small. Larger samples were obtained in Miller's study of the Scots electorate, Madgwick's study of Cardigan politics, Rose's study of Northern Ireland, and Husband's study of National Front sympathies. Targeted studies need to be encouraged, and not just geographically targeted ones. More attention should also be given to a multi-subgroup design, as distinct from a uniform national sample on the one hand, and a single-target sample on the other. The drawback with single-target surveys is that they lack internal contrast, though national benchmark surveys may provide some basis for measuring deviance. Multi-subgroup designs are a further realistic step towards a classic factorial design: we define the range of subgroups of interest, and then ensure sufficient rather than proportionate samples in each.

Large samples, unclustered samples, and targeted samples do not exhaust the possibilities for varying traditional sample design, but they are especially appropriate for surveying a heterogeneous polity.

11.4 *Surveys for causal analysis*

A major objective of the early behaviouralists was to move on from description to causal explanation. And a major criticism of survey work advanced alike by practitioners themselves and by anti-behaviouralist critics has been that survey analysis proved, in the event, to be insufficiently causal. No one would demand an end to description, nor deny its importance, nor under-estimate the subtlety and delicacy it can achieve; but superb descriptions do not substitute for causal explanations.

Causal analysis requires some attention to topics wider and deeper than the froth of current rhetoric. It requires some effort to state hypotheses, devise explicit models, integrate the current survey with previous work, and not least to tie the survey design and survey variables closely to the model being tested. Too often a few survey-based percentages are dribbled into a text to illustrate the argument, but no more. However, individual pieces of research must be judged on their merits and I can make no general recommendations about appropriate survey designs for causal analysis, save one—that time appears to be the essence of causal analysis. If there is no time dimension built in to the design, the chances are that any causal investigation will be weak and inconclusive.

At the simplest, a time dimension requires regular repeated surveys to establish trends and identify turning points. Many variables in political analysis are uninteresting and uninterpretable in so far as they have only a level. What does it mean if we find that 40 per cent claim they 'usually trust the government to do what is right'? or 'feel that a party keeps its promises? Little or nothing! But when the levels giving these replies suddenly or systemically change, it does tell us something. Thus the swift collapse of approval for the government's record, and for the prime minister in particular, that occurred between November 1978 and February 1979 strongly suggested that the 'Winter of Discontent' was a major cause of the government's subsequent general election defeat and probably also a major cause of its smaller than expected majority in the Scotland Act referendum.

One requirement for useful trend analysis is that surveys are sufficiently frequent to allow us to identify turning points sufficiently precisely. For example, a trend series that is confined to regular election surveys fails to distinguish the effects of an election campaign—Goldwater's 1964 campaign in the USA is a good example—from those of various events that occurred at other times in the inter-election periods. Worcester's conclusion that Labour won the 1979 campaign but lost the election illustrates the difficulty (Worcester 1979). While media polls supply one source of regular monthly trends, the academic contribution to fine-chop trend information is virtually non-existent, while their use of such information is considerable. The danger here is that academic analysts are merely making use of available data and failing to make any intellectual contribution to the nature of those data. So possibilities for using high frequency trend designs are almost unexplored: the range of series information collected by the media polls is not very great and does not include many of the variables academics have stressed in their own surveys.

But monthly trend surveys are an insufficient basis for causal analysis. We may find that support for the Conservatives goes up at the same time as support for EEC membership. Yet purely trend data would not allow us to examine the connection in any greater detail. It is entirely possible that those who switch to the Conservatives are different people from those who switch to supporting EEC membership. Coincident trends may not be evidence of any causal link.

Even trends in the correlation between attitudes are insufficient for causal analysis. During the late seventies there was an increasingly close fit between attitudes to Scottish devolution and political partisanship. But comparisons between separate surveys cannot tell us whether attitudes influenced partisanship, or vice versa. We need panel surveys for causal analysis. Only panel surveys come close to quasi-experimental designs. Panel analysis suggests, in this Scottish example, that the tension between attitudes and partisanship was resolved in favour of partisanship for Conservative and Labour partisans; but in favour of attitudes amongst SNP partisans whose party identification was more recent and less rigidly held (W. L. Miller 1983).

Several features of panel surveys make them very expensive. First, repeated interviews with the original respondents mean that named individuals have to be sought out for interview. Quota-style substitution is impossible. Secondly, it is so expensive to make contact with a named individual, whether in a panel or in a random sample survey, that each contact has to be treated to a full-length interview to justify the contact cost. Third, contact rates decline sharply with time: over the full length of a parliament, experience with the Butler/Stokes and later election surveys suggests that only around two-fifths of the original panel can be reinterviewed. Now apart from the problems of sample bias—which proved extreme in Himmelweit's panel—this means that the sample size for panel analysis can be very low, even when the original sample was quite large. Moreover, there are problems other than expense: panels appear to increase political participation, especially if the reinterviews occur with any frequency—a point that was noted with Crewe and Särlvik's February 1974 –October 1974–June 1975 inter-electional panel, and with MORI's 1979 campaign panel, for example.

Yet despite all these problems of data collection, and despite some problems of analysis (see Kessler and Greenberg 1981), panels remain the best route to causal analysis, and the difficulties must just be overcome. Using the new technology described in the next chapter, the cost of recontacting respondents becomes trivial, the pressure to engage in a long interview each time is eliminated, the whole process becomes less obtrusive to the interviewee and hence may alter his or her participation rate rather less, and large samples can be traded against shorter interviews. Hence the economics of panel analysis can be changed radically.

We need several kinds of panel surveys: first, large-sample long-term rolling panels, big enough to leave the panel, as distinct from the initial sample, with enough respondents for sensitive analyses of long-term changes in attitudes to governments, parties, and issues or changes in personal circumstances. They must be continuously topped-up with new respondents to replace those with whom contact is lost. It might be best to operate on at least an annual frequency, rather than a full parliamentary term, so as to catch change as it occurs. The original Columbia method of dividing the initial sample and reinterviewing random subsamples at different time intervals could be a useful way of keeping costs down and keeping the surveillance unobtrusive. This was the method used between 1966 and 1974 by the Conservative party for its long-term panel.

Secondly, most recent elections have shown the importance of the campaign, and a high frequency campaign panel with interviews at least once a week during the three-or four-week campaign would be of enormous help in causal analyses of campaign effects.

Thirdly, we need a quasi-experimental panel-survey approach to *all* causal investigations. Examples come readily to mind: one might be a panel survey of children coming up to school-leaving age and beyond. At present anything up to half of them might end up unemployed. The panel survey could analyse the causal impact of unemployment on political partisanship, on support for violent direct action, and on political attitudes to the regime, the government, the parties, social groups, and issues. There really is no point in attempting to measure the impact of unemployment by surveying people only after they have become unemployed. Another possible quasi-experimental panel could look at a current example in social engineering: the sale of council houses. It would be necessary to design the sample so as to catch people before they changed tenure, milieu, or both; yet catch them in sufficient numbers to make the conclusions quantitative. It would centre on the interplay of partisanship affecting housing change and vice versa; it would distinguish tenure change from a change in social milieu. Drawing such a sample would be difficult but not impossible. No doubt the reader can think of many more examples. The essential point is to spot groups or times where one important change is likely to occur; then to investigate the consequences of that change by starting a panel survey before the anticipated change has happened. Sometimes we may guess wrongly, but very often significant changes in causal variables can be anticipated sufficiently well to start the survey before the event, instead of after.

12 The new technology

Clearly, many of my suggestions for the future of political surveys require either an enormous increase in funds during a period of economic constraint, or they require vigorous adoption of new techniques. If we need, as I believe we do, a lot more interviews spread more widely throughout the country, then the cost per interview has to be reduced. There are at least five ways of collecting survey data more cheaply than using the traditional Butler/Stokes methodology, but several have significant drawbacks. I will discuss them in reverse order of utility.

12.1 *Five ways of doing cheap surveys*

The most restrictive, and generally the least useful, is to use local samples concentrated in the vicinity of the survey director's university. Since the field staff of commercial fieldwork agencies are spread around the country in anticipation of national coverage, a highly concentrated location may increase rather than decrease costs or, indeed, may be quite beyond the competence of professional agencies. The only really good reasons for local surveys are the availability of cheap or even free student labour—and it is not so readily available now as in the fifties—or a special interest in the locality for its own sake. Thus the Columbia methodology adopted by British universities in the fifties is far more difficult to justify than that used by Madgwick in Cardigan. Local surveys must be justified in terms of topic, not technique.

I have stressed the need for a time dimension in survey design, and one implication of this is the need to monitor levels of certain political indicators at fairly frequent time intervals. One inexpensive way of doing this is to use the commercial pollsters' 'carrier' or 'omnibus' surveys. These are monthly or even weekly general-purpose surveys in which a few political questions can be included at a charge of so much per question. Since we purchase only the right to include a few specific questions, rather than a complete survey interview, the cost is low. This is an inexpensive way to set up time series and also, by aggregating successive samples, an inexpensive way to interview very large samples of the electorate or substantial samples of small subgroups. So far academics have tended to use these omnibus surveys, but only for reanalysis, accepting the pollsters' questions as given. Academics have not made much use of this technique for asking their own questions. By contrast, both Labour and Conservative party analysts use it regularly.

Omnibus surveys present some special problems. The interviews may involve abrupt changes of topic, and we cannot control the influence of other topics, like detergent sales perhaps, that are being investigated in the same omnibus interview. The method only remains cheap if we specify relatively few special questions and are content to analyse them alone or in conjunction with the pollsters' own questions on political attitude and social background. But it is not so restrictive as passively accepting the pollsters' questions as the only possible ones.

Commercial pollsters also run 'omnibus panels' consisting of as many as 60,000 respondents who have already been interviewed and have agreed to further interivews. Because their social background characteristics are already known and are held on computer files, it is very easy to select a subset of the omnibus panel for special purposes. For example, the computer can list panel members who are unemployed, or who are working wives. Hence certain targeted samples can be contacted quite cheaply. There is an obvious danger that these panels are so voluntary that their members are effectively self-selected and unrepresentative of the general population even when they join the panel. Then their experience on the panel may turn them into 'gentlemen of opinion'. Though new respondents are added to the panel and old ones dropped every week, people still stay on these panels for a lengthy period. None the less the method provides cheap targeted samples and, if telephones are used to recontact panel members, it also provides very speedy targeted samples.

If we insist on a more extensive range of variables, necessitating a separate independent survey, we could mail postal questionnaires to a named sample, or accept interviews with a quota rather than a random sample. There is little control of any kind over postal questionnaires. They may even be filled up by someone other than the supposed respondent, and any degree of length or complexity may have severe effects on the response. The method may be more acceptable with élite samples who have a high level of interest in the subject and a high level of competence in form-filling (see Kavanagh 1970; and Parkin 1968) but it is less acceptable with mass samples. Crewe and Särlvik achieved a very high response rate of 80 per cent in a postal questionnaire to their panel survey shortly after the 1975 EEC referendum, but their sample had already been personally interviewed twice in 1974 and their postal questionnaire was very short—two sides of A4-sized card (Särlvik et al. 1976). Levine and Robinson (1976) sent out a much lengthier postal questionnaire to their 1975 sample of the New Zealand electorate and were unable to filter and motivate respondents by prior personal interviews. They achieved only a 38 per cent response rate—1,604 questionnaires were returned, out of 4,200 sent out— and they found a strong social and partisan bias in the achieved sample. Postal surveys would appear to be at their best when used either for élite studies, or when used in conjunction with other techniques. Crewe and Särlvik's postal questionnaire which added another time point, but very few extra variables, to their on-going panel illustrates the method at its most effective.

Quota sampling rather than random sampling might not effect a massive reduction in cost if it was done properly. If complex interlocking quotas are applied, the number of interviewers may have to be increased, and the greatest advantage of quota over random samples may lie in speed rather than cost. Some so-called quota samples are actually quota-weighted analyses of unsystematic samples. In addition, academic surveys requiring perhaps an hour, or an hour and a half, of interview might entail interviewers making acceptable contacts but then having to call back later for the full interview. Media pollsters need quota samples because experience —in 1948 and 1970 especially—has shown that political attitudes and partisanship change so rapidly that they can forecast voting patterns accurately only if they poll a day or so before election day. Although academics want after-the-event polls to record votes rather than intentions, political memories decay after election day and political attitudes go on changing, not least in reaction to the new government's political acts. Thus time and speed are as important in academic political polls as in media polls. It is absurd to use political attitudes a month or two after an election to explain the vote at the election itself. Hence, if quota sampling could speed up the data collection process, even when lengthy interviews were necessary, then it could be valuable.

But by far the best prospect for improvement in political surveys lies in a switch away from face-to-face and towards telephone interviewing. Some leading British pollsters have described the difference between telephone and face-to-face Survey Methods to me as 'merely a matter of cost—use the cheapest.' That is a Luddite response. If the difference between phone and face-to-face surveys was purely a matter of cost, I would relegate it to a paragraph or two; but it is not.

12.2 *Better and cheaper: the CATI method*

Telephone interviews form an essential part of what I will call the *new technology norm*, which differs from the traditional survey norm of the 1930s in a variety of interconnected ways. It is the *combination* of several interlocking changes that makes the new technology norm excitingly different from the old. (For a fuller introduction to the new technology see Dillman 1978; or Groves and Kahn 1979; or McDonald and Bowles 1981).

As with the old norm, all sorts of variants around it are possible to deal with special survey problems or financial constraints. Good work could be done with cheap approximations to the norm, but all three elements of the norm are required for the method to realise its full potential. They are:

1 interviews are still personal, but done by telephone instead of by physically transporting the interviewer to the respondent's home;
2 all the interviewers work in an 'interviewing factory' under the continuous control of a supervisor and in contact with other interviewers;
3 a computer flashes questionnaire items on to a screen for the interviewer to read; the interviewer enters the responses directly into the computer; and the computer also carries out a number of 'housekeeping' tasks which may include phoning up the next person to be sampled, but will certainly include automatic selection of respondents, question filtering, randomisation of response option sequences, plus checks on errors and consistency.

Centralisation in a factory style environment allows production-line efficiency: personal briefings for all interviewers; instant and continuous supervision of interviewers; reduction of interviewer bias; independent monitoring by supervisors listening in; immediate tactical decisions by controllers and supervisors; and computerisation of questionnaire presentation and data entry. From the interviewer's standpoint, centralisation allows the interviewer to get immediate response to any queries; continuous on-the-job training; well-defined shifts, but probably in the evenings and at weekends; greater flexibility in distributing assignments; and the ability to hand respondents over to a supervisor or research director when the respondent so demands.

Respondents can be allocated randomly to interviewers, and interviewers who suffer relatively high refusal rates, for whatever reason, can be dropped. *Ad hoc* labour, like students, can be used, because evening work suits them, because they are under tight supervision, and because they are not exposed to personal danger.

This methodology has some very important consequences. First, it means an end to the old necessary evil of clustering. Beyond a thirty mile radius, phone calls to anywhere in Britain are subject to the same uniform cost. In America the WATS system (Wide Area Telephone Service) provides a similar facility. So there is no need to cluster, no advantage even in clustering. Interviews north of the Highland Line become feasible and, indeed, a study of rural politics becomes as inexpensive as a study of urban areas. The location of the interviewing centre has very few cost implications: siting it in Glasgow, London, Edinburgh, Birmingham, Liverpool, or Manchester—the six so-called Director Systems whose dialling codes begin with zero—would increase the number of local-rate calls, but a telephone interviewing unit can lease lines into all six of these exchanges, and then approximately one third of all its calls would be at the local rate. (It is not necessary to be located in London, or even in England, to have a London telephone number.) Tight control of phone bills is also possible by centralisation.

Secondly, the new technology makes the cost of call-backs insignificant. That makes it peculiarly suitable for random sampling or for panel sampling or any other sample design in which it is necessary to make contact with specific, named individuals. And as a corollary, the near-zero cost of call-backs means that three twenty-minute interviews cost the same as a single one-hour interview. Consequently there is no pressure to pad out the interview with enough questions to justify the high cost of going to meet the respondent. There is a simple, perfect trade-off between sample size and questionnaire length. There is the possibility of collecting trend data or even panel data for no more cost than collecting the same amount of data from the same number of respondents in a single-wave cross-sectional survey. The interview is no longer effectively a unit, but a collection of questions which can be distributed over time at almost no extra cost. Zero-cost call-backs also make it easy to switch interviewers in an attempt to persuade reluctant respondents to agree to an interview. Experience has shown this can have a large effect on improving response rates.

Computer control of questionnaire presentation and data entry also has important implications. Much more complex filtering can be used in the questionnaire design, because the interviewer is never troubled with anything more than the next appropriate question appearing on the screen in front of him. We can be certain that answer categories really are permuted to avoid bias. Direct entry of the responses as they are made means that inconsistencies and errors can be brought to the attention of the interviewer immediately, and referred back to the respondent. The computer can also control the sampling of subgroups by automatically truncating the interview when enough representatives of the particular type of respondent have been interviewed. Continuous analysis is also possible and makes sequential sampling a practical possibility for the first time: as early interviewing results accumulate, the research directors can decide to terminate the survey or boost the sample in certain geographic areas or in certain subgroups of the population. And it no longer requires an enormously expensive computer to service a battery of display screens and direct entry terminals, since the cost of computer hardware is falling rapidly.

Centralisation also makes for speed. A survey questionnaire can be developed on the computer—no printed copy need ever exist; the assembled interviewers can be briefed and interviews commenced immediately. The first hundred can be treated as a pilot study, the questionnaire adjusted, and the main survey continued. All the relevant people can be in one room all the time. Supervisors and directors assessing the adequacy of the questionnaire can be listening in to interviews without even the need to wait for a report back from the interviewers. Interviews can easily be taped for teaching and research purposes.

Hyett (1981) has estimated that, in Britain, telephone surveys to mass samples cost between two-thirds and three-quarters of the cost of equivalent face-to-face surveys. A large scale comparative test at the University of Michigan found that the number of man-hours spent on a phone survey was only 40 per cent of those spent on a face-to-face survey (Groves and Kahn 1979). Pre-testing, interviewer training, materials, control and supervision were also much cheaper in the phone survey. Against all these savings there is the increased cost of communication with respondents, though phone bills for interviews have to be set against quite substantial transport and communications costs for interviewers and supervisors with the traditional Survey Method. But cost, it must be reiterated, is not the main reason for advocating telephone surveys.

Of course there are problems with telephone surveys. Until recently they were not practicable in Britain for the simple but sufficient reason that relatively few people were accessible by telephone. What now makes phone surveys an exciting prospect is that phone penetration in Britain has now reached the threshold where the problems of phone surveys no more than balance the problems associated with any other survey methodology.

Critics of telephone surveys in Britain point to the contrast between Britain and America, where phone surveys have become widely established. The current Nuffield Election Study, published after the 1979 election, took a relatively favourable view: 'because Britain has only 60 per cent saturation of telephone ownership, heavily biased towards the better-off, such an approach needs far more delicacy in use than in the USA or Australia, where there is 90 per cent telephone saturation, (but) more will undoubtedly be heard of political telephone surveys in Britain (Butler and Kavanagh 1980). Indeed it will, and partly because the figures quoted by the Nuffield study are long out of date. Argument rages over whether current telephone access covers 73 per cent or 83 per cent of the adult population. However even British Telecom, which takes a conservative view, forecast coverage to be 76 per cent in 1982, rising to 82 per cent by 1984 and 89 per cent by 1988. The British Telecom figures do not take account of the high number of business phones in private households, nor the tendency for phone-renting households to be larger than those without phones. Telephone saturation in Britain will certainly be high enough by the end of the eighties to make telephone interviewing a reasonable method, perhaps supplemented by some face-to-face interviews; and in the nineties telephone access will be so widespread that phone surveys will be the norm. It is none too soon, perhaps even rather late already, to begin serious studies on the methodological difficulties and opportunities offered by phone surveys. It seems likely that in their media political polls, the commercial polling agencies will not take full advantage of the opportunities presented by telephone polling and will use it merely to do polls on the cheap.

12.3 *New opportunities, new problems*

There are special problems as well as special opportunities presented by telephone Survey Methods. Some of the most obvious, however, do not turn out the most serious. Psychological studies and comparative tests suggest that communication over the phone is good, as much because of the impersonality and poor sound quality of the medium as in spite of it (Champness 1981). Interviews up to eighty-five minutes long have been sustained, and there is no correlation between the length of interview and the refusal rate (McDonald and Bowles 1981). Most refusals occur immediately after the interviewer has finished his or her introductory remarks. Just why some interviewers consistently achieve 90 per cent acceptance rates and others 70 per cent is not clear (Cannell 1981), but by randomising the allocation of respondents to interviewers, the unacceptable interviewers can be identified and dropped. With the current state of the art, refusal rates are only around 5 per cent to 10 per cent higher than using traditional methods, but even this may reflect a lack of experience with the new technology. Telephone interviewing seems to be better for questions on sensitive, embarrassing, or conflict-ridden topics (Cannell 1981; Champness 1981). With open-ended questions telephone interviewing cuts the quantity of response, but only amongst those groups that usually give the greatest volume of response: so that the phone evens out the response given to open-ended questions by different social groups. Multiple response questions or visual, show-card techniques are difficult to use over the phone, but they have been developed specially for face-to-face interviewing. Alternative methods of eliciting the same underlying information by more verbal means are usually available. Generally, phone interviews run faster than face-to-face interviews. The overall conclusion must be that the medium of telephone interviewing is inherently no worse, and possibly better, than the medium of face-to-face interviewing, but that it needs an equivalent degree of development and attention to detail. Voice, for example, becomes important, while appearance ceases to matter at all. Both British and American telephone pollsters have found out-of-work actors particularly useful as phone interviewers.

Access is something of a problem. Even in America, overall telephone coverage in excess of 90 per cent masks variations down to 77 per cent for the state of Mississippi and right down to 50 per cent amongst non-urban blacks. Sampling presents problems, since almost a fifth of American telephone numbers are ex-directory. Hence the American tendency to use random digit dialling techniques, rather than sampling from telephone directories. On the other hand, America is an extremely violent society, and physical access by unknown survey interviewers to guarded apartment blocks is frequently refused. Americans feel physically safer talking to strangers over the phone. Conversely, American interviewers no longer have the incentive to avoid contact with dangerous-looking areas or individuals when they interview by phone: the society described in Michael Frayn's *A Very Private Life* now exists in wide areas of America. America is also so large that personal briefing of interviewers is prohibitively expensive if they have to travel to central locations for the briefing and then disperse across the land to conduct their interviews. And the American telephone network's WATS system (Wide Area Telephone Service) provides leased lines into different parts of the USA, and so relatively inexpensive phone charges.

How does Britain compare on these critical aspects of phone techniques? First, the regional and social variation of phone coverage is no worse in Britain than America, and probably better. Phone coverage is highest in London and the South-East—but Eastern England, South-West England, and Scotland all come within 5 per cent of the average for Great Britain. The Midlands, Northern England, and Wales have fewest telephones but even the worst region, Wales, has only 11 per cent fewer than the GB average. Those in lower occupational strata and those who do not own their houses tend to have fewer telephones. Skilled manual workers have as many phones as the GB average. The group who lack phones to a significant extent are the pensioners and welfare recipients. For that reason the SSRC's Designated Research Centre for survey work, SCPR (Social And Community Planning Research) has no immediate interest in phone techniques, because most of its work is aimed at those sections of society which do not rent phones. The situation is quite different for those interested in the electorate as a whole, and in its most politically active sections in particular.

Hyett uses NOP data published in May 1981 to show that in addition to a class bias in telephone coverage, there is a political bias within classes between those who do and those who do not rent phones. The Conservative lead over Labour within each social stratum is about 18 per cent larger among those who have phones than among those who do not—though a control for house ownership would reduce this. This 18 per cent difference has been remarkably constant over the years (compare Rose 1974d), but it gets less significant as the numbers without telephones decline. Thus, in 1981 the NOP figures showed that their telephone renters gave a Conservative lead only 11 per cent greater than the whole NOP sample, simply because there were so few without phones, and if the telephone renters were weighted by class, the Conservative lead in the class-weighted phone sample was only 5 per cent greater than in the full NOP sample. Weighting by house ownership would reduce this discrepancy still further, but we should still need to make periodic checks on the difference between phone renters and others.

British telephone directories are much more inclusive than American. Ex-directory numbers are probably around 5 per cent of the total, rising to 10 per cent in London, though precise data are not available. Thus sampling from directories is more feasible in Britain, especially since the upper-class characteristics of the ex-directory people probably balance those who do not have phones at all and bring the social and political characteristics of directory people closer to the national average.

At present, the commercial pollsters in Britain use two main sampling methods. One is to take a systematic sample of directory entries and impose a running quota on the interviews as obtained. This is fast and cheap and used for media polls. The second is to work with an omnibus panel, recruited by face-to-face interview, all of whose phone numbers, socio-economic background, and convenient phone-call times are stored on computer. The whole panel or any defined subset can be accessed quickly for a particular survey. The panel is recruited by traditional omnibus face-to-face surveys and suffers from all their defects—quota selection and clustering, as well as a high degree of self-selection for re-interview.

For academic purposes the full potential of the new technology will require careful sample construction, and perhaps a mix of methods. (The Canadian 1974–79–80 panel survey used telephones for the 1980 wave: see LeDuc 1983). Biases in the phone sample must be recognised and adjustments made where necessary. But biased samples—provided that the bias is explicitly recognised—are less of a problem in academic research than in media polls. The media pollster wants to predict an election 'right' in the sense of estimating the right levels of voting percentages. The academic wants to analyse patterns, and a well-understood systematic bias may cause little trouble. For example, my own re-analysis of the May 1981 NOP data used by Hyett shows that class polarisation—measured by the difference between the Conservative lead among middle-class ABC1s and among working-class C2DEs—was 58 per cent in the sample as a whole, 53 per cent among telephone renters alone, and 55 per cent among telephone renters weighted to adjust the ratio of C2 : DE to their numbers in the full sample. Now estimating the Conservative lead wrongly by 5 per cent when, in a close election, the true figure is close to zero could be disastrous for a media poll. But estimating class polarisation wrongly by only 3 per cent, when the true figure is 58 per cent, should not change any academic conclusions, especially if we have accumulated some understanding of phone bias.

Britain is nowhere near so violent a society as America, and there may be less of a tendency for residents to refuse entry to interviewers or for interviewers to shrink from physical contact with significant numbers of potential respondents. None the less, interviewers do avoid certain city-centre neighbourhoods, even in Britain. When quota samples are used, we have no means of knowing whether interviewers are avoiding certain groups: getting the right number of blacks, or young, or unemployed, or C2DEs is no real check when quota interviewers may well have picked the more peaceable-looking members of these groups. Though the problem is less in Britain than in America, it is growing. What makes it worse is that evening interviewing is necessary unless the sample is to be biased towards the housebound and the more publicly accessible trades.

Personal briefing has been more the norm in compact Britain than in the USA. But transport costs are likely to rise faster than telecommunications costs and collecting face-to-face interviewers together for a briefing incurs a time delay which is particularly unacceptable in political surveys. The whole British telephone system is equivalent to a single area of America's WATS system and, in addition, leased 'FX tie-lines' to the six 'Director Systems' in the British network puts a third of the electorate within reach of the cheapest local-charge call.

In short, the argument that phone interviewing is peculiarly suited to the American electorate and unsuited to the British is one whose validity is fading fast.

Telephone methods eliminate many of the problems caused by distance.

That is true for cross-national research as well as single-country surveys. From a single interviewing factory we can phone respondents in many developed countries. At least one Dutch survey research organisation routinely polls several thousand respondents throughout Europe, using a multi-lingual team of interviewers in a single location. Transatlantic interviewing is also economically feasible. Obviously cross-national surveys raise special problems of questionnaire design, as much because of cultural and institutional variations as because of language differences. While international interviewing may be technically and economically possible, international telephone polling could be insensitive and misleading, But despite the obvious dangers, the new possiblities for tightly controlled, fully comparable, relatively inexpensive, and speedily mounted cross-national surveys must present exciting opportunities.

12.4 *The Hillhead experiment*

Some of the ideas in this chapter and the preceding one must seem either impractical or impossibly expensive. So let me give a concrete example to show how cheap and effective they can be.

At the end of 1981 the sitting Conservative MP for the constituency of Glasgow Hillhead died and Roy Jenkins, leader of the new Social Democratic Party, announced he would contest the by-election, whenever it occurred. With a certain lack of historical perspective, Hillhead was billed by the media as the 'by-election of the century'. Without much difficulty I persuaded BBC-Scotland and the *Sunday Standard* to fund an experiment in using the new survey technology.

We did not know when the by-election would occur, but decided to do a four-wave panel study with the first wave in the first week of February 1982. Each wave would consist of interviews on Tuesday, Wednesday, Thursday, and if necessary Friday evening, with full computer analyses and interpretations to be delivered on the Saturday morning for publication in Sunday papers and television programmes. The panel was to start with approximately 500 respondents. For a total cost, including telephone charges, of less than two thousand pounds (say $3,000) we carried out a four-wave panel study with 537 respondents over an eight-week period, checking the main panel study with another 504 interviews of non-panel respondents.

Generally we followed the methodology set out in Dillman (1978) and found Scottish conditions remarkably similar to Dillman's description of America.

Hillhead is close to the BBC and to Glasgow University campus, the best educated constituency in Britain, a middle class constituency in a working class city. Several conventional surveys suggested that between 80 per cent and 90 per cent of Hillhead electors had telephones. The constituency was divided into four wards: Anniesland in the North West, Kelvinside in the North East, Scotstoun in the South West, and Partick in the South East. Census figures were available by ward. They showed that the two northern wards were relatively middle class, while the two southern ones were more working class; the two eastern wards, nearer the city centre, housed more transient populations, while the two more suburban wards in the west housed more settled populations. So the map looked like a two-by-two table of class by mobility. Anniesland contained the owner-occupied villas and semi-detached houses; Scotstoun the socialised council-rented property; Partick the privately rented flats and a mobile population mainly shifting around the Glasgow connurbation; Kelvinside was the nearest to the BBC and the University, a mixture of owner-occupied and privately rented prestige flats and terraces with a mobile, professional population, many of them shifting around Britain as a whole. Kelvinside was the only ward that contained many English-born residents.

Given this social background, we expected that Anniesland would vote Conservative, Scotstoun Labour, Kelvinside Social Democrat, and Partick would be more evenly split. Ward breakdowns were clearly important for monitoring the survey methodology.

For the first wave we randomly selected Hillhead telephone numbers from the directory and used the Troldahl and Carter (1964) method for randomly selecting a respondent within the household. Survey results then had to be weighted by the number of adults in the household. To get to our target of over 500 respondents in four evenings of interviewing (with only eight interviewers) we had to issue 920 phone numbers. Of these 58 per cent gave a successful interview, 18 per cent refused, and in 24 per cent of cases we made no contact with the person selected for interview, even if we did succeed in getting through to the household. Non-contacts ran at 21 per cent in both the stable western wards, irrespective of class; and at 27 per cent in both the mobile eastern wards, again irrespective of class. Refusal rates as a percentage of contacts did not differ significantly between wards.

Three weeks after the first wave we tried to recontact the panel. Fully 84 per cent gave a second interview; 9 per cent were away, 2 per cent were not issued because they had been too old or ill on the first wave, and only 5 per cent refused. Three weeks after that we carried out a third wave, with a fourth wave a week later. Of the original panel, 74 per cent gave interviews in the third wave, 67 per cent in the fourth, and 80 per cent responded in one or other of these third and fourth waves.

Taking all four waves together, we put 112 questions to panel respondents. These included 'open-ended' questions on which issues were important and on why respondents 'would *not* vote for' each of the parties. There were 'panel' questions, i.e. the same question repeated at different times, on vote intention, images of the parties, contact with canvassers, and attendance at election rallies. There was 'distributed' questioning on social background with questions on class, age, sex, religion, papers read, trade union membership, and house tenure, spread over the first three waves. As many as a dozen calls were made to a phone number in order to contact a panel member. Reluctant respondents were persuaded to cooperate by the supervisor taking over the phone before handing back to the interviewer for the actual interview. During the fourth wave one of our best interviewers was assigned the task of ringing back the 'don't knows' to find out whether 'don't know' meant 'won't say' or indeed whether a better interviewer could extract more information.

The supervisor listened in to interviews and gave advice immediately any problem occurred. We did not use computer control of the interviewers, but checked each interview schedule for coding errors within minutes of the interview. We began the survey with half the interviewers drawn from field-forces of the major British commercial polls, the other half being untrained students or office staff. Because each interviewer received a random stream of respondents, it was relatively easy to continuously monitor individual interviewers and the two groups of interviewers. They were monitored for the number of interviews achieved, the partisan breakdown in their interviews, and the 'don't know' rate. The untrained (but not unbriefed) interviewers were less confident at first, but more flexible in adapting to the requirements of new Survey Methods. They scored just as well for numbers of interviews achieved and were no different on the party breakdowns. At first they produced significantly higher levels of 'don't know' responses, but this was detected within two hours of the start of interviewing and corrected. Open-ended questions were coded as part of this check on interviewers and all coding was done during the interviewing time.

Because telephone interviewing allowed interviews to be done in a random sequence, we could regard each evening's interviews as a random subsample of the panel. So computer analysis started the morning after the first evening of interviewing. Preliminary conclusions were drawn, and a revised format for computer-produced tables were specified. The next day the preliminary conclusions could be checked against the by-now-larger random subsample, and so on. Patterns and conclusions usually stabilised before the final evening's interviewing: so that a final analysis and interpretation could be produced an hour or two after the last interview.

Clearly this experiment showed that the new technology could be applied by a fairly inexperienced team, that it was cheap, that it was very fast, and that it worked outside America as well as within. I would also argue that the design had substantive as well as technological advantages.

Because the design allowed an unclustered sample, its sampling variance was much less than for conventional polls with 500 respondents. In particular, spatial breakdowns to estimate party activity and support in different parts of the constituency were more reliable than with a clustered sample. While I cannot pretend that a sample size of only 500 is anywhere near enough for highly detailed analyses, at least we did not add quota and cluster problems to those of small sample size.

The panel format meant that our estimates of political trends during the campaign were better than with a sequence of separate surveys, and we could measure volatility as well as net change. Early in the campaign support for the Social Democratic Party was specially volatile—only two-thirds of original SDP supporters stayed SDP in the second wave; but thereafter SDP support was no more volatile than that for other parties. The panel also revealed the extent to which vote intentions switched between Conservative and SDP, between Labour and SDP, and from the Scottish National Party to SDP, but not between Labour, Conservative, and SNP.

Perhaps the most interesting finding occurred unexpectedly: the survey was not designed to detect it, but an ongoing panel coped well with the unexpected. One feature of the campaign was the very large meetings and rallies held in the constituency by both SDP and Labour parties. The biggest rally was a Labour one, but the audience was not entirely local, for our fourth-wave survey showed that three times as many respondents had attended an SDP rally as attended any other—fully 16 per cent of our sample (and that was with another week to go before polling day; so that ultimately as many as a quarter of the electorate probably attended an SDP rally). Because our survey was a panel survey, we could compare respondents' voting intentions before and after attending rallies. Those who went to SDP rallies were already relatively favourable to the SDP before they went: 51 per cent of SDP-rally attenders had been SDP inclined before the rally, compared with only 26 per cent SDP support among those who did not go to a rally. But while those who did not go to an SDP rally remained stable in their voting intentions (26 per cent SDP in wave one, 24 per cent of SDP in wave four), those who went to an SDP rally became even more pro-SDP than they had been before (51 per cent SDP in wave one, but 65 per cent SDP in wave four). Given the large numbers who went to SDP rallies both during our survey and in the final week of the campaign, this is striking evidence of the resurgence and effectiveness of old-style political campaigning for a new political party, and helps to explain the SDP's repeated achievement in picking up a significant amount of support right at the end of each by-election campaign. There would be no way of detecting this campaign effect without a *panel* design. And in practice a panel design requires fast and cheap methods for calling back on respondents.

A full report of the findings in the Hillhead Telephone Survey is given in W. L. Miller (1982). During the Falklands crisis that occurred soon after the Hillhead by-election, telephone methods were adopted by several polls in order to assess fast-changing public opinion on support for a military response to the Argentinian action.

12.5 *Programmatic organisation of surveys*

When it comes to commissioning surveys, there is an important distinction to be drawn between commissioning a single survey and undertaking a programme of survey research. Much of the detailed knowledge and skills required in survey research can be acquired only through some degree of practical experience. Kavanagh (1981) has contrasted the lack of cumulation in American party pollsters' work with the growth of expertise in European parties: 'in the decentralised American system the national committees of the two main parties do relatively little polling. Pollsters work directly for candidates in the primary elections and then in the general election. There are a myriad of pollsters working for state, congressional, and local candidates. Since the organisations and the data do not belong to parties *per se*, there is little cumulation of knowledge. In Germany, Sweden, Britain, and other countries where the same pollsters work regularly and systematically for the central party office, they can do research, relate current results to past ones, and advise on strategies to improve the party situation over a five or ten-year period.' The same view has been put both by media men who commission polls and pollsters who get commissioned. BBC officials recognise the disadvantage of their large bureaucratic structure for commissioning polls. So many different editors and producers commission particular polls for particular programmes that they are always amateurs in the hands of polling agencies' experts. Polling agencies have their own commerical objectives, and their expertise does not embrace all the subjects on which they carry out surveys. ITN has developed a much better relationship with these agencies. It looks, not for the lowest competitive tender, but for a satisfactory continuing relationship in which standards must be maintained or improved; in which ITN's commissioning agents develop a high level of expertise in polling techniques; and in which the polling agency is committed to an innovative and successful survey design by having more than a single survey contract at risk and by facing a client with an identity and a memory. Pollsters have made the same point from the opposite side of the table: a competitive tender system does not encourage the polling agency to make full use of its accumulated expertise when the ideas produced in its tender bid may end up incorporated in a marginally cheaper rival's contract.

Unfortunately the pattern of academic political polls in Britain has followed the norm set by American candidates, rather than British parties. Whereas American academic surveys have been organised within the continuing organisational frameworks of Survey Research Centres like those at Michigan or Chicago, no comparable British institution as emerged (the nearest equivalent is SCPR), and British political surveys have been planned largely as one-off enterprises. In addition, Britain's constitution guarantees that the final planning and execution of any parliamentary election survey has to be undertaken in something of a crisis atmosphere because neither the date, the issues, nor the political climate can be known in advance. (See Perry 1975 or Crawford and Perry 1976 on the British SSRC and its short-lived Survey Unit.)

There is a case for thinking more in terms of programmes of survey research and less in terms of survey. An alternative to the 'big-bang' approach would encourage the steady cumulative development of political themes, survey technology, and operational skills.

The first advantage of a survey programme is cumulation. One major difference between academic and non-academic political polls in Britain is the lumpiness of the way money is spent. Over a five-year period non-academic analysts might spend no more money, but spend it in a much larger number of smaller amounts. Academics should consider programmes of survey research that cost no more than a single academic survey does at present, but in which the survey work would be distributed across several relatively inexpensive surveys, with some opportunity for reflection and analysis between one survey and the next. This links in with the new technology: just because a telephone interview for ninety minutes costs the same as six interviews of fifteen minutes each, the new technology presents a radically new opportunity to break surveys down into sequences of less expensive surveys.

A sequential approach can allow a better integration of methodological and substantive research through development of survey questions and instruments specifically designed for the task in hand. It can encourage the development of personal skills, and provide a good environment for teaching them. Studies can be developed routinely in the context of previous work. The new technology not only provides an opportunity for such a programme, it also necessitates one. No one imagines that telephone surveys will be done very well at first. Face-to-face interviewing has been intensively developed over the last half-century. The new pattern of sample construction and interviewer/respondent communication must be capable of development and improvement for some time to come.

The second advantage of a survey programme is that it allows a much more causal approach, through the incorporation of a time dimension. Single-wave surveys are not particularly informative, and the quality of the information they provide seems worse the more closely we look at it. A programme approach facilitates regular surveys and panels.

A third advantage of a survey programme is that the quality of the field-force, the interviewers, is very important, and continuity is an important way of achieving this. Leading British pollsters have noted that even with their well-trained interviewers, response rates can be up to 20 per cent higher on social rather than political surveys; and, moreover, it seems likely that this does not reflect variations in mass co-operation so much as in interviewer motivation. At present there is no 'politics-only' survey organisation in Britain. For most major polling agencies, political surveys account for only around 5 per cent of their work. Response rates and general political interviewing might be improved by a field-force which concentrated mainly on political surveys. A similar case could be made for subject specialisation in other subjects.

Finally, since retrospective survey research is not really possible, important phenomena and changes have to be researched at the time they occur. This is much easier in the context of an on-going programme where finance and procedures allow some discretionary ability to take decisions fast. One function of a continuing survey programme should be to spot gaps, look closely at developing situations, and take a survey initiative.

I am arguing that academics should dispense with the notion of a survey as a piece of research, and focus instead on the idea of survey research as an ongoing process. The nature of political inquiry demands such a change of perspective, and the new technology permits it. With that new technology, which has ended the tyranny of space and distance, we can do a certain amount of interviewing (rather than 'a survey'); then after an analysis of this initial quantum of data, we can easily go back to the same people to ask more questions on new topics, or in greater depth on the same topics, or simply to monitor change. Alternatively we can augment the sample size, even if that requires only a relatively few interviews very widely scattered across the nation. Or again, we can go back to some previous respondents to persuade the 'don't knows' to co-operate. Or we can break off an interview and call back for the remaining information at a more convenient time for the respondent. There are no longer rigid inflexible boundaries to a survey, either in terms of the number of contacts and call-backs, or the number of respondents in the sample, or the number of questions asked of each respondent. The cycle of research question and data analysis is no longer limited to recurrent analyses of the same questions and individuals.

In one sense there is nothing new in this approach. The sequence of election surveys can be viewed as an iterative survey research process—but on a macro-scale of time and funds. There is now the possibility of cycling round between data analysis and data collection on a very short time scale and with a modest budget. A micro version of the process which formerly linked a sequence of surveys over a period of decades can now operate within a single survey research project.

References

Abramowitz, A. I. (1980) 'The United States: political culture under stress', in *The Civic Culture Revisited*, eds. G. A. Almond and S. Verba (Little Brown, Boston).

Abrams, M. (1951) *Social Surveys and Social Action* (Heinemann, London).

Abrams, M. (1960) in *Encounter*, 14, May 1960.

Abrams, M. (1969) 'Attitudes of the British public', in *Colour and Citizenship: a Report on British Race Relations*, ed. E. J. B. Rose *et al.* (Oxford University Press, Oxford).

Abrams, M., R. Rose, and R. Hinden (1960) *Must Labour Lose?* (Penguin, Harmondsworth).

Adorno, T. W. (1969) 'Scientific experiences of a European scholar in America', in *The Intellectual Migration*, eds. D. Fleming and B. Bailyn (Belknap Press, Cambridge, Mass), Chapter 7.

Adorno, T. W., E. Frenkel-Brunswik, D. J. Levinson, and R. N. Sanford (1950) *The Authoritarian Personality* (Norton, New York).

Alderman, G. (1978) *British Elections: Myth and Reality* (Batsford, London).

Alford, R. (1963) *Party and Society* (Rand McNally, Chicago).

Almond, G. A. (1980) 'The intellectual history of the *Civic Culture* concept', in *The Civic Culture Revisited*, eds. G. A. Almond and S. Verba (Little Brown, Boston).

Almond, G. A. and S. Verba (1963) *The Civic Culture: Political Attitudes and Democracy in Five Nations* (Princeton University Press, Princeton).

Almond, G. and S. Verba (eds.) (1980) *The Civic Culture Revisited* (Little Brown, Boston).

Alt, J. E. (1979) *The Politics of Economic Decline* (Cambridge University Press, Cambridge).

Andersen, J. G. (1983) 'Class Voting in Disguise: the Political Role of Women and the Decline of Class Voting in Denmark'. (Paper to ECPR Conference, Freiburg).

Annan (1977) *Report of the Committee on Broadcasting: Cmnd 6753* (HMSO, London).

Anwar, M. (1980) *Votes and Policies: Ethnic Minorities and the General Election 1979* (Commission for Racial Equality, London).

Anwar, M. and D. Kohler (1975) *Participation of Ethnic Minorities in the General Election, October 1974* (Community Relations Commission, London).

Arneson, B. A. (1925) 'Non voting in a typical Ohio community', *American Political Science Review*, 19, 816–25.

Barbrook, A. (1975) *Patterns of Political Behaviour* (Martin Robertson, London).

Barnes, S. H. and M. Kaase (eds.) (1979) *Political Action: Mass Participation in Five Western Democracies* (Sage, Beverly Hills).

Barry, B. M. (1970) *Sociologists, Economists and Democracy* (Collier-Macmillan, London).

Bealey, F., J. Blondel, and W. P. McCann (1965) *Constituency Politics: a Study of Newcastle-under-Lyme* (Faber, London).

Bean, L. H. (1948) *How to Predict Elections* (Knopf, New York).

Belknap, G. and A. Campbell (1951) 'Political party identification and attitudes towards foreign policy', *Public Opinion Quarterly*, 15, 601–23.

Benewick, R. J., A. H. Birch, J. G. Blumler, and A. Ewbank (1969) 'The floating voter and the liberal view of representation', *Political Studies*, 17, 177–95.

Beniger, J. R. (1976) 'Winning the presidential nomination: national polls and state primary elections, 1936–1972', *Public Opinion Quarterly*, 40, 22–38.

Benney, M. and P. Gleiss (1950) 'Social class and politics in Greenwich', *British Journal of Sociology*, 1, 310–27.

Benney, M., A. P. Gray, and R. H. Pear (1956) *How People Vote: a Study of Electoral Behaviour in Greenwich* (Routledge, London).

Berelson, B. R., P. F. Lazarsfeld, and W. N. McPhee (1954) *Voting: A Study of Opinion Formation in a Presidential Campaign* (University of Chicago, Chicago).

Berelson, B. and G. Steiner (1964) *Human Behaviour: an Inventory of Scientific Findings* (Harcourt, New York).

Bilton, M. and S. Himelfarb (1980) 'Fleet Street', in *The British General Election of 1979*, eds. D. Butler and D. Kavanagh (Macmillan, London).

Birch, A. H. and P. Campbell (1950) 'Voting in a Lancashire constituency', *British Journal of Sociology*, 1, 197–208.

Birch, A. H. *et al.* (1959) *Small-town Politics: a Study of Political Life in Glossop* (Oxford University Press, Oxford).

Blewett, N. (1972) *The Peers, the Parties and the People: the General Election of 1910* (Macmillan, London).

Blondel, J. (1963) *Voters, Parties and Leaders* (Penguin, Harmondsworth).

Blumler, J. G. (1977) 'The intervention of television in British politics', Appendix E of the *Report of the Annan Committee on Broadcasting*, Cmnd 6753 (HMSO, London).

Blumler, J. G. and D. McQuail (1968) *Television in Politics: Its Uses and Influence* (Faber, London).

Blumler, J. G., D. McQuail, and T. J. Nossiter (1975) *Political Communication and the Young Voter 1970–71* (Report to SSRC, London).

Blumler, J. G., D. McQuail, and T. J. Nossiter (1976) *Political Communication and the Young Voter in the General Election of February 1974* (Report to SSRC, London).

Bochel, J. M. and D. T. Denver (1983) 'Candidate selection in the Labour Party: what the selectors seek', *British Journal of Political Science*, 13, 45–70.

Bonham, J. (1952) 'The middle class elector', *British Journal of Sociology*, 3, 222–30.

Bonham, J. (1954) *The Middle Class Vote* (Faber, London).

Booth, C. (1892–97) *Life and Labour of the People of London* (Macmillan, London).

Bowley, A. L. (1913) 'Working class households in Reading', *Journal of the Royal Statistical Society*, 78, 672–701.

Bowley, A. L. (1915) *Livelihood and Poverty* (Bell, London).

Bowley, A. L. (1925) *Has Poverty Diminished?* (King, London).

Brewster-Smith, M., J. S. Bruner, and R. W. White (1956) *Opinions and Personality* (Wiley, New York).

Brown, A. and J. Gray (1977) *Political Culture and Political Change in Communist States* (Holmes and Meier, New York).

Budge, I. (1970) *Agreement and the Stability of Democracy* (Markham, Chicago).

Budge, I., J. A. Brand, M. Margolis, and A. L. M. Smith (1972) *Political Stratification and Democracy* (Macmillan, London).

Budge, I., I. Crewe, and D. Farlie (eds.) (1976) *Party Identification and Beyond* (Wiley, London).

Budge, I. and D. Farlie (1976) 'A comparative analysis of factors correlated with turnout and voting choice', in *Party Identification and Beyond* eds. I. Budge, I. Crewe, and D. Farlie (Wiley, London).

Budge I. and D. Farlie (1977) *Voting and Party Competition: a Theoretical Critique and Synthesis Applied to Surveys from Ten Democracies* (Wiley, London).

Budge, I. and D. W. Urwin (1966) *Scottish Political Behaviour: a Case Study in British Homogeneity* (Longmans, London).

Burdick, E. and A. J. Brodbeck (eds.) (1959) *American Voting Behaviour* (Free Press, Glencoe).

Burnham, W. D. (1974) 'The United States: the politics of heterogeneity', in *Electoral Behaviour: a Comparative Handbook*, ed. R. Rose (Free Press, New York).

Butler, D. (1955) 'Voting behaviour and its study in Britain', *British Journal of Sociology*, 6, 93–103.

Butler, D. (1958) *The Study of Political Behaviour* (Hutchinson, London).

Butler, D. (1962) 'The study of political behaviour in Britain', in *Essays in the Behavioural Study of Politics*, ed. A. Ranney (University of Illinois, Urbana), p. 209.

Butler, D. and D. Kavanagh (1974) *The British General Election of February 1974* (Macmillan, London).

Butler, D. and D. Kavanagh (1975) *The British General Election of October 1974* (Macmillan, London).

Butler, D. and D. Kavanagh (1980) *The British General Election of 1979* (Macmillan, London).

Butler, D. and A. King (1966) *The British General Election of 1966* (Macmillan, London).

Butler, D. and U. Kitzinger (1976) *The 1975 Referendum* (Macmillan, London).

Butler, D. and M. Pinto-Dushinsky (1971) *The British General Election of 1970* (Macmillan, London).

Butler, D. and A. Ranney (1978) *Referendums: a Comparative Study of Practice and Theory* (American Enterprise Institute, Washington).

Butler, D. E. and R. Rose (1960) *The British General Election of 1959* (Macmillan, London).

Butler, D. and D. Stokes (1969, 1974) *Political Change in Britain: The Evolution of Electoral Choice* (Macmillan, London).

Campbell, A., P. E. Converse, W. E. Miller, and D. E. Stokes (1960) *The American Voter* (Wiley, New York).

Campbell, A., P. E. Converse, W. E. Miller, and D. E. Stokes (1966) *Elections and the Political Order* (Wiley, New York).

Campbell, A. and P. E. Converse (eds.) (1972) *The Human Meaning of Social Change* (Russell Sage, New York).

Campbell, A., G. Gurin, and W. E. Miller (1954) *The Voter Decides* (Row Peterson, Evanston).

Campbell, A. and R. L. Kahn (1952) *The People Elect a President* (Survey Research Centre, Michigan University, Ann Arbor).

Campbell, P., D. Donnison, and A. Potter (1952) 'Voting behaviour in Droylesden 1951', *Manchester School*, 20, 62–4.

Cannell, C. (1981) 'Methodological work in telephone surveys', in *Telephone Research*, ed. Market Research Development Fund (Market Research Society, London).

Cannon, I. C. (1967) 'Ideology and occupational community', *Sociology*, 1, 165–85.

Champness, B. (1981) 'The psychology of telephone interviewing', in *Telephone Research*, ed. Market Research Development Fund (Market Research Society, London).

Christie, R. (1956) 'Some abuses of psychology', *Psychology Bulletin*, 53, 439–51. (See also the rejoinder by Eysenck.)

Cleary, E. J. and H. Pollins (1953) 'Liberal voting at the General Election of 1951', *Sociological Review*, 1, 27–41.

Cohen, A. (1964) *Attitude Change and Social Influence* (Basic Books, New York).

Coleman, J. S. (1959) 'Relational analysis: a study of social organisation with survey methods', *Human Organisation*, 17, 28–36.

Coleman, J. S., E. Katz, and H. Menzel (1957) 'The diffusion of an innovation among physicians', *Sociometry*, 20, 253–70.

Community Relations Commission—see Anwar.

Conradt, D. P. (1980) 'Changing German political culture', in *The Civic Culture Revisited*, eds. G. A. Almond and S. Verba (Little Brown, Boston).

Converse, P. (1964) 'The nature of belief systems in mass publics', in *Ideology and Discontent*, ed. D. Apter (Free Press, New York) 206–61.

Converse, P. E. (1972) 'Change in the American electorate', in *The Human Meaning of Social Change*, eds. A. Campbell and P. E. Converse (Russell Sage, New York).

Converse, P. (1974) 'Comment: the status of non-attitudes', *American Political Science Review*, 68, 650–60.

Converse, P. E., A. R. Clausen, and W. E. Miller (1965) 'Electoral myth and reality: the 1964 election', *American Political Science Review*, 59, 321–36.

Converse, P. E. and G. Dupeux (1962) 'Politicisation of the electorate in France and the United States', *Public Opinion Quarterly*, 26, 1–23.

Craig, A. L. and W. A. Cornelius (1980) 'Political culture in Mexico: continuities and revisionist interpretations', in *The Civic Culture Revisited*, eds. G. A. Almond and S. Verba (Little Brown, Boston).

Craig, F. W. S. (1968, 1971, 1976) *British Electoral Facts* (Macmillan, London).

Crawford, E. and N. Perry (1976) *Demands for Social Knowledge: The Role of Research Organisations* (Sage, London).

Crewe, I. (1972) 'Do Butler and Stokes really explain political change in Britain?' *European Journal of Political Research*, 2, 47–92.

Crewe, I. (1975) 'Two cheers for Parliament: the Granada Survey of public attitudes to Parliament', in *Adversary Politics and Electoral Reform*, ed. S. E. Finer (Wigram, London).

Crewe, I. (1976) 'Party identification theory and political change in Britain', in *Party Identification and Beyond*, eds. I. Budge, I. Crewe, and D. Farlie (Wiley, London).

Crewe, I. (1981a) 'Why the Conservatives won', in *Britain at the Polls 1979*, ed. H. R. Penniman (American Enterprise Institute, Washington).

Crewe, I. (1981b) 'Why the going is now so favourable for a centre party alliance', *The Times*, 23 March 1981.

Crewe, I., T. Fox, and J. Alt (1977) 'Non-voting in British General Elections 1966–October 1974', in *British Sociology Yearbook Vol. 3*, ed. C. Crouch (Croom Helm, London).

Crewe, I. and B. Särlvik (1976) *Report to SSRC on EEC Referendum Panel Study* (SSRC, London).

Crewe, I., B. Särlvik, and J. Alt (1977) 'Partisan dealignment in Britain 1964–1974', *British Journal of Political Science*, 7, 129–90.

Crick, B. (1959) *The American Science of Politics* (Routledge, London).

Curtice, J. and M. Steed (1980) 'An analysis of the voting', in *The British General Election of 1979*, eds. D. Butler and D. Kavanagh (Macmillan, London).

Curtice, J. and M. Steed (1982) 'Electoral choice and the production of government: the changing operation of the UK electoral system since 1955', *British Journal of Political Science*, 12, 249–98.

Dennis, J. (ed.) (1973) *Socialisation to Politics* (Wiley, New York).

Denver, D. T. and J. M. Bochel (1973) 'The political socialisation of activists in the British Communist party', *British Journal of Political Science*, 3, 53–71.

Dicey, A. V. (1914) *Law and Public Opinion in England* (Macmillan, London).

Dillman, D. A. (1978) *Mail and Telephone Surveys: the Total Design Method* (Wiley, New York).

Dogan, M. and S. Rokkan (eds.) (1969) *Quantitative Ecological Analysis in the Social Sciences* (MIT Press, Cambridge).

Doorn, L. van, W. L. Saris, and M. Lodge (1983) 'Discrete or Continuous Measurement: What Difference Does it Make? (Paper to ECPR Conference, Freiburg).

Downs, A. (1957) *An Economic Theory of Democracy* (Harper, New York).

Dunleavy, P. (1979) 'The urban basis of political alignment: social class, domestic property ownership and state intervention in consumption processes', *British Journal of Political Science*, 9, 409–44.

Dunleavy, P. (1980a) 'The political implications of sectoral cleavages and the growth of state employment: part 1, alternative approaches to production cleavages', *Political Studies*, 28, 364–83.

Dunleavy, P. (1980b) 'The political implications of sectoral cleavages and the growth of state employment: part 2, cleavage structures and political alignment', *Political Studies*, 28, 527–49.

Easton, D. (1969) 'The new revolution in political science', *American Political Science Review*, 63, 1051–61.

Eijk, C. van der, and K. Niemoller (1983) *Electoral Change in the Netherlands: Empirical Results and Methods of Measurement* (CT Press, Amsterdam).

Eijk, C. van der, and J. Outshoorn (1980) 'Too hot to handle. Abortus als strijdpunt in de Nederlandse politiek', in *Gestalten van de dood*, eds. G. A. Banck, L. Brunt, B. van Heerikhuizen, H. Hilhorst, and J. Ijzermans (Ambo, Baarn).

Eldersveld, S. J. (1964) *Political Parties: a Behavioural Analysis* (Rand McNally, Chicago).

Eulau, H. (1962) *Class and Party in the Eisenhower Years* (Free Press, New York).

Eulau, H. (1963) *The Behavioural Persuasion in Politics* (Random House, New York).

Eulau, H. (ed.) (1969) *Behaviouralism in Political Science* (Atherton Press, New York).

Farah, B. G., S. H. Barnes, and F. Heunks (1979) 'Political dissatisfaction', in *Political Action: Mass Participation in Five Western Democracies*, eds. S. H. Barnes and M. Kaase (Sage, Beverly Hills).

Fielder, L. A. (1959) 'Voting and voting studies', in *American Voting Behaviour* eds. E. Burdick and A. J. Brodbeck (Free Press, Glencoe).

Firth, R. (1939) 'An anthropologist's view of Mass Observation', *Sociological Review*, 31, 166–93.

Fitton, M. (1973) 'Neighbourhood and voting: a sociometric examination', *British Journal of Political Science*, 3, 445–72.

Fleming, D. and B. Bailyn (1969) *The Intellectual Migration* (Belknap Press, Cambridge).

Frayn, M. (1968) *A Very Private Life* (Fontana, Glasgow).

Gallup Poll (1972) *Public Opinion 1935–1971* (Random House, New York).

Glock, C. Y. (1967) *Survey Research in the Social Sciences* (Russell Sage, New York).

Goldthorpe, J. H., D. Lockwood, F. Bechhofer, and J. Platt (1968–69) *The Affluent Worker: Vol. 1. Industrial Attitudes and Behaviour, Vol. 2. Political Attitudes and Behaviour, Vol. 3. The Class Struggle* (Cambridge University Press, Cambridge).

Golembiewski, R. T., W. A. Welsh, and W. J. Crotty (1969) *A Methodological Primer for Political Scientists* (Rand McNally, Chicago).

Goodhart, C. and R. Bhansali (1970) 'Political Economy', *Political Studies*, 18, 43–106.

Gosnell, H. F. (1927) *Getting Out the Vote: an Experiment in the Stimulation of Voting* (University of Chicago Press, Chicago).

Grant, A. (1982) *The American Political Process* (Heinemann, London).

Groves, R. M. and R. L. Kahn (1979) *Surveys by Telephone: a National Comparison with Personal Interviews* (Academic Press, New York).

Hakim, C. (1982a) 'Secondary analysis and the relationship between official and academic social research', *Sociology*, 16, 12–28.

Hakim, C. (1982b) *Secondary Analysis in Social Research* (Allen and Unwin, London).

Hall, C. (1975) *How to Run a Pressure Group* (Dent, London).

Halsey, A. H. and I. M. Crewe (1969) *Social Survey of the Civil Service* (Report to Fulton Committee, HMSO, London).

Harrison, T. (1978) *Living Through the Blitz* (Penguin, Harmondsworth).

Harrop, M. (1980a) 'Social research and market research: a critique of a critique', *Sociology*, 14, 277–81.

Harrop, M. (1980b) 'The urban basis of political alignment: a comment', *British Journal of Political Science*, 10, 388–402.

Harrop, M., J. England, and C. T. Husbands (1980) 'The bases of National Front support', *Political Studies*, 28, 271–83.

Hess, R. D. and J. V. Torney (1967) *The Development of Political Attitudes in Children* (Aldine, Chicago).

Himmelweit, H. T. and R. Bond (1974) *Voting Stability and Change: a Developmental Study from Adolescence to Age Thirty Three* (Report to SSRC, London).

Himmelweit, H., P. Humphreys, M. Jaeger, and M. Katz (1981) *How Voters Decide* (Academic Press, London).

Hindess, B. (1971) *The Decline of Working Class Politics* (MacGibbon and Key, London).

Hodder-Williams, R. (1970) *Public Opinion Polls in British Politics* (Routledge, London).

Hoinville, G. and R. Jowell (1977) *Survey Research Practice* (Heinemann, London).

Houghton Committee (1976) *Report of the Committee of Inquiry on Financial Aid to Political Parties: Cmnd 6601* (HMSO, London).

Husbands, C. T. and J. England (1979a) 'The hidden support for racism', *New Statesman*, 11 May 1979, 674–76.

Husbands, C. T. and J. England (1979b) *The Dynamics of Racist Voting* (ECPR Joint Sessions, Brussels).

Hyett, G. P. (1981) 'Telephone interviewing', in *Telephone Research*, ed. Market Research Development Fund (Market Research Society, London).

Hyman, H. H. (1972) *Secondary Analysis of Sample Surveys: Principles, Procedures and Potentialities* (Wiley, New York).

Hyman, H. H. (1973) 'Surveys in the study of political psychology', in *Handbook of Political Psychology*, ed. J. N. Knutson (Jossey Bass, San Francisco).

Inglehart, R. (1971) 'The silent revolution in Europe: intergenerational change in post-industrial societies', *American Political Science Review*, 65, 991–1017.

Inglehart, R. (1977) *The Silent Revolution: Changing Values and Political Styles among Western Publics* (Princeton University Press, Princeton).

Inglehart, R. (1979) 'Value priorities and socio-economic change', and 'The impact of values, cognitive level, and social background', in *Political Action: Mass Participation in Five Western Democracies* eds. S. H. Barnes and M. Kasse (Sage, Beverly Hills).

Inglehart, R. and A. Hochstein (1972) 'Alignment and dealignment of the electorate in France and the United States', *Comparative Political Studies*, 5, 343–72.

Inglehart, R. and D. Sidjanski (1976) 'The left, the right, the establishment and the Swiss electorate', in *Party Identification and Beyond*, eds. I. Budge, I. Crewe, and D. Farlie (Wiley, London).

Ions, E. (1977) *Against Behaviouralism* (Blackwell, Oxford).

Irvine, J., I. Miles, and J. Evans (eds.) (1979) *Demystifying Social Statistics* (Pluto, London).

Jahoda, M., P. F. Lazarsfeld, and H. Zeisel (1933, 1972) *Marienthal: the Sociography of an Unemployed Community* (Tavistock, London).

Janowitz, M. (1960) *The Professional Soldier* (Free Press, Glencoe).

Janowitz, M. and W. E. Miller (1952) 'The Index of Political Predisposition in the 1948 election', *Journal of Politics*, 14, 710–27.

Jennings, M. K. and R. G. Niemi (1968) 'The transmission of political values from parent to child', *American Political Science Review*, 62, 169–84.

Jensen, R. (1969) 'American election analysis: a case history of methodological innovation and analysis', in *Politics and the Social Sciences*, ed. S. M. Lipset (Oxford University Press, New York).

Jones, D. C. (1931) 'The Social Survey of Merseyside', *Journal of the Royal Statistical Society*, 94, 218–50.

Jones, D. C. (1948) *Social Surveys* (Hutchinson, London).

Kaase, M. (1976) 'Party identification and voting behaviour in the West German election of 1969', in *Party Identification and Beyond*, eds. I. Budge, I. Crewe, and D. Farlie (Wiley, London).

Kaase, M. and A. Marsh (1979) 'Political action: a theoretical perspective', 'Political action repertory: changes over time and a new typology', and 'Distribution of Political Action', in *Political Action: Mass Participation in Five Western Democracies*, eds. S. H. Barnes and M. Kaase (Sage, Beverly Hills).

Kavanagh, D. (1970) *Constituency Electioneering in Britain* (Longmans, London).

Kavanagh, D. (1980) 'Political culture in Great Britain: the decline of the *Civic Culture*', in *The Civic Culture Revisited*, eds. G. A. Almond and S. Verba (Little Brown, Boston).

Kavanagh, D. (1981) 'Public opinion polls', in *Democracy at the Polls: a Comparative Study of Competitive National Elections* (American Enterprise Institute, Washington) pp. 196–215.

Kessler, R. C. and D. F. Greenberg (1981) *Linear Panel Analysis* (Academic Press, New York).

Key, V. O. and F. Munger (1959) 'Social determinism and electoral decision: the case of Indiana', in *American Voting Behaviour*, eds. E. Burdick and A. J. Brodbeck (Free Press, Glencoe).

Kilbrandon (1973) *Commission on the Constitution: Cmnd 5460* and especially, *Research Paper 7. Devolution and Other Aspects of Government: An Attitudes Survey* (HMSO, London).

Kirkpatrick, N. (1962) in *Essays in the Behavioural Study of Politics*, ed. A. Ranney (University of Illinois, Urbana), Chapter 1.

Komarovsky, M. (ed.) (1957) *Common Frontiers of the Social Sciences* (Free Press, New York).

Kovenock, D. M., J. W. Prothro, and Associates (1973) *Explaining the Vote: Presidential Choices in the Nation and States 1968* (University of North Carolina, Chapel Hill).

Kruskal, J. B. and M. Wish (1979) *Multidimensional Scaling* (Sage, Beverly Hills).

Lazarsfeld, P. (1949) '*The American Soldier*: an expository review', *Public Opinion Quarterly*, 13, 377–404.

Lazarsfeld, P. F. (1957) 'The historian and the pollster', in *Common Frontiers of the Social Sciences*, ed. M. Komarovsky (Free Press, New York).

Lazarsfeld, P. F. (1969) 'An episode in the history of social research: a memoir', in *The Intellectual Migration*, eds. D. Fleming and B. Bailyn (Belknap Press, Cambridge).

Lazarsfeld, P. F., B. Berelson, and H. Gaudet (1944) *The People's Choice: How the Voter Makes up his Mind in a Presidential Campaign* (Columbia University, New York).

LeDuc, L. (1983) 'Is there Life after Dealignment? Partisan Change in Three National Panel Studies' (Paper to ECPR Conference, Freiburg).

Leiserson, A. (1958) *Parties and Politics* (Knopf, New York).

Lemieux, P. H. (1977) 'Political issues and Liberal support in the February 1974 British general election', *Political Studies*, 25, 323–42.

Leonard, R. L. (1968) *Elections in Britain* (Van Nostrand, London).

Levine, S. and A. Robinson (1976) *The New Zealand Voter: a Survey of Public Opinion and Electoral Behaviour* (Price Milburn, Wellington).

Lipset, S. M. (1960) *Political Man: The Social Bases of Politics* (Doubleday, New York).

Lipset, S. M. (ed.) (1969) *Politics and the Social Sciences* (Oxford University Press, New York).

Lipset, S. M. and S. Rokkan (eds.) (1967) *Party Systems and Voter Alignments: Cross-national Perspectives* (Collier-Macmillan, London).

Lodge, M. (1981) *Magnitude Scaling: Quantitative Measurement of Opinions* (Sage, Beverly Hills).

McCallum, R. B. (1955) 'The study of psephology', *Parliamentary Affairs*, 8, 508–13.

McClosky, H. (1967) 'Survey research in political science' in *Survey Research in the Social Sciences*, ed. C. Glock (Russell Sage, New York), pp. 63–143.

McClosky, H. (1969) *Political Inquiry: The Nature and Uses of Survey Research* (Macmillan, London).

McClosky, H., P. J. Hoffman, and R. O'Hara (1960) 'Issue conflict and consensus among party leaders and followers', *American Political Science Review*, 54, 406–27.

McDonald, C. and T. Bowles (1981) 'Telephone surveys: a review of research findings', in *Telephone Research*, ed. Market Research Development Fund (Market Research Society, London).

McKenzie, R. and A. Silver (1968) *Angels in Marble: Working Class Conservatives in Urban England* (Heinemann, London).

Madgwick, P. J. (1973) *The Politics of Rural Wales: A Study of Cardiganshire* (Hutchinson, London).

Madgwick, P., D. Balsom, and D. van Mechelen (1983) 'The Red and the Green: patterns of partisan choice in Wales', *British Journal of Political Science*, 13, 299–325.

Maine, H. *The Nature of Democracy* (quoted in Milne and Mackenzie, 1958).

Market and Opinion Research International (1979) *British Public Opinion: General Election 1979 Final Report* (Market and Opinion Research International, London).

Market Research Development Fund Conference (1981) *Telephone Research* (Market Research Society, London).

Market Research Society (1971) *Public Opinion Polling on the 1970 Election* (Market Research Society, London).

Markus, G. B. (1979) *Analysing Panel Data* (Sage, Beverly Hills).

Marsh, A. (1974) 'Explorations in unorthodox political behaviour: a scale to measure protest potential', *European Journal of Political Research*, 2, 107–29.

Marsh, A. (1977) *Protest and Political Consciousness* (Sage, Beverly Hills).

Marsh, A. and M. Kaase (1979) 'Measuring political action', and 'Background of political action' in *Political Action: Mass Participation in Five Western Democracies*, eds. S. H. Barnes and M. Kaase (Sage, Beverly Hills).

Marsh, C. (1979) 'Opinion polls—social science or political manoevre', in *Demystifying Social Statistics*, eds. J. Irvine, I. Miles, and J. Evans (Pluto, London).

Marsh, C. (1982) *The Survey Method: The Contribution of Surveys to Sociological Explanation* (Allen and Unwin, London).

Martin, F. M. (1952) 'Social status and electoral choice in two constituencies (Greenwich and Hertford)', *British Journal of Sociology*, 3, 231–41.

Mass Observation (1938) *First Year's Work 1937–38* (Lindsay Drummond, London).

Maud (1969) *Report of the Royal Commission on Local Government in England and Wales: Cmnd 4040* (HMSO, London).

Mayhew, H. (1862) *London Labour and London Poor; a Cyclopaedia of the Conditions and Earnings of those that will Work, those that cannot Work, and those that will not Work* (Griffin and Bohn, London), Vol. 4.

Merriam, C. E. and H. F. Gosnell (1924) *Non-voting: Causes and Methods of Control* (University of Chicago Press, Chicago).

Merritt, A. J. and R. L. Merritt (1970) *Public Opinion in Occupied Germany* (Univeristy of Illinois Press, Urbana).

Merritt, R. L. and S. Rokkan (eds.) (1966) *Comparing Nations: The Use of Quantitative Data in Cross-National Research* (Yale University Press, New Haven).

Miller, A. H. (1978) 'Partisanship reinstated? a comparison of the 1972 and 1976 US Presidential elections', *British Journal of Political Science*, **8**, 129–52.

Miller, W. E. (1956) 'One-party politics and the voter', *American Political Science Review*, **50**, 707–25.

Miller, W. E. and T. E. Levitin (1976) *Leadership and Change: Presidential Elections from 1952 to 1976* (Winthrop, Cambridge).

Miller, W. E. and J. M. Shanks (1982) 'Policy directions and presidential leadership: alternative interpretations of the 1980 presidential election', *British Journal of Political Science*, **12**, 299–356.

Miller, W. E. and D. Stokes (1966) 'Constituency influence in Congress', in *Elections and the Political Order*, eds. A. Campbell, P. Converse, W. E. Miller, and D. Stokes (Wiley, New York).

Miller, W. L. (1975) 'The Scottish voter', *Scotsman* 14, 15, 16 October.

Miller, W. L. (1977a) *Electoral Dynamics in Britain since 1918* (Macmillan, London).

Miller, W. L. (1977b) 'The connection between SNP voting and the demand for Scottish self-government', *European Journal of Political Research*, **5**, 88–102.

Miller, W. L. (1978) 'Social class and party choice in England: a new analysis', *British Journal of Political Science*, **8**, 257–84.

Miller, W. L. (1979) 'Class, region and strata at the British General Election of 1979', *Parliamentary Affairs*, **32**, 376–82.

Miller, W. L. (1981a) *The End of British Politics? Scots and English Political Behaviour in the Seventies* (Clarendon Press, Oxford).

Miller, W. L. (1981b) 'Beyond two-party analysis: some new methods for linear and log-linear analysis in three-party systems', *Political Methodology*, **7**, 1–41.

Miller, W. L. (1982) *A Panel Survey of the 1982 Hillhead By-election Campaign* (Telephone Survey Research Unit, Strathclyde University, Glasgow).

Miller, W. L. (1983) 'The denationalisation of British politics: the re-emergence of the periphery', *West European Politics*, forthcoming.

Miller, W. L., J. Brand, and M. Jordan (1981) 'Governing without a mandate: the Conservative Party in Scotland', *Political Quarterly*, **52**, 203–13.

Miller, W. L., J. Brand, and M. Jordan (1982) 'On the power or vulnerability of the British press: a dynamic analysis', *British Journal of Political Science*, **12**, 357–73.

Miller, W. L. and M. Mackie (1973) 'The electoral cycle and the asymmetry of government and opposition popularity', *Political Studies*, **21**, 263–79.

Miller, W. L., P. J. Madgwick, *et al.* (1982) *Democratic or violent protest? attitudes towards direct action in Scotland and Wales* (Strathclyde University Studies in Public Policy No. 107, Glasgow).

Milne, R. S. and H. C. Mackenzie (1954) *Straight Fight 1951* (Hansard Society, London).

Milne, R. S. and H. C. Mackenzie (1958) *Marginal Seat 1955* (Hansard Society, London 1958).

Minkin, L. (1978) *The Labour Party Conference* (Allen Lane, London).

Moodie, G. (1964) *The Government of Great Britain* (Methuen, London).

MORI—see Market and Opinion Research International.

Moseley, P. (1982) *The British Economy as Represented by the Popular Press* (Strathclyde University Studies in Public Policy No. 105, Glasgow).

Moser, C. A. and G. Kalton (1958, 1971, 1981) *Survey Methods in Social Investigation* (Heinemann, London).

Moss, L. (1981) *Attitudes towards Government* (Report to SSRC, London).

Mosteller, F., H. Hyman, P. J. McCarthy, E. S. Marks, and D. B. Truman (1949) *The Pre-Election Polls of 1948* (Social Science Research Council, New York).

Moxon-Browne, E. (1979) 'The Northern Ireland Attitudes Survey 1978'. (Queens University mimeo, Belfast).

Moxon-Browne, E. (1983) *Nation, Class and Creed in Northern Ireland* (Gower, Aldershot).

Mueller, J. (1970) 'Presidential popularity from Truman to Johnson', *American Political Science Review*, 64, 18–34.

Muller, E. N. (1979) *Aggressive Political Participation* (Princeton University Press, Princeton).

Nie, N. H., S. Verba, and J. R. Petrocik (1976) *The Changing American Voter* (Harvard University Press, Cambridge).

Niemi, R. G. (1973) 'Collecting information about the family: a problem in survey methodology', in *Socialisation to Politics*, ed. J. Dennis (Wiley, New York).

Noelle-Neuman, E. (1974) 'The Spiral of Silence: a Theory of Public Opinion', *Journal of Communication*, 24, 43–51.

Noelle-Neuman, E. (1979) 'Public Opinion and the classical tradition: a re-evaluation', *Public Opinion Quarterly*, 43, 144–56.

Nordlinger, E. A. (1967) *The Working-Class Tories: Authority, Deference and Stable Democracy* (MacGibbon, London).

Nuffield Studies—see D. Butler.

Parkin, F. I. (1968) *Middle-class Radicalism: the Social Bases of the British Campaign for Nuclear Disarmament* (Manchester University Press, Manchester).

Pateman, C. (1970) *Participation and Democratic Theory* (Cambridge University Press, Cambridge).

Pateman, C. (1980) 'The *Civic Culture*: a philosophic critique', in *The Civic Culture Revisited*, eds. G. A. Almond and S. Verba (Little Brown, Boston).

Penniman, H. R. (ed.) (1981) *Britain at the Polls 1979* (American Enterprise Institute, Washington).

Perry, N. H. (1975) *The Organisation of Social Science Research in the United Kingdom* (SSRC Survey Unit, London).

Perry, P. (1979) 'Certain problems in election survey methodology', *Public Opinion Quarterly*, 43, 312–25.

Pilgrim Trust (1938) *Men without Work: A Report Made to the Pilgrim Trust* (Cambridge Universtity Press, Cambridge).

Pinto-Dushinsky, M. (1981) 'Financing the British General Election of 1979', in *Britain at the Polls 1979*, ed. H. R. Penniman (American Enterprise Institute, Washington).

Polsby, N. W. (1960) 'Towards an explanation of McCarthyism', *Political Studies*, 8, 250–71.

Pomper, G. (1975) *Voters' Choice: Varieties of American Electoral Behaviour*, (Dodd Mead, New York).

Posner, M. (1982) 'Foreword', in C. Hakim, *Secondary Analysis in Social Research* (Allen and Unwin, London).

Powell, G. B. (1980) 'Voting turnout in thirty democracies: partisan, legal and socioeconomic influences', in *Electoral Participation: a Comparative Analysis*, ed. R. Rose (Sage, Beverly Hills).

Przeworski, A. and H. Teune (1970) *The Logic of Comparative Social Inquiry* (Wiley, New York).

Putnam, R. (1973) *The Beliefs of Politicians: Ideology, Conflict and Democracy in Britain and Italy* (Yale University Press, New Haven).

Rabier, J. R. (1970 onwards) *Euro-Barometer Surveys*: Detailed titles include *Europeans and European Unification* (1970); *European Opinion on Regional and Agricultural Policy* (1971); *Satisfaction with Conditions of Life in the European Community* (1973); *Europe as seen by Europeans* (1973); *Euro-Barometer* (1974 onwards); *European Men and Women* (1975); *European Consumer* (1976); *The Perception of Poverty in Europe* (1977); *Science and European Public Opinion* (1977); *Attitudes of the Working Population to Retirement* (1978); *The European Public's Attitudes to Scientific and Technical Development* (1979);

European Men and Women (1979); *Unemployment* (1979); *Europeans and their Children* (1979); *European Women in Paid Employment* (1980); *Europeans and their Regions* (1980). (All published by the Commission of the European Communities, Brussels.)

Rabier, J. R. (1981) 'Les études comparatives des publics Européens', *Etudes de Radio-Television* (Brussels).

Ranney, A. (ed.) (1962) *Essays in the Behavioural Study of Politics* (University of Illinois, Urbana).

Robinson, C. E. (1934) 'The straw vote', in *Encyclopedia of the Social Sciences*, 14, 417–9 (Macmillan, New York).

Robinson, W. S. (1950) 'Ecological correlation and the behaviour of individuals', *American Sociological Review*, 15, 351–71.

Rokkan, S. (1962) 'The comparative study of political participation', in *Essays on the Behavioural Study of Politics*, ed. A. Ranney (University of Illinois, Urbana).

Rokkan, S. (1964) 'Review of *The Civic Culture*', *American Political Science Review*, 58, 677.

Rokkan, S. (1967) 'Geography, religion and social class: cross-cutting cleavages in Norwegian politics', in *Party Systems and Voter Alignments*, eds. S. M. Lipset and S. Rokkan (Collier-Macmillan, London).

Rokkan, S. (ed.) (1968) *Comparative Research across Cultures and Nations* (Mouton, Paris).

Rokkan, S. (1970) *Citizens, Elections, Parties: Approaches to the Comparative Study of the Processes of Development* (Universitetsforlaget, Oslo).

Rose, E. J. B. (1969) *Colour and Citizenship: a Report on British Race Relations* (Oxford University Press, Oxford).

Rose, R. (1968) 'Class and party divisions', *Sociology*, 2, 129–62.

Rose, R. (1971) *Governing without Consensus: an Irish Perspective* (Faber, London).

Rose, R. (1974a) *Politics in England Today* (Faber, London).

Rose, R. (ed.) (1974b) *Electoral Behaviour: a Comparative Handbook* (Free Press, New York).

Rose, R. (1974c) 'Comparability in electoral studies', in *Electoral Behaviour: a Comparative Handbook*, ed. R. Rose (Free Press, New York).

Rose, R. (1974d) 'Britain: simple abstractions and complex realities', in *Electoral Behaviour: a Comparative Handbook*, ed. R. Rose (Free Press, New York).

Rose, R. (1980a) *Class Does Not Equal Party* (Strathclyde University Studies in Public Policy No. 74, Glasgow).

Rose, R. (ed.) (1980b) *Electoral Participation: a Comparative Analysis* (Sage, Beverly Hills).

Rose, R. (1981) 'Toward normality: public opinion polls in the 1979 election', in *Britain at the Polls 1979*, ed. H. R. Penniman (American Enterprise Institute, Washington).

Rossi, P. (1959) 'Four landmarks in voting research', in *American Voting Behaviour*, eds. E. Burdick and A. J. Brodbeck (Free Press, Glencoe).

Rowntree, S. (1902) *Poverty: A Study of Town Life* (Longmans, London).

Rowntree, S. (1941) *Poverty and Progress* (Longmans, London).

Rusk, J. G. (1976) 'Political participation in America: a review essay', *American Political Science Review*, 70, 583–91.

Sani, G. (1980) 'The political culture of Italy: continuity and change', in *The Civic Culture Revisited*, eds. G. A. Almond and S. Verba (Little Brown, Boston).

Särlvik, B., I. Crewe, J. Alt, and A. Fox (1976) 'Britain's membership of the EEC: a profile of electoral opinions in the spring of 1974 with a postscript on the referendum', *European Journal of Political Research*, 4, 83–113.

Särlvik, B. and I. Crewe (1983) *Decade of Dealignment* (Cambridge University Press, Cambridge).

Sartori, G. (1969) 'From the sociology of politics to political sociology', in *Politics and the Social Sciences*, ed. S. M. Lipset (Oxford University Press, New York).

Schuur, W. H. van (1983) 'Perception and Evaluation of Political Problems' (Doctoral Thesis, University of Groningen, Groningen).

Scotsman (1979) 'Opinion Research Centre Devolution Surveys 1974–79', (*Scotsman* 28 September 1979, Edinburgh).

Searing, D. (1978) 'Measuring politicians' values: administration and assessment of a ranking technique in the British House of Commons', *American Political Science Review*, 72, 65–79.

Sharpe, L. J. (1962) *A Metropolis Votes* (London School of Economics, London).

Smith, H. L. (1928) *New Survey of London Life and Labour* (King, London).

Steed, M. (1966) 'An analysis of the results', in *The British General Election of 1966*, eds. D. E. Butler and A. King (Macmillan, London).

Steed, M. (1971) 'The results analysed', in *The British General Election of 1970*, eds. D. Butler and M. Pinto-Dushinsky (Macmillan, London).

Steed, M. (1974) 'The results analysed', in *The British General Election of February 1974*, eds. D. Butler and D. Kavanagh (Macmillan, London).

Steed, M. (1975) 'The results analysed', in *The British General Election of October 1974*, eds. D. Butler and D. Kavanagh (Macmillan, London).

Stouffer, S. (1955) *Communism, Conformity and Civil Liberties* (Wiley, New York).

Stouffer, S. A. *et al.* (1949) *The American Soldier*: *Vol. 1. Adjustment During Army Life*, *Vol. 2. Combat and its Aftermath* (Princeton University Press, Princeton).

Survey Research Centre (1980a) *National Election Studies Data Sourcebook 1952–78* (Havard University Press, Cambridge).

Survey Research Centre (1980b) *Social Attitudes Data Sourcebook 1947–78* (Harvard University Press, Cambridge).

Survey Research Consultants International (1981) *Index to International Public Opinion 1979–80* (Greenwood, Westport).

Taylor, H. (1970) 'The power of the polls', *New Society*, 19 March 1970, 477–9.

Teer, F. and J. D. Spence (1973) *Political Opinion Polls* (Hutchinson, London).

Thomassen, J. (1976) 'Party identification as a cross-national concept: its meaning in the Netherlands', in *Party Identification and Beyond*, eds. I. Budge, I. Crewe, and D. Farlie (Wiley, London).

Tingsten, H. (1937, 1963) *Political Behaviour: Studies in Election Statistics* (Bedminster, Totowa).

Todd, J. and B. Butcher (1982) *Electoral Registration in 1981* (Office of Population Censuses and Surveys, London).

Trenaman, J. and D. McQuail (1961) *Television and the Political Image* (Methuen, London).

Troldahl, V. C. and R. E. Carter (1964) 'Random selection of respondents within households in phone surveys', *Journal of Marketing Research*, 1, 71–6.

Truman, D. (1969) in *Behaviouralism in Political Science*, ed. H. Eulau (Atherton, New York).

Tuchman, S. and T. E. Coffin (1971) 'The influence of election night television broadcasts in a close election', *Public Opinion Quarterly*, 35, 315–26.

Verba, S. (1980) 'On revisiting *The Civic Culture*: a personal postscript', in *The Civic Culture Revisited*, eds. G. A. Almond and S. Verba (Little Brown, Boston).

Verba, S. and R. A. Brody (1970) 'Participation, policy preferences and the war in Vietnam', *Public Opinion Quarterly*, 34, 325–32.

Verba, S. and N. H. Nie (1972) *Participation in America: Political Democracy and Social Equality* (Harper and Row, New York).

Verba, S., N. H. Nie, and J. Kim (1971) *The Modes of Democratic Participation: a Cross-National Comparison* (Sage, Beverly Hills).

Verba, S., N. H. Nie, and J. Kim (1978) *Participation and Political Equality: a Seven Nation Comparison* (Cambridge University Press, New York).

Wallas, G. (1908) *Human Nature in Politics* (Constable, London).

Webb, N. and R. Wybrow (1981) *The Gallup Report 1980* (Sphere, London).

Weber, M. (1922, 1978) 'The Nature of social action', in *Max Weber: Selections in Translation*, ed. W. G. Runciman (Cambridge University Press, Cambridge).

Welch, S. (1975) 'Dimensions of political participation in a Canadian sample', *Canadian Journal of Political Science*, 8, 553–9.

Wheatley (1969) *Report of the Royal Commission on Local Government in Scotland: Cmnd 4150* (HMSO, London).

Whiteley, P. (1981) 'Who are the Labour activists?', *Political Quarterly*, 52, 160–70.

Wiatr, J. J. (1980) 'The *Civic Culture* from a marxist sociological perspective', in *The Civic Culture Revisited*, eds. G. A. Almond and S. Verba (Little Brown, Boston).

Williams, P. (1982) 'Electoral studies and the 1980 election in the United States', *Electoral Studies*, 1, 347–54.

Worcester, R. M. (1979) 'How the Tories lost the campaign and won the election', *British Public Opinion*, 1, 18–36.

Worcester, R. (1980) *Political Opinion Polling: an International Review* (Market and Opinion Research International, London).

Worcester, R. M. and R. T. Stubbs (1978) 'Ascertaining the opinions of workers: a critique of ACAS survey techniques', *Market Research Society Conference Papers*, 357–66.

Worcester, R. M. and R. T. Stubbs (1980) 'Ascertaining the opinions of workers: Corrigendum', *Journal of the Market Research Society*, 22, 60–4.

Wright, J. D. (1976) *The Dissent of the Governed: Alienation and Democracy in America* (Academic Press, New York).

Wright, V. (1978) 'France', in *Referendums: a Comparative Study of Practice and Theory*, eds. D. Butler and A. Ranney (American Enterprise Institute, Washington).

Index

Note: Where a year appears in brackets after a name, the index entry refers to a publication. Full details of the publication can be found in the list of references. The index entry indicates the place in the text where the publication is cited. The publication may also be discussed in the text at other places than those given in this index.

A name without a year in brackets indicates that a person, rather than a publication, is discussed in the text.